MW01039470

Spirit of Hope

THE YEAR AFTER THE JOPLIN TORNADO

RANDY TURNER
JOHN HACKER

Drop Cap Publishing

ISBN-13: 978-1477523407
ISBN-10: 1477523405

Printed in the United States of America

Book design by David Hoover
Copy editing by Kristin Hacker-Hickman

This book is dedicated to the people of Joplin, Missouri.
Thank you for showing the world the Spirit of Hope.

CONTENTS

REPORTS

PREFACE

By Mitch Randles | Joplin Fire Chief

On May 22, 2011, at 5:41 p.m., the City of Joplin and its residents underwent a life-changing event. A tornado of such fury and destruction laid a path of devastation through our city leaving it scarred and unrecognizable. As I first surveyed the damage from the storm, I was fearful that our city would never recover and be the hometown that we had all grown comfortable with and accustomed to.

Emergency responders and volunteers descended upon Joplin to aid in search and rescue, the removal of debris, demolition and reconstruction of homes. They were like angels from heaven. Without all of the assistance that was received I have no doubt that we would not be as far along in our recovery efforts are we are today. I believe that everyone from Joplin, the four-state area, and possibly the entire country felt the effects of the tornado, not just those in the tornado's path. I don't think there is a single resident of the Four States that didn't know someone who had lost a loved one, their home or their place of employment. It affected each and every one of us in some way.

As we continue with recovery and rebuilding efforts there have been several times when people have asked about a single individual who has made a significant difference either in the rescue or the recovery efforts, and I cannot come up with a single name or even a group. There was no one person or group that stood out. We all stood out; we were a community of people who were placed in an extraordinary situation and each one of us stepped forward. This was a group effort from the moment the storm struck the city. No one put himself or herself first — we all looked to help others no matter how bad the individual circumstances were. We all believed that our friends and neighbors needed assistance first. I have never in my life been more proud of our city, our citizens, our friends, and our neighbors. We were united in a cause as never before, and I believe that Mayor Mike Woolston summed it up perfectly when he said, "We aren't going to let some F5 tornado kick our a**."

With the one-year anniversary of the storm quickly approaching, I find the city still working feverishly on the recovery and rebuilding efforts, working on getting back to normal. But I believe that the normal we knew on May 21, 2011, was forever taken from us on May 22, 2011. I once thought that things would go back to being the same, but shortly after moving into our new home, my wife and kids were talking about having the family out to our new home for the annual holiday celebrations. That is when my daughter Sabrina looked at me and said, "This is our house, it isn't our home. That was taken away from us." Reality really came crashing back to me. I thought about how many other residents must feel the same. I think that Sabrina got it right; we will never go back to the normal we knew before. We are currently creating the "New" normal with each piece of debris that is removed and every building and home that is rebuilt.

Looking forward I know that the buildings and homes will be replaced and that our city will recover. Our community is too strong not to have that happen. But I pray that each and every one of us affected and touched by this tragic event are able to find closure and have the "New Normal" which I long for. For each of us that will come in our own time as the emotional scars heal. For me, I wait for the day when Sabrina looks at me and says, "Daddy, I'm home."

1. SPIRIT OF HOPE

BY RANDY TURNER

I am not one of those who shrugged off the tornado warnings that sounded in Joplin on May 22, 2011.

I knew better.

Maybe at one time I would have ignored the warnings. After all, what everyone said in the aftermath of May 22 was correct — the sirens were a given in Joplin during certain times of the year, almost as much of a fixture in the background music of life as the roar of the trains that always stopped traffic at the most inopportune times on 20th and 15th streets.

It was the tornadoes that hit the area in May 2008 that caused me to pay greater heed to the sirens. None hit anywhere near my Joplin apartment, but I was watching television as I heard that a tornado warning had been issued for the Newtonia-Stark City area, approximately 30 miles east of Joplin.

Even though my parents live in Newtonia, I didn't think anything of it. Tornado watches and warnings were always being issued. About 30 minutes later, I received a phone call I will never forget.

Jodie and Christina Neal sift through the wreckage of their home in Duquesne.
PHOTO BY RANDY TURNER

I heard my mom's voice, but I had never heard it like this before.

"The house is gone," she said.

Despite hearing the tornado warning, I didn't immediately understand what she was saying. "The tornado," she added.

She told her story. The neighbors had offered to let my parents share their shelter and they were headed across the street with Mom carrying her dog, Zoey, when they saw the tornado coming. They could not find Woody, their 12-year-old cat.

"Bill said we'd better get back in the house." They crouched down in the living room behind the sofa as the tornado hit the building that had been home for them since 1952.

The damage was not as serious as Mom initially thought. Part of the room that had been my bedroom was gone, as was the front portion of the living room. The garage, which held many boxes of memories and Christmas decorations that had been collected for years, was stripped from the ground.

Mom, Dad, and Zoey were safe. Mom suffered a bump on the head, but otherwise, she was safe. Woody was nowhere to be found and that upset Mom more than anything.

Thankfully, as our conversation continued, I heard the cat make his presence known. Apparently, he had been sleeping under my old bed and though he was considerably inconvenienced by the tornado, he was all right.

I drove down the next day, getting through a National Guard checkpoint to go to my parents' home. Neighbors were already there helping and I quickly joined in, though in retrospect, I don't think there was anything I did over the next eight or nine hours that really helped.

I had to do something. This had always been my home.

My parents were able to remain in the house, not even having to stay away one night due to the tornado. Today, their house has been rebuilt and is better than ever, and now has a tornado shelter.

The people of Newtonia were fortunate. Though half of the homes in the community of 200 were destroyed, not one person was killed or injured. The tornado came on a Saturday night, shortly after 6 p.m. and the homes that were totally destroyed were almost all empty when the storm hit.

The community, however, was not so fortunate. Most of the people who were displaced by the forces of nature never returned. Many were relative newcomers who had not established an attachment to Newtonia and used the town as a bedroom community, coming home at night while working at jobs in Joplin or Neosho.

If you drive into Newtonia today, you still see the shattered remnants of homes that have never been replaced and have never been torn down. Some buildings have been cleared away and where once children played, or older couples sat on porch swings whiling away summer evenings, there is only emptiness.

So when the tornado sirens sounded in Joplin on May 22, 2011, I took them seriously, but like so many others, I had no place to go. Ironically, I had visited my parents earlier that day and instead of staying at a place that had a tornado shelter, I drove back to Joplin to get home before the storm hit.

On the way home, I listened to KZRG, which had already suspended its regular programming to provide listeners with wall-to-wall coverage of the weather, a service it would continue for several days.

The words of the announcer were growing more and more ominous as I pulled into the parking lot of my apartment complex. I ran into my apartment, turned on the radio, and heard within a few moments that a tornado had touched down at 7th and Range Line, only a few blocks from where I live.

I grabbed some pillows and blankets from my bed, dropped to the floor, covered my head, and waited for the winds to blast through my apartment.

A few minutes later, it was all over. Apparently, the report of a tornado at 7th had been erroneous. The tornado had missed my apartment by a few blocks. No one who had the radio tuned to any of the Zimmer stations that afternoon will ever forget the impact of a clearly affected reporter driving through town, giving us the first glimpse of the horror that had befallen Joplin.

"The high school is gone," he said.

He had to be in shock, I thought. The high school couldn't be gone. But then he continued, giving a list of places that had been vibrant parts of the Joplin community, which simply were no more.

It wasn't long before we learned that St. John's, one of the two major hospitals serving the city, had been another tornado victim, though Freeman just across the street had been spared, fortunately for a community which desperately needed one of its hospitals to be fully functioning.

The storm passed, leaving a brownish sky, a sight no one who was there on that day will ever forget. Within a few hours, darkness fell on a crippled city, the high piercing sounds of sirens punctuating the horror.

In *5:41: Stories from the Joplin Tornado*, John Hacker and I collected some stories and wrote others about the night that forever changed Joplin. One third of the city was gone, more than 160 people killed, in the most devastating tornado that hit the United States in six decades.

One thing became evident right from the first — Joplin was not going to be a Newtonia. The May 22 tornado was not going to be the death of this city. This book tells the story of some of the heroes who made sure Joplin was not going to become just another footnote in history.

We write about the ones who have been the center of many reports on the tornado: Mayor Mike Woolston, City Manager Mark Rohr, Rob O'Brian, director of the Joplin Area Chamber of Commerce, Joplin

Schools Superintendent C. J. Huff, and the man who was gracious enough to provide the introduction to this book, Fire Chief Mitch Randles.

No book will ever be big enough to name all of the heroes, the people who came from all over the U. S. and the world to lend us a hand in our time of need, the Joplin residents who pitched in to help their neighbors, and those who were most affected by the tornado, the ones who were in the path of its devastation and who were fortunate enough to live to tell their stories.

I have had the opportunity to address a number of groups over the past few months talking about *5:41*, and I always mention the unnamed heroes whose contributions have impressed me the most.

In John Hacker's story about Samaritan's Purse in our first book, he wrote about the people whose homes had been hit by the tornado, but who came in asking how they could help others who were in worse shape.

That is the spirit of hope. That is the spirit of Joplin.

2. HISTORIC STORM, HISTORIC RECOVERY

By John Hacker

Wow, what a year.

The clichés all apply to the Joplin tornado, historic storm, storm of epic proportions, storm of the century, pull them all out, they all work here.

As terrible and deflating as the tornado of May 22, 2011, was, the recovery of the year since that day has been almost as magnificent and inspiring.

While no community could ever be prepared to take a direct hit from a storm the magnitude of the one that hit Joplin, probably no area of the country has had more practice at recovering from weather disasters as we here in the Four States have.

All that practice, from the tornado that hit 32nd Street in Joplin in 1997, to the Parsons, Kan., tornado in 2000, to the tornadoes that hit Barton and Lawrence counties in December 2002. Who could forget May

This monument, in Cunningham Park in Joplin, lists the 161 people killed in the May 22, 2011, tornado. Inside this monument is a time capsule containing a variety of items related to the storm and the people who died in it.

PHOTO BY JOHN HACKER

4, 2003, when four tornadoes lashed at Cherokee County and Franklin, Kan., and Carl Junction, Stockton and Pierce City, Mo.? More than 20 people died that day.

There were the ice storms of 2007. Remember? There were two of them.

There was the Mother's Day tornado of 2008 that put the last nail in the coffin of the already dying community of Picher, Okla., then devastated a section of rural Newton County, Mo. More than two dozen people died that day.

As terrible as those events were, it just seems like Mother Nature was warming up.

But so were we. The residents of this region learned from all those events. As Joplin Emergency Management Director Keith Stammer once said, weaknesses are strengths pushed too hard.

Even though we were in shock at the magnitude of the devastation, we also knew we had been here before. This was exponentially worse than those earlier storms, but we had rebuilt our communities — Parsons, Kan., Carl Junction, Mo., Franklin, Kan., Stockton, Mo., Pierce City, Mo.

Mother Nature scaled up the destruction, so we just had to scale up the reconstruction.

My journey that day started in the parking lot of what had been the Peace Lutheran Church at 20th and Wisconsin, maybe that's why I have a special affinity for that little church, why I returned on May 29, 2011, and again on May 20, 2012. Maybe that's why that church has an entire chapter dedicated to it in this book, but that church represents dozens who may be struggling, but who vow to overcome and rebuild even a year after the storm.

Personally, as I walked through the devastation east of Joplin High School at 6:30 p.m. on May 22, 2011, I was torn.

When do I put the camera and notebook down and help? But I'm not trained to help — my training is in recording events. Is that really important now? Is that a dead person over there?

I was able to do both that day. Many I talked to on that day were eager to talk. I was able to give them some information I had gleaned from the radio before getting out of my car. They needed to talk, as if it somehow validated and confirmed that they had just gone through a terrible ordeal and come out alive.

I was also able to play a small part in prying two women who had survived the heart of that EF5 monster out of the car that had been destroyed around them.

As I walked that neighborhood between Wisconsin and Indiana Avenues, and 20th and 24th streets, the smell of natural gas was everywhere. The air felt heavy — and it was. It was full of the dust and debris that had been people's lives only an hour before.

I recalled visiting Barbara Wells' home, at 22nd Street and Indiana Avenue just 18 hours before. Jeff Wells, a great friend and long-time colleague had been up with his wife, Melissa DeLoach Wells, visiting his childhood home and I came down and met with them for a few hours on May 21, 2011.

Now here I was in that same place on May 22, 2011, and I couldn't find Barbara Wells' home — I couldn't find 22nd Street. It was covered in debris.

This couldn't be the place I had visited a few hours before.

That area is cleared of debris now and construction is evident everywhere. I've had the great pleasure of covering many of the construction projects, thanks to my job with *The Carthage Press* and thanks to Lee Radcliff, who owns *Show Me the Ozarks Magazine*.

Thanks to her assignments, I've spent more time in Joplin than I ever would have without them. Joplin, our story is still being written.

A new chapter is added every time a house is finished or someone who was made homeless returns or every time a business or school reopens.

Every person who has helped to clean up and rebuild their home or business is a character in this story, and their roles continue, into a future filled with promise.

It's only been a year since the tornado and there is much to do, but we are off to a great start.

Joplin Mayor Melodee Colbert-Kean leads the crowd down 20th Street between Range Line Road and Connecticut Avenue on the May 22, 2012, Unity Walk marking the one-year anniversary of the tornado that killed 161 people.
PHOTO BY JOHN HACKER

3. ONE YEAR, ONE COMMUNITY, ONE DIRECTION

BY JOHN HACKER

Like the tornado, it started small, on one end of town, with a few hundred people gathering at the roundabout at 20th Street and Duquesne Road and moving west.

Like the tornado, it grew quickly into a powerful wave with thousands of people joining them at 17th Street and Range Line Road.

Like the tornado, thousands of people formed an unstoppable force sweeping across Joplin.

Unlike the tornado, this force came not for destruction but for construction, not for death but for life, not for an end but for a beginning — a new beginning for two cities ripped asunder exactly one year before.

The Unity Walk on May 22, 2012, marked exactly one year after the Joplin tornado with a march in the opposite direction that the tornado traveled.

"It was symbolic," said Joplin City Manager Mark Rohr as he prepared to lead the crowd west from 17th and Range Line. "We're walking against the wind toward Cunningham Park and we're doing it as a group. The purpose of the Unity Walk and the Day of Unity is to stay together. That's what's been the secret to our success so far and led us to the point where we're at and that's what's going to take us home in terms of completing the rebuilding process. We thought it was important to highlight that, to remind people of that and to urge them to continue to work together until we reach the point where we're rebuilding the city."

EARLY WALKERS

Duquesne Mayor Denny White estimated that between 300 and 350 people gathered at the Duquesne Road roundabout for his city's portion of the walk.

Duquesne is a much smaller city than Joplin, but proportionately, it might have suffered even more than its larger neighbor.

The tornado destroyed more than 40 percent of the structures in Duquesne, between 300 and 400 homes damaged beyond repair.

One of them belonged to Cindy Sundy.

"This walk is, it's hard to put it into words, but this walk is victory," Sundy said as she walked west on 20th Street toward Range Line Road. "It means that we've come through on the other side of what should have been the worst day of my life, but I actually realize it was the best day of my life because my son, my husband and I were trapped in my house, the walls exploded around us. Any one of us, or all of us could have lost our lives and we didn't. So it really puts it into perspective what's important. The stuff, everyone says it was stuff. It was important stuff. There's stuff I miss, but not near as bad as I would have missed my husband or my son or my best friend who lived across the street, or my dog, who wouldn't come in the bathroom with us, but still managed to survive. So it's victory."

Sundy said she heard that the weather was going to be bad, so she took a shower because "I don't like to shower in a thunderstorm."

"I flipped the TVs over to local channels when I saw the sky to the west get dark," Sundy said. "They were showing their weather cam, you could see transformers blowing and they said there was a tornado on the ground, but it was rain-wrapped. It didn't look like a funnel cloud, but it was a tornado and we should take cover. At this point it was on the west side of town. It was west of the TV stations so I went and got my husband and told him, they say there's a tornado on the ground. He, being a man, wanted to go see, so we went and stood on the driveway and we talked about where we wanted to go, do we want to go in the tub in the bathroom, or do we want to go under the house. Well there are spiders under the house; I'm not going there. So we chose to go to the tub."

As the winds tore at her house, she, her son and husband huddled in their bathroom. The tornado hit and demolished the home.

"It sounded like there was a 747 parked in our driveway with all of its engines on at once," Cindy Sundy said. "And then we were in the eye of it. At first I thought it was over, we had made it, and then when the other wall hit, I remember praying with everything I had because I didn't think there was enough house left to protect us. When the roof went, my husband immediately laid on top of my son and me, we had both felt the suction and if he hadn't done that, there's no telling what could have happened. A bathroom wall fell on us and that's what kept us in.

"My husband crawled out and the dog was waiting for him. She was fine, covered with leaves, covered with debris, but she was fine. Our house and neighborhood were completely gone. It was surreal, but like I said, I've come to realize that was the best day of my life."

Sundy was joined by people who didn't live in the tornado's path, but were affected nonetheless.

"We're here because some parts of me feel guilty because we didn't lose our home and I just want to be with those that did and let them know that we're behind them," said Joyce Wall, who walked the Duquesne walk with her niece, Adison Wright, and Adison's mother Amy Wright.

"We were lucky enough that our home wasn't hit, but we had a graduation party going on in our house for Amy's daughter and Adison's sister," Wall said. "If they hadn't been in our house at that time having a graduation dinner, there might have been some injuries or deaths. We had about 22 people in the house; some that lived up by the hospital and some that lived down in Duquesne."

"I'm basically here just to show the strength and power behind our community," Adison Wright added. "And to show that, yeah, our entire town got wiped out but still, after all of this and after all the volunteers leave, our community is still going to be here to rise up and walk to show that we're still strong and we're still going to be here even if it happens again. We're still here and we're going to have that strength."

Duquesne Mayor Denny White said the one-year anniversary was an important milestone for residents of the entire area.

"It's been a very tough year," White said. "There's been a lot going on but we've worked hard to rebuild and we're happy to be here today and have this moment. In the beginning, Joplin had more of the limelight than we did, but as time went on, we got our fair share and we're not unhappy about anything. We're just happy to be here."

Joplin City Council Member Mike Woolston, who was mayor of Joplin at the time of the tornado, walked with the Duquesne crowd as they moved to meet the Joplin contingent of the walk. Woolston said Joplin and Duquesne are partners in the reconstruction and must work together to reach out to all who have helped and all who still need help.

"That's why I'm here with Denny, I called him to ask him a couple of days ago if he'd mind if I started the walk with them," Woolston said. "Because it is a partnership and I think the community needs to see that and I hope they buy into it because our futures are more or less intertwined in terms of going forward. As a percentage, Duquesne probably took a greater loss than Joplin did in terms of houses and those kinds of things and many people don't recognize that I don't think.

"It's a long walk and it'll be difficult for some people, but I think it's symbolic of the difficulty that we've encountered in the past year since the tornado, but just as we have overcome in that area, we'll overcome today. I think the walk is symbolic to a lot of people in terms of how we conquered the tornado, we'll conquer this walk today as a symbol of our resiliency and the spirit of today."

SECOND BEGINNING

The beginning of the walk for a majority of participants was almost three-quarters of a mile into it for those who started at the Duquesne Roundabout.

Thousands of people gathered at the 17th Street entrance to the Walmart parking lot as police prepared to clear the path for the Unity Walk.

For Jody Kirk, Joplin, the walk was a deeply personal event. She walked the distance carrying a sign honoring her father, Stan Kirk, who died in the 15th Street Walmart when it was hit.

"It's very much a part of my healing process," Jody Kirk said. "Seeing all these people out here today is so comforting and therapeutic for, I don't think just me personally, but as a community. We've all lost something whether it's a relative or a house; we've all lost a part of our community so I think it helps with the healing process for everyone. This is a beginning. Even from May 23, in Joplin we showed what coming together as a community was like, and we are, as a community, so strong and we'll continue to be strong. This is the beginning of a new future. Thank you so much for everyone coming out."

Myra Pickering, Duquesne, remembers the path the Unity Walk would take and what it looked like a year earlier.

"A year ago today, it was a path of total destruction," she said. "Today it's a path of everyone being together, working hard, showing the partners that we made that you can't keep us down. I'm here just to show that we can overcome anything if we work together. I think it's a good idea, this walk."

Laura Pyle, Carthage, had relatives who lived on the path she and her family planned to walk on May 22, 2012.

"We have a lot of friends and family that are in Joplin," Pyle said. "Joplin is part of where we grew up so we've just come out and helped a lot throughout the year so we're here to support and keep going. I think the walk is a good way to bring everyone back together and just have that day to all get together and walk through everything, see what's changed, see what's come back, what's new, what's different and get the perspective a year later on how much it's grown back and become one again.

"It is so different, the cleanup was quick, they're rebuilding quickly and amazingly and bigger and better and everybody just seems to continue to come back and change things ... and make things happen."

Ann Ingram, Carthage, said she may not live in Joplin, but everyone in the area was affected by what happened on May 22, 2011. That's why she decided to participate in the walk.

"I was in Joplin with my family in Academy less than an hour before the tornado," Ingram said. "So its one of those things where there's not a whole lot in Carthage to do on a Sunday, it's a gorgeous weekend, you want to get out and do something and you're probably going to get out and go to Joplin. This is a chance for us to show our support for them. If anything ever happened in Carthage, I know it would be the same way, Joplin would come out and show their support for us."

Joplin City Manager Mark Rohr walked with residents from Walmart to Cunningham Park. Rohr said the anniversary brought out many different emotions in him and everyone participating in the event.

"It's a day to walk together, it's a day to be unified," Rohr said. "We'll see what comes after this, but today we're all coming together and we're all sharing some experiences together. The emotions have to do with the attitude with which we've approached our recovery process. Undoubtedly it was a horrible thing and a lot of things were lost, a lot of lives were lost. There's two ways to approach it, to sit and worry about what happened to you or to work on improving things and that's what we chose to do."

Rohr said Joplin's reconstruction and can-do spirit is part of the attitude shown by people throughout the area.

"I think not only Joplin is unique, but the whole area is unique and Carthage is part of the area," Rohr said. "I think we've demonstrated a toughness and resiliency that is the nature of the area and Carthage has been an important part of helping recover, we appreciate their efforts and their contributions and we hope to be there, God forbid, if anything ever happened to Carthage. If they need our help, we're going to pay it forward. We've already done that in certain situations where other people have experienced tornadoes here recently and we're prepared to share our knowledge and our efforts to help other people if they ever find themselves in a similar situation."

STEEPLE RAISING AND GROUND BREAKING

A little more than 2.5 miles into the walk, residents paused to mark two major reconstruction efforts which reached milestones on the first anniversary of the tornado.

The Joplin School District marked the day with groundbreakings at several schools, including Joplin High School, during the Unity Walk.

Across Indiana Avenue from the old Joplin High School site, the Church of Jesus Christ of Latter Day Saints (LDS) raised a big white steeple on its Joplin Stake office, which replaces the one destroyed in the tornado.

The steeple-raising ceremony at the LDS Church featured a talk by Lee Allphin, one of nine people who were in the church and rode out its destruction in a women's bathroom.

Next to him stood Ruby McBryde, who was 8 and the youngest person in the building at the time of the storm.

"Ruby is a very special young lady," Allphin said. "A lot of our children in our area suffered this tragedy, but as the savior said, 'Suffer the little children that they should come unto me, forbid them not for such is the Kingdom of Heaven.' I believe we can learn a lot from the youth and the young people who have suffered and had experiences here. But this is not a time of sorrow but a time of rejoicing and rebuilding. There were eight of us who crowded into a small women's restroom here in the former building. The building went down around us. Debris was flying everywhere. Smells and sounds, many of you experienced that the same as we did. There were hundreds of stories just like ours, but we felt protecting hands guarding us."

LDS Stake President Creed Jones, who lost his home in the tornado, also spoke at the steeple raising. He said he hoped the reconstruction of the LDS church would serve as beacon to other churches struggling to rebuild.

"We recognize that there were 27 or 28 churches that were destroyed," Jones said. "I'm told that there were about 48 places of worship that were affected one way or another through the tornado so this is just symbolic of one for many here."

He talked about how the Constitution protects the right to practice one's religion, and then he described the history of the LDS Church on Indiana Avenue.

"This property was all owned by Kelsey Norman," Jones said. "Behind you there were no houses, it was prairie areas, chat piles. This block from 22nd to 20th, Indiana to Wisconsin, there were a couple of shanties on here and some open mine shafts, and Kelsey Norman, after the school was being built, said he wanted to have something positive across the street from the school. He said he wanted a light on a hill to be a positive influence to the school. So he made this property available to our church. He had a lot of respect for our church and maybe the fact that it was full of chat piles and mine shafts made him make such a good deal on it, I don't know. We acquired the property and then we filled in all those shafts and later we sold different portions of this lot to Harmony Baptist Church and Peace Lutheran Church and Burt Realty and so forth.

"Finally, a church was built and dedicated here in 1961. We're pleased that we can rebuild here and that we have the significance of this church and this event representing all the churches here."

He also talked about the significance of the steeple as workers used a crane to place the spire on top of the building.

"Steeples are pretty common on religious buildings," Jones said. "You see them on cathedrals, you see them on a lot of churches, they're wider at the bottom and they go to a point. And the purpose and the symbolism of that is to draw your attention upward to direct your eyes toward Heaven. It reminds us that we are all children of God and we are all dependent on the Lord for his tender mercies that he gives us. To us, in our church, it also reminds us of the living Christ who ascended from the tomb, resurrected Christ and ascended into heaven."

Rick Nugent, another who survived the tornado and attended the steeple raising one year later, said the event was "certainly bringing back memories that have been there all along."

"It's a great moment to think that I can be here with my friends and I'm still here, alive and we were spared that night," Nugent said. "It's a great moment to see Joplin the way it's been rebuilt and how it's been rebuilding and all the people that have stepped up to make that happen.

"It's pretty awesome to have all these people here. It's great to feel all that support. It's been inspiring to see how people have stepped up and all the volunteers that came in and everybody helped each other."

WALK ENDS AT A PARK AND A SYMBOL

The massive river of people left the high school grounds and headed west on 24th Street and across Main Street to the grounds of the old Irving Elementary School.

There, organizers set up a fair of sorts, with food and games for the kids. All along the route, bottled water was available for free and handed out by volunteers.

The walk then moved south to 26th Street and approached its end at two symbols of the tornado — the ruined St. John's Regional Medical Center building and Cunningham Park.

Crews have been tearing down the nine-story St. John's building since January, a long and painstaking process made necessary because of the mine shafts that lace the ground under this part of Joplin.

The shell is still recognizable and was used as a background by media and residents for photos and video on May 22, 2012, just as it was in the days after May 22, 2011.

Joplin's oldest park, Cunningham Park, was also destroyed in the tornado. The iconic bandstand in the middle of the park was erased, the pool destroyed and hundreds of old trees, some dating back to 1898 when it was known as Cunningham's Grove, were blown down.

Thomas W. Cunningham, Joplin's mayor in 1897, gave the grove to the city to be used as a park. Since the tornado, it has become a gathering place for events such as the 10th anniversary of the 9/11 attacks on America and the six-month anniversary of the tornado on Nov. 22, 2011.

It would serve that role again on May 22, 2012, as thousands gathered in lawn chairs and on the grass for the unveiling of a brass monument to the 161 people who died in the tornado.

Duquesne Mayor Denny White was at Cunningham Park to greet the throng that had grown from that modest gathering a few hours before, four and a half miles away at the Duquesne roundabout.

"It couldn't be any better than this," White said. "If you expect better than this, your expectations are too high. Just look out ahead of you, there's still a sea of people approaching and there's been a sea going the other way already. It's been well worth it to be part of this, it really has. I haven't seen a sad face out here today, and that's a testimony to the people of this area. These people are tough; they've gotten right back in and gotten back with their lives and everything. We couldn't ask for more than what we had today."

Jeff Piotrowski is a storm chaser from Oklahoma who followed the storm into Joplin with video camera in hand. He has returned to Joplin many times since the storm and has produced a video of his experience.

He stood on 26th Street watching the crowd file by and remembered.

"Twelve months later and you think of the biggest tornado in U.S. history that took a heavy toll in Joplin," Piotrowski said. "Now we're here ... and you think about all the rebuilding. Here's a whole community, 6,000-plus buildings, and all the people that live here, people from around the country are here in Joplin, just as I am, and it's a celebration of moving forward. Twelve months of unbelievable things these people have been faced with. Here today we had the two school dedications, the high school dedication, we had the church steeple raising, and we had businesses opening up and just look at Cunningham Park. Look at the people. We see 8,000 or 9,000 people here it's unbelievable. It's just a great moment in history that I don't think will ever repeat itself, ever."

PEOPLE GATHER

Thousands of people gathered on the lawn at Cunningham Park at around 5:15 p.m. for the final ceremony of the anniversary day.

The program included speeches, people placing items in a time capsule and the unveiling of the brass plaque featuring the names of the 161 people who died.

Mark Norton, father of Will Norton, the student who graduated from Joplin High School on May 22, 2011, then was killed minutes later while on his way home with his father, placed one container of items into the time capsule, set in the base under the plaque honoring the tornado victims.

Mark Norton suffered serious injuries when the vehicle he and his son were riding in was caught up in the tornado on Schifferdecker Road and destroyed.

"Physically, I'm pretty much healed up," Mark Norton said. "I was much luckier than so many people that got hurt and I didn't have internal injuries like so many people did. Mine was all structural, but its nothing compared to the emotional things people suffered. I'm doing fine."

Mark Norton said he was deeply moved by the care shown by the community to him and his family after the storm and by the turnout for the anniversary ceremony.

"I think it's an accomplishment to get through this first year," Mark Norton said. "Now we can see so many good things that have happened and in the midst of the tragedy. It's a really warm feeling to see all these people here with all the love and kindness and support shown by the vol-

Mark Norton, father of Will Norton, the 2011 Joplin High School graduate who died in the tornado minutes after graduating, carries an item relating to Will Norton to the time capsule set up in the monument in Cunningham Park that features the names of the 161 people who died in the tornado.
PHOTO BY JOHN HACKER

unteers. It's touching to us to see what's happened to this community."

Norton said faith was helping his family cope with its tragic loss as he healed physically from the terrible wounds he suffered.

"They say you take one day at a time, but sometimes I think you take one hour at a time or one minute at a time," he said. "You have difficult days, but you just get through. We know we'll see our son again someday and so now you just go through life and look to that time. We have strong faith and we know he's in a better place and we still have a son, he's just not here with us today, physically."

Brian Mora also survived the Joplin tornado and attended the May 22, 2012, service.

"I was downstairs in my office and I started hearing the sirens going off," Mora said. "I started hearing the winds getting louder and louder. My mother got into the downstairs laundry room and I got into the down-stairs hot water closet. After the horror was done, my mother and I went outside and we saw the devastation — houses all over the place, windows broken out, some houses were completely leveled, there were cars flipped like pancakes."

Mora and his mother lost their home and both their cars, but they came out of it with an introspective outlook on life.

"We have to rebuild in order to really move on with our lives," Mora said. "We really do need, at some point, to start rebuilding ourselves and renewing ourselves and making efforts to think about what we've done in our lives. If there are things we haven't done or we would like to do, it's a good idea to get out and do them. There are a lot of wonderful things and we have to learn to get out and appreciate life. I've spoken with a cowboy church pastor in Texas about some of the problems affecting us and there are a lot of things you need to get out and do."

As he did one week after the tornado and six months after the torna-do, City Manager Mark Rohr spoke about the people who died in the tor-nado and how they will be remembered in Cunningham Park.

"We lost 162 fellow citizens as a result of the devastating storm that struck Joplin Missouri at 5:41 p.m. on May 22, 2011," Rohr said. "Although no longer here in body, they surround us and envelop us in spirit. Their names will be forever commemorated on the plaque that we dedicate here today. Their earthly presence will be reflected in the 161 trees planted in Cunningham Park and their spirits infuse and permeate our daily lives and our efforts to rebuild our city."

Rohr spoke again about the "Miracle of the Human Spirit," a phrase he used to describe what was happening in Joplin in the wake of the tornado.

"We gather amongst the 130,000 registered volunteers that have helped us clear away the debris from the storm and have helped us in the process of rebuilding our community," Rohr said. "Mere thanks are not enough but please know you are part of the miracle of the human spirit and a very special movement that has occurred here now, and you will forever be an important part of the city of Joplin."

The keynote speaker at the anniversary event was Hal Donaldson, co-founder and president of the Springfield-based Convoy of Hope, a group that has played a big role in helping victims since the day after the storm.

Convoy of Hope has committed to building a number of homes and, in fact, dedicated the first of these completed homes on May 22, 2012.

"Twelve months ago, we began a journey from uncertainty to hope," Donaldson told the crowd. "But as you know we have not traveled this road alone. People from across the country have joined with us by giving of their time and their resources and offering their prayers. I know tonight on this one-year anniversary, I speak for thousands and thousands of Americans when I say, tonight we stand together with you as one, proud to call this our adopted home."

He talked about how Joplin and Duquesne had shown the nation three principles for overcoming disaster and paving the way for healing and restoration:

• Finding solutions is more important than fixing blame.

• Focusing attention on a common vision works better than "being enslaved by division."

• Either find the courage to persevere or wallow in pity.

"The future of Joplin, Missouri will be built upon your brave shoulders and rest assured the same faith and character and values that have carried you through this crisis will be there to help you navigate the challenges of tomorrow," Donaldson said. "I'll close with this. There's no denying this has been a long and arduous journey but my friends, through it all, we are stronger, we are united and we are determined that this city will soon be better than ever. God Bless You."

4. I'M PROUD OF JOPLIN

By Mark Rohr

City Manager Mark Rohr made the following speech at the Day of Unity in Cunningham Park May 22, 2012

There's not too many things I'm sure of in an uncertain world, but what I am sure of is that I'm very proud of the city of Joplin. You should be proud of yourselves. Welcome everyone, we thank you for joining us here today on this very important moment in Joplin's history. We gather here today to look back on what happened on this fateful day in 2011 and we gather to reflect on the journey we have traveled since that time.

We lost 161 fellow citizens as a result of the devastating storm that struck Joplin, Missouri, at 5:41 p.m. on May 22, 2011. Although no longer here in body, they surround us and envelop us in spirit. Their names will be forever commemorated on the plaque that we dedicate here today. Their earthly presence will be reflected in the 161 trees planted in Cunningham Park and their spirits infuse and permeate our daily lives and our efforts to rebuild our city.

We gather amongst the 130,000 registered volunteers that have helped us clear away the debris from the storm and have helped us in the process of rebuilding our city. Mere thanks are not enough, but please know you are part of the miracle of the human spirit and a very special movement that has occurred here now, and you will forever be an important part of the city of Joplin.

One of the things we'd like to do, as a city, to acknowledge the effort that the volunteers brought forward in demonstrating the miracle of the human spirit, is a sculpture that will be located in the middle of the four concentric circles in the volunteer memorial to our right.

We've started a fundraising drive and we are selling these t-shirts that the memorial committee here today has on, and city council up in the tent on the hill there (has on), with the proceeds going to the memorial sculpture in acknowledgement of the efforts of the volunteers.

We gather today to not only look back, but also cast an eye to the future, for out of bad good things can happen, and Joplin will be better and stronger than it was when our task is complete. At this point in time, the one-year anniversary of the storm, I'm pleased to announce that 67 percent of the 7,500 homes impacted by the storm are already under permit or have been rebuilt or repaired, and are currently being occupied — more than two-thirds of the homes impacted by the storm.

I'm told, based on the analysis that the Chamber of Commerce has done for us, that some 85 percent of the 553 businesses impacted by the storm are already under operations or are in the process of being rebuilt, and five percent of that number, 553, are brand new businesses that have come to the city of Joplin after the storm.

Now I speak of the importance of one. The obvious reference is the duration of time since the storm hit. But if you look closer at the design of the one on the shirts that the memorial committee and city council are wearing here this evening, you can see the one is comprised of many individuals who come together to form the number. It is symbolic of the unity of purpose and effort that has made Joplin the standard of excellence in disaster response in our country, and is a reminder of the entire city's effort necessary to complete the rebuilding of our town.

5. GOD WAS WITH ME

By Randy Turner

The smile never vanished from Sarah Kessler's face as she listened to the names of one student after another being called onstage to receive their diplomas.

It takes a while to go through 431 names. Fortunately for Sarah, her name was closer to the beginning of the alphabet so she would have to stand in line for much less time than some of her classmates.

It had been an exciting evening for the tall, slender ("I'm a beanpole," she says) senior. About an hour and a half earlier she had been in a room with the President of the United States. It was not her voice that said, "Oh, my God, the leader of the free world." That was a classmate, but she could understand the awe.

The Joplin High School Class of 2012 listened to seemingly endless speeches- from High School Principal Kerry Sachetta, Superintendent C. J. Huff, Gov. Jay Nixon, and yes, from President Barack Obama "the leader of the free world," in a ceremony that started a few minutes late.

All of the speakers had praised Sarah and her classmates. "You are an

PHOTO COURTESY THE WHITE HOUSE

inspiration," the president had said, but somehow Sarah did not feel like an inspiration. As she waited, she thought back over the past year, the path that led her from the most horrifying moments of her life, some spent in this same building, the Leggett & Platt Center on the Missouri Southern State University campus, to where she was today, a few moments from receiving her diploma — her ticket into adulthood.

It still brought a shudder to her every time she thought about the events of May 22, 2011.

That weekend had been a big one for the Kessler family. A day earlier, the wedding of Sarah's older sister, Kate, had taken place. Sarah and her brother, Will, had provided music for the occasion — Sarah on her beloved violin, Will on guitar.

"My entire family was in town," Sarah recalled. The family stayed for another big event the next day, Will Kessler's graduation with the Joplin High School Class of 2011.

The family watched with pride as Will received his diploma, had pictures taken afterward, and then Will left. "He had a party he was going to, so he left before the rest of us," Sarah said. It was shortly after Will left that the tornado siren sounded.

As the rest of the Kessler family was about to leave, a security guard stopped them. "He told us we had to go to the basement. We didn't have a choice. We were all wanting to leave."

The guard escorted the family to the locker room area with five or six other families to wait out the storm. "We were down there for a quite a while," Sarah said. It was there that they received word that Home Depot had been hit. "That's when we started to get nervous about my brother because we live a block from the high school. One of the easiest ways to get from the college to my house was down 20th."

Scaring the Kesslers even more was their inability to contact Will. There was no phone coverage in the locker room. "That was the scariest 30 minutes in my life, not knowing where my brother was, or even if he was still alive."

Finally, they were able to contact Will. He had been driving through the heart of the storm. "He said he prayed the whole time he was in the car. He just got a new car and he is a good driver. Thank God for both of those things. He said was dodging flying cars, flying trees," Sarah lowered her voice, "flying people."

Will Kessler ended up at a church at 26th and Connecticut.

Now that they knew Will was all right, the family piled into two cars to head toward their home, which they now knew had been in the path of the tornado.

"We went down Range Line, but that wasn't going to happen. It was mass chaos everywhere, so we drove down side streets. It was terrifying; the closer we got to home, the worse the destruction. We wondered if home was going to be there."

As what would normally be a 15-minute trip had already taken more than a half hour, Sarah's dad received a call from Will.

"Where are you?" her father asked.

"Home."

"Do we have a home left?"

"Sort of."

Still seven blocks from home, Sarah's dad stopped the car, jumped out and began walking. Sarah's cousin took the wheel. After what seemed an eternity, Sarah was close enough to see her house.

Joplin High School graduate Sarah Kessler greets Missouri Gov. Jay Nixon and Joplin Superintendent C.J. Huff at the May 21, 2012, graduation ceremony.
PHOTO BY MIKE GULLETT

"I will never be able to forget that. We were on Indiana and I can remember driving up to 20th Street. I could see clear to the hospital. There was nothing there. I saw the school, then I looked slightly to the left. Our house was built a little better than the ones around us. It was the least damaged. The lower level was still standing. You could see a part of the upper story where my brother's room was."

The first words she said when she saw what was left of her home will be forever burned into her memory. "I remember looking at it, crying, and saying to my cousin, 'That's my house. That's my house.' All I could think was it was gone."

At that point, Sarah got out of the car, stepping over downed power lines, walking between cars. "I walked the path between the school and my house, the same as I had done every day since my freshman year."

She spotted Will and ran to him, hugging him. The two stood crying. They checked on neighbors to make sure they were all right and then went

Quinton Anderson (middle) who was nearly killed in the tornado that ravaged Joplin a year ago, blushes as President Barack Obama retells his story of recovery during commencement exercises Monday, May 21, 2012, for the graduating seniors at Joplin High School.

PHOTO BY RICH SUGG

into their house to see what had survived.

Much of the family's irreplaceable sentimental items, including photo albums and papers, were unharmed since they were under their parents' bed in the lower level. "We were able to salvage quite a bit," Sarah said. "We were fortunate."

And the one possession that Sarah cherished above all others — her violin — was also undamaged, as was her brother's guitar. "We had played my sister down the aisle at the wedding and when we got home, we left the instruments downstairs in the hallway." Had they taken the instruments upstairs where they were normally kept, they would have been swept away.

"That was about the only happy thing that happened that night. I love playing the violin. It has always been special to me."

For the next few weeks after the tornado, Sarah and her family stayed with Matt Proctor, president of Ozark Christian College, his wife, Katie, and their six children. Some of the time Sarah stayed with Rebecca McMillin, her best friend since kindergarten.

The Kessler family lost some of its animals, but "we found two of our rabbits and two of our cats." The family also had two dogs, Hank, a yellow lab, and Rusty, a golden retriever.

After a few days, Rebecca McMillin talked Sarah into going to the Humane Society to see if her dogs were there. "I didn't want to go. I was afraid I wouldn't find them." When they walked into the building with the dogs, "I saw Rusty right off the bat. I went up to the cage and he started barking." When he was released, he ran into Sarah. "Basically, he almost knocked me over. It was so good to see him."

Sarah was never able to find Hank.

A new home had to be found for Rusty after the Kesslers moved into an apartment, where they would have to stay for quite a while before their house could be rebuilt.

In the days following the tornado, many friends helped the Kessler family through its ordeal, including some they had never met before. "The people from our church (Central City Christian Church) were there for us. They helped us with our house and helped us move into our apartment."

The summer was a blur for Sarah. After a couple of weeks dealing with the aftermath of the worst night of her life, Sarah had an opportunity to get away from it all for a short time, as she traveled with Ozark Christian College's Highest Praise Choir, playing her violin. "It was nice to get away," she said. "It was such an encouraging environment."

When she returned, it was not to the home she had known for her whole life, but to a place she had never seen before. "I didn't quite have a room. My room was full of boxes, so I stayed on the couch in the living room for a while, but that was OK. It took us quite a while to get everything put in its place. It was mass chaos."

It was also not the home she knew. "We had just remodeled our house, spent the last two or three months before the tornado just totally redoing it. We had a beautiful new deck. I told everyone that next year, we would have to have all of our study parties at my house.

"Obviously, that didn't happen."

Sarah threw herself into volunteer work, helping Forest Park Baptist Church's Mission Joplin. Sarah's plans to spend her summer looking for colleges were tossed aside. That would have to wait.

Before she knew it, it was time for her senior year of high school to begin, not at the historic building she could walk to every morning, but in a box store at Northpark Mall. "I thought it would be poorly put together. When school actually started, it was so much better than I could have possibly imagined. It's not the best, obviously, because it is not a permanent facility, but it worked."

Sarah will never forget the first day of school at Northpark Mall. "It was all hugs and laughter and smiles. Even with people you barely knew, it was like, 'Oh, my goodness. I know you. You're alive.'"

That spirit continued throughout the school year. "The student body seemed to be closer. There is something that links us all together."

As the school year passed, there were many positive moments such as using another tornado survivor, her violin, to earn a I rating at state and being a part of the Prom Court. "That was something totally unexpected." Her fourth year as a member of Key Club, a service organization, was also a highlight. Sarah was lieutenant governor on the Missouri/Arkansas Board.

And while she didn't have a deck for study parties, she had something even better. "We have a roof at our apartment," she said. "The other night my dad and I had a candlelight dinner of beans and weenies on our roof."

Even though the Kessler family will soon move back into a house, Sarah confided, "I kind of like our little apartment. We all secretly kind of like it."

The experience of living through the tornado has helped strengthen Sarah Kessler's faith. "I'm a Christian. I'm very proud of that. One of the biggest lessons I have learned is to trust in Him no matter what. No matter what the situation is, He will take care of you."

God helped provide for her family, Sarah said, with everything from saving her brother Will the day of the tornado to helping them to cope with the aftermath of the storm.

"I went through, maybe not quite depression, but I wasn't my normal, bouncy self for a while," Sarah said. "When that happened, I needed to reconnect with Him. I learned that the more I make an effort in my relationship with God, the more joyful and hopeful I was, the more content I was."

By this time, Sarah had moved to near the front of the line. In a few moments, her name would be called and she would leave Joplin High School forever. The next stop for Sarah will be Missouri State University in Springfield where she will study music education.

"I've always wanted to be a teacher since I was little. I like helping other people learn and I have a lot of patience. Teaching comes naturally to me."

"Sarah Kessler."

A smile spread across her face and there was a spring in her walk as she stepped forward to receive her diploma. She turned to her family in the audience and smiled, then she took a brief moment to give thanks.

The path to graduation had not been an easy one for Sarah Kessler, but the moment had arrived and she knew this was never something she could have done alone.

"One big lesson I have learned this year is that even when you can't feel God's presence, that doesn't mean He's not there. God has promised us He will never leave us."

This time, Sarah felt His presence.

6. "ST. JOHN'S HAS BEEN HIT THAT'S ALL WE KNOW FOR SURE"

By Rebecca Williams
May 22, 2011, 7:26 p.m.
First Joplin Tornado Info post

We heard the KSN news anchors beg people to take cover, and then take cover themselves ... it was obvious Joplin was being hit by a tornado. Neosho and Joplin are close-knit communities and only 16 miles apart. How bad was it in Joplin? A friend that works at St. John's Hospital posted on Facebook it had been hit. How could we find accurate information about what was going on? We searched the internet and found virtually nothing of help. We don't remember for certain how it happened but within the hour at my coffee table using an iPhone, Joplin Tornado Info (JTI) was born. When the page was started we had no idea we had just signed on as a communication link for one of the worst natural disasters in U.S. history. By sunrise the morning of the 23rd, the breadth and scope of what

The remains of St. John's Regional Medical Center loom in the background of this uprooted tree where a child's toy fire truck came to rest after the May 22, 2011, tornado in Joplin.

PHOTO BY DAVID HOOVER

had happened became clear.

Across town, unbeknownst to us, an acquaintance Joel Clark had launched joplintornado.info website. None of us can remember exactly how we connected and merged JTI Facebook with joplintornado.info but it happened within the first 48 hours.

People ask what was different about the Joplin response and what led FEMA to applaud the rescue and recovery. I would say the can-do and help-your-neighbor attitude of the people of the area, the on the spot response of area faith-based organizations, the overwhelming support of the people of the region and the nation, and the presence of social media were deciding factors. This is the story of one social media outlet: Joplin Tornado Info.

The tornado hit at 5:41 p.m. At 7:36 p.m. Joplin Tornado Info Facebook page made its first post, went viral, began connecting dots between needs, resources, transportation, storage and dispersal and had become a trusted, timely news source.

The first days and even weeks after the tornado remain a blur, we have pulled out the worn legal pads that were JTI, (as it came to be called in those early days) and watched YouTube videos of the KSN tower cam footage and Red Cross volunteer Marie Colby's video among others and talked about how it was at JTI after the tornado, to remember. Almost a year has passed and there are still not words to express what happened during Joplin's early recovery. The dazed look on the faces of survivors is haunting.

We quickly reached over 49,000 fans. It all happened so fast and just as fast there were people helping us. Several groups and individuals such as the group of people that went to the computer lab at Crowder College and continuously posted critical information to JTI were unofficial admins of the page and vital to our efforts.

From the beginning we relied on the JTI community to post and repost for the good of the Joplin effort. Jennifer and Michelle both reached out from Alabama that first night to help. Volunteer admins signed on and others just took it upon themselves to help. JTI was a community page and early on people responded. Within hours we also had admins and or points of contact from all of the utility companies.

Relief organizations, churches and news sources began posting on our site as well. We made every effort to read and answer every post. JTI pages moved so fast at one time that it was necessary to repost vital information often or it became lost in the Facebook newsfeed. We monitored all available news sources and reposted to JTI.

We didn't sleep much during those first few weeks. We devoted every waking minute to JTI and coordinating efforts to connect the dots for the next two months. We were not alone in this; many people in our area put their lives and livelihoods on hold to do what they could for Joplin. There was such an overwhelming response to the need in Joplin and supplies came in so fast that FEMA, the Red Cross, and other major organizations quickly became overwhelmed. Through JTI, overflow storage was coordinated by Royce at the Galena High School Football Field. Royce became a vital part of JTI as we routed donations to area storage and dispersal locations. Solace, a youth-based church on the fringe of ground zero with an average age of 24 and attendance of less than that, went from evening service to relief center in the blink of an eye. People of the area did what they could, when they could. Back in the day, if your neighbor's barn was on fire you dropped what you were doing and ran to help your neighbor put the fire out. Joplin's barn was on fire and area people responded as they had for generations.

In the beginning, many of the community posts were people searching for missing loved ones, asking about shelter and water. One memorable post was the joy we had notifying people that huge water trucks were pulling in to Memorial Hall, to bring containers and get what you need. Water was off throughout Joplin and these trucks were such a blessing. JTI was not about fluff. Many survivors were literally hand to mouth. As we posted, food, water, bandage, clothing locations people texted our posts to survivors at ground zero who relied on cell phones texts for all outside communication. We accepted no donations, endorsed no specific church, charity or organization.

JTI, a community page with no affiliation or loyalty to any group or entity, made every effort to post timely, concise, accurate, unbiased information.

My daughter, Genevieve, and I came to realize that in this region none of us are more than a degree of separation from someone who lost their life in the tornado.

We all know someone who died personally or we know someone who knew someone.

When locals speak of the tornado now, we don't ask "were you affected?" We have come to realize that this was a regional tragedy; we were all affected.

Our mourning for those we lost will go on as long as we do. Out of our grief and necessity, the tornado aftermath has given birth to change, innovation, invention, entrepreneurship, volunteerism and philanthropy that many of us were unaware was within us. Folks in the area take the tornado and recovery in stride and continue to look for ways to help those in need. Joplin and area folks are reaching out today to our neighbors, Branson, and the several other communities hit by the Leap Day Storm, doing what we can and lending our experience. David Burton who has been an admin on JTI since nearly the beginning from University of Missouri-Extension had the foresight to set up three tornado info Facebook pages in advance. One of these pages was Branson Tornado Info which by sad coincidence was put into use in the 2012 Leap Day Storm and quickly went viral with over 16,000 fans in 48 hours. Genevieve, David, Joel and I are working to make the story of JTI, our operating guidelines and tips, available worldwide. Wouldn't it be great if every municipality and county had a major disaster social media preparedness plan?

As of this writing, the beginning of meteorological spring March, 1, 2012, JTI has had 87,112,786 post views from over 20 countries and languages. After peaking at just over 49,000 nine months after the tornado, JTI retains 47,754 of its original fans.

Joplin Tornado Info was created and managed by 23-year-old Genevieve Williams, Neosho, Mo., less than two hours after the May 22, 2011, tornado. JTI was honored as one of seven nominees for a 2011 Mashable Award in the Social Good Cause Campaign Category. Ms. Williams and her mother, Rebecca Williams, who wrote this story, have been the driving forces behind Joplin Tornado Info.

7. A LAZY AFTERNOON

BY BRENNAN STEBBINS

We were at the intersection of 26th and Main Street when the first sirens went off.

I was with two close friends, Isaac Duncan and Corey Waterman, and we were spending the afternoon driving around in my car and listening to the Kansas City Royals play the St. Louis Cardinals on the radio.

Earlier, knowing severe storms were forecast for the day, I had looked up to the sky to the west and saw the clouds steadily building. Now, with the ominous drone of the sirens in the background, I looked back to the west and saw the sky darkening.

It's been said many times by many people in the year since May 22, 2011, but upon hearing the tornado sirens, none of us worried because it's such a common occurrence in the Midwest in May. If anything, it excited us and made the drive more interesting.

We drove east on 26th Street, then turned north on Wisconsin past dozens of old ranch-style homes in the neighborhood near Joplin High School.

Looking out my window to the left, I noticed the red brick home at 2314 Wisconsin, with its large Pin Oak swaying in the breeze. The sky was still growing darker, and the front yard of the house was dark, except for the old gas lamp.

I turned into the parking lot at the high school, and I remember looking up at the tall pine trees at the back of the lot before we pulled out and continued our meandering. A few minutes later, we were driving on Connecticut, and then east on 24th Street into my old neighborhood. We drove past the Rosedale swimming pool, and then past the cream-colored house at 2302 S. Florida where I grew up.

Still listening to the baseball game, we were driving north on Texas when drops of rain began kissing the windshield, and we turned to a local news station to get an update on the weather. There were reports of large hail just west of town. We turned west on 12th Street and then headed north on Florida, crossing Seventh Street and then passing behind the Ozark Memorial Park Cemetery.

Coming up on Newman Road, we decided to go to the Sonic Drive-In near 20th Street to park the car under something sturdy. As we turned onto Newman and drove to Range Line Road, we heard radio reports of people panicking and fleeing the Joplin High School graduation just east of us at Missouri Southern.

The quickest route to Sonic was to turn right on Range Line and drive south for a few miles, and we would surely beat the hail. I felt like making things interesting, though, and we were curious to see what was going on at the college, so we pulled up to the red light at Newman and Range Line and waited to go straight instead of turning right.

It was the longest red light.

Soon we were all talking about how strange it was to be stopped at a red light for so long.

"I should have just turned right and we'd already be there by now," I said.

Finally, the light changed to green and we continued towards Missouri Southern, where we planned to turn south onto Duquesne Road, drive over to 20th Street and then on to the Sonic and our respite from the weather.

You could feel the tension in the air by now, and we knew the hail was probably just blocks away from us, but it gave us a rush. There was nothing going on at the college; everybody had already left, so we drove on Duquesne to the intersection of Seventh Street when we began hearing radio reports of a tornado on the ground at Seventh and Schifferdecker, and then reports of a tornado on the ground at Seventh and Range Line, just barely west of us.

I looked to my right and thought the radio reports must be wrong, so I turned onto Seventh Street and drove west, but didn't get far before my friends urged me to turn the car around.

We turned back onto Duquesne and drove south.

Driving the stretch of road from Seventh Street to 20th Street through Duquesne, the radio reports really started to get spooky. We all started to feel for the first time that this was a really serious storm. As we circled the roundabout at 20th and Duquesne, we saw a white Duquesne police car speeding out of the Fastrip parking lot and driving north.

"That guy was sure going somewhere fast," someone said.

Something inside me said this was as far as we were going to go, and I pulled into the lot and parked. We just sat there wondering what to do. Should we go inside the store and wait it out? Should we keep driving? Which direction should we be driving?

We decided to wait in the car and see what happened. The sky to the west was almost black by now, and it was raining heavily. There was another car parked under the roof above the gas pumps, which gave us comfort knowing we weren't the only ones waiting outside.

Within a minute, though, we saw the passengers jump out and sprint to the door of the gas station. Almost simultaneously, the three of us got out of the car and ran to the doors behind them, where Ruben Carter, the Fastrip clerk, let us inside.

I almost slipped and fell when I took a few steps onto the wet tile inside, and there were already about 20 people sitting on the floor in the back of the store, so we joined them.

It was then that Isaac pulled out his cell phone and began recording the video that would go viral within hours, not because of what is seen, but because of what is heard.

***

A small child asks her mother if she can go to the bathroom, but the mother says no because the bathroom is at the front of the store.

"Hey, where do you want me to put everybody?" Ruben asks someone on the phone. "At least probably 10 or 12."

A woman counts out loud.

"There's probably 18 or 19," she says.

Isaac tells a woman about the radio reports of a tornado on the ground at Seventh and Range Line.

"Yeah, but there's one coming this way on 20th," she says.

"Dude, s*** is getting real," Isaac says.

Then, more people come to the door, and Ruben walks across the tile to let them in.

It's almost pitch black in the store because the power has already gone out, and I hear a girl crying and her mother trying to soothe her while I look out the window at the roof above the gas pumps looking very weak as it rocks up and down in the wind.

"Is that the tornado, is that what that roar is?" someone asks.

Ruben tells everybody to get down and huddle on the ground.

"Jesus, Jesus, Jesus," a woman says. "Where's it at?"

Now we can all hear debris pelting the back of the building, and any thoughts that this storm might miss us are gone.

"Let's get inside that ... what is that room right there?" Corey asks, looking at the walk-in beer cooler.

Another woman asks Ruben if we can get in the beer cooler, but he doesn't have a chance to answer before the windows blow in and everybody knows we're getting in the beer cooler.

The entire group tries to get through the door to the cooler, and it's a mad dash at first before people calm down and wait their turn.

"Jesus, heavenly Father."

"Come on, go. Everybody move inside."

"God? God? GOD?"

"Jesus, Heavenly Father."

Kids are crying and people get separated, but everybody makes it inside and I know what Isaac means when he says s*** is getting real. There's just a single light bulb hanging from the ceiling and the walls are lined by shelves of cold beer.

Everybody gets on the floor and huddles together.

I can hear that tell-tale sound of a freight train, and it sounds like a dozen of them are running across Range Line. Slowly, they're moving this way.

"We're good, we're good, we're good," Isaac says, trying to comfort everybody. "I think we're going to do it."

With those words, everyone hears the growing roar outside, and we get hit.

"Heavenly Father. Jesus Jesus Jesus. Oh heavenly Father. Jesus Jesus Jesus."

"I love everyone," Isaac says. "I love everyone, man."

"Yeah, I love all you guys," Corey responds.

I feel my glasses get sucked off my face, and I start feeling around on the floor for them. Eventually I find them, still on my face.

"Jesus Jesus heavenly Father. Thank you Jesus."

"Are you guys all OK?"

"Yeah we're alright."

"Stay down. Stay down."

Isaac asks if everyone is OK below him.

"I'm trying not to lay on someone," he says.

"Somebody's on my back."

"Am I hurting anybody?"

Bottles begin breaking. The roof has collapsed and is resting on the shelves of beer, which are holding up the weight but beginning to buckle. Bottles are sliding off and shattering on the floor and people below.

"We need to call somebody," Corey says. "Who should I call?"

"Be careful, there's glass on your back," somebody else says.

The storm passes, and we can see daylight shining through holes in the walls. I'm sitting with my legs under one of the shelving units, which I notice is leaning toward me at nearly a 45 degree angle, and I look between some bottles of beer and see a tree a few feet away. I run my hands down my legs and arms to make sure nothing is missing.

***

The plan is to just stay put and wait for help. Nobody figures the tornado has hit as many areas as it has, and we all assume the fire department will arrive shortly to help us out.

People are calm at first, but it doesn't take long for everyone to get restless. There's no way to stand up and most can't extend their legs. People are getting cramps and sitting on broken glass.

I can see Isaac and we make eye contact briefly, but I can only hear Corey's voice from the back end of the cooler.

People begin wondering out loud whether we should look for a way out. A few people try to crawl to the holes where they see daylight, but they just end up crushing people underneath them.

I sit and look toward the shelves in front of me, wondering what has happened to my car on the other side. There's a strong smell of fuel in the air.

When we start smelling smoke from an electrical fire somewhere in the rubble, people start panicking. Corey, who sits on the west end of the building, is the first person to find a way out, and he relays the good news. It's probably a 10-foot climb up a piece of the metal wall of the cooler, which is at a steep angle, so people stack cases of beer at the bottom as a makeshift ladder.

I was sitting on the east end of the cooler, so I was one of the last people to climb out. I made it to the top of the wall and stood up to jump down to the ground behind the building, and I will never forget looking around and seeing absolute devastation for 360 degrees.

All of us stand there for a few moments, unsure of what to do or where to go. My car is sitting upright in the middle of the store, around where the cash register was just a few minutes earlier. The next day I drove it across the street on flat tires, but a forklift picked it up to move it again and it didn't run after that.

There was gasoline spewing out of the ground, and the strong scent of fuel was now joined by the sickly smells of plowed earth and old, musty lumber. There were no hugs and really no words said at all after everyone was out of the cooler. Gradually people just began walking west on 20th Street, toward a horizon with plumes of black smoke and piles of wet carnage.

I got a call from my father who said my grandpa in Duquesne was fine, but his barn had been destroyed and his house damaged. He hadn't yet reached my grandmother, who lived at 2314 Wisconsin, and I could hear in his voice he was nervous. Later, I would find her walking down her street with a cat carrier in one hand and my stepfather walking beside her.

But in the moments after we emerged from the gas station, there was really only one thing we could do.

So, we began walking west.

8. LOVE LED ME THROUGH

BY ANDREA THOMAS

Our journey through the aftermath of the storm appears to be ending. Three weeks ago, almost nine months from the day of the storm, my husband, Joe and I, moved home again. As I work to make our house feel like the home that it was before the storm, I reflect on the journey we traveled to get to this point. We faced trials and heartache along the way, but as I think back, I am overwhelmed with joy and gratitude. I feel like I've been handed an incredible gift and that I should make an acceptance speech thanking each person who supported us and our God who was faithful to us. The gift is not our home; although we are overjoyed to be back and in many ways our home symbolizes our great treasure. The real gift is a mysterious peace, an understanding that in the darkest of times, love still reigns.

The evidence of love's supremacy came to us almost immediately after the winds quieted down on that fatal evening of May 22. As Joe and I were searching for neighbors, and then, trying to decide how to leave our home, my grandparents — Hal and Darlene Roper — were trying to make their way through our ravaged city to get to us. The storm had destroyed towers and with so many trying to text or call loved ones in the minutes and hours after the storm, communication via phones was almost completely halted. My grandparents couldn't call us, and they didn't know how they would find us — injured or worse. They just knew they had to get to us, and they did. In the midst of chaos, my grandparents appeared on our driveway, and I felt an indescribable peace. I didn't know then that I would only have two more months with my grandmother on earth — she went to sleep one night in July following the celebration of my cousin's wedding and never woke, but my memory of her on that day is a treasure of a love. She and my grandfather came to find us that night because they loved us, and the evidence of their love gave me hope to start the journey that was still ahead.

The day following the storm Joe and I returned to our home to salvage what we could. The mess of our city, of our neighborhood, and of our home was almost too overwhelming for me. And in addition, we knew more storms were on their way; the knowledge of the storms added a miserable nervousness to my already overwhelmed emotional state, but as we arrived in our neighborhood, another example of love's supremacy brought me renewed peace. The son of one of our elderly neighbors had arrived after rescue teams had swept through the area, and he had stayed the night in his truck in front of what used to be his mother's home. He had stayed in the neighborhood to guard it from looters. He had chosen to put himself in the midst of the devastation out of love for his mother and for her neighbors.

When the skies grew too dark and a storm rolled in on May 23, we had to abandon our neighborhood for shelter. The task of trying to salvage items from our home was also abandoned. We returned to the task of salvaging on the morning of May 24. When we first arrived, I really didn't know what to do. The task of sorting through items covered in tornado debris and trying to decide what could be saved, and what could not, seemed impossible to me. But then love won again. Family, friends, and strangers — people who knew friends or friends of friends — showed up to help. My parents, Mark and Terry Taylor, along with my brothers, Grant and Logan, and one of their friends, came. Joe's parents, Tom and Tonna Thomas, along with his sister, Lisa, came. My mom's friend, Teri Byrd and her two grown children, Jennifer and Taylor, arrived. A friend, Will

Hedrick, I had taught with at East Middle School, a school that was hit by the tornado, came. My friend Kristen Swadley came. She brought a friend, Dusty Neill. Dusty brought her cousin. More family came. My uncle, Lindy Taylor, and cousin, Kellen arrived. These amazing people lovingly went through my debris-littered home and yard and made decisions about what could be salvaged, cut trees, or covered the badly damaged roof with more tarps. Later, two family friends, Sarah and Jane Honeywell, helped re-sort the items that were salvaged and packed them away for us. My uncle and aunt, Cindy and Dennis Rice, who drove from their home several hours away, helped with additional cleanup. Every action that was taken that day, and in the ones that followed, by those who came was a blessing to me. I wanted to wilt and weep; they gave me courage and took care of the mess.

In the weeks and months that followed the storm, we experienced highs and lows. Our neighbors on all sides settled with their insurance companies and made decisions not to return to the neighborhood, to start fresh in other places. When an insurance adjuster finally arrived on our property, two weeks after the storm, to walk through our home, we experienced one of the first of the biggest lows. We learned we would not be like our neighbors. We would need to stay, gut the remaining mess, and rebuild using the same foundation and floor plan. Although the homes on either side of us, not even ten feet from our home, were totaled, our insurance refused to consider our home totaled. We learned that apartments, or other structures that would have changed the culture of our neighborhood, might be built near us. I felt incredible grief. When the storm raged around us, we lost a sense of security. In the days after the storm, we also learned a neighbor had not survived the brutality of the tornado. We grieved knowing so many others had also experienced the loss of life. We lost our home — it was too damaged to live in — and many belongings. We lost a sense of normalcy as we were forced to develop new routines in response to what the storm had destroyed, and we were learning that we might lose the wonderful peaceful neighborhood we had known. I felt the hope I had held — that we would be like our neighbors and have the chance to start new — slip away. I felt like anything good I could have imagined — a fresh start, for example — slip away in those moments, but again, love reigned.

Love proved itself again and again elevating me from my place of despair. One of the first places I experienced the gift of love after I felt incredible despair was at Mission Joplin, a distribution center sponsored by my church, Forest Park, and started by my aunt, Misty Frost. Incredibly, Misty and a team had gathered a week before the storm to pray about starting a mission to help meet the needs of the Joplin community. She and the team prayed because they didn't know how to find and connect with people in need or where supplies would come from to meet the needs. They had no way of knowing that a storm was coming, and that the storm would create obvious needs, and an overwhelming response from around the country in the way of supplies. Misty also wouldn't know, the day she prayed with her team, that Mission Joplin would be a key to my personal healing. I began serving at Mission Joplin the week of the storm, when it was forced to move directly from an idea to a literal place. On the Wednesday following the storm, May 25, I helped unload a semi full of supplies and personally helped a woman load her car with food and other basic provisions. Following that week, and the next, and the news from our insurance that we would not be helped as our neighbors had been helped, I spent more time serving at Mission Joplin. I helped families fill their cars with items that met physical needs. I listened to stories that were similar or more heartbreaking than mine and tried to meet emotional needs. I welcomed volunteers from around the country. And as I saw others show love to my community, and as I showed love to my community, I began to feel hope again.

Hope also came in the way of tangible gifts that reminded me of God's love for me. He wanted me to know He could meet each of my needs and quiet all of my fears. Two incredible gifts came from people I will never be able to thank because I don't know who gave the gifts; I just know the gifts helped me. One of the gifts was a broom and a dustpan. Joe and I had been given a dustpan with a long handle attached to it as a wedding gift; it survived the storm, but while I was using it to clean up debris, the pan snapped off of the handle. It wasn't a huge loss, but I felt the loss was significant because it was in addition to every other loss I felt. While serving at Mission Joplin, though, I learned that someone had donated a similar dustpan. I hadn't felt I needed to take from Mission Joplin before as I had family members who were helping to meet our needs, but the dustpan was exactly what I needed, and it was given exactly when I needed it. I really felt that God was using a small, seemingly insignificant thing — a new

Trucks haul some of the more than three million cubic yards of debris.
PHOTO BY U. S. ARMY CORPS OF ENGINEERS

dustpan — to remind me that He was taking care of me. He could handle the little losses and the big ones too.

The other gift that reminded me of His love was given by a lady who stopped at my house one day as my mom and others were working to clear out more debris. I was feeling overwhelmed by the tasks of preparing my home for rebuilding and had stayed away for the day. The lady was a complete stranger, but she approached my mom and handed her five twenty-dollar bills. She said simply, "I feel led to give this to you." The lady didn't want thanks; her gift was simply another way God wanted to tell me He loved me, that I shouldn't worry about the insurance's view of my situation, that He would take care of me.

And I believe God did take care of us. He sent many people to show us love. Terry and Sandy Marrow, along with a crew from St. Louis, came and blessed us. Although they were strangers to us before the storm, we now consider them our champions and friends. Neil Kurtz, a college friend, traveled from California to Missouri to show his support for us and to serve at Mission Joplin. A group from FBC in Union, Mo., came and helped us with debris removal. Local friends set aside their schedules to show us love. Chad Doss, Lauren and Greg Walker, Tim and Lisa Hall, and James Richards were faithful to encourage us and support us. Even recently, a group of college students from St. Joseph, Mo., came to work on our yard giving us free labor and providing what insurance did not cover. There were many others, including our church and every member of our families, who gave in many ways — too many to recount. My grandmother, Jacque Taylor, hauled debris and offered other support; Joe's uncle, Terry Tracy, guided us through much of the rebuilding process, giving us good advice; my aunt and uncle, Tammy and Rick Brown, who also lost their home in the tornado, offered support and empathized with us. We're blessed by a large family and by each act; truly, again, too many to recount. I also know that God cared for us as He responded to each of my fears; for example, our neighborhood is returning to the peaceful place it once was, and we are meeting new neighbors, starting fresh with them.

Truly the last few months of my life have been filled with trial, loss, and uncertainty, but love proved stronger. Love held me together. Love led me through.

9. PANCAKES, PRAYERS AND PROGRESS

By Rick Nichols

I've enjoyed pancakes with maple syrup, pancakes with strawberries, and pancakes with chocolate chips, but I'm now convinced beyond a shadow of a doubt that pancakes go best with a heaping helping of heartfelt prayer.

A light rain had already begun to fall when the car carrying my half-starved sister and my mother and I pulled into the parking lot at the IHOP in Joplin, Mo., shortly after 5 p.m. Sunday, May 22. The gray clouds seemingly miles away to the west of us hinted at the possibility of heavier rain in the hours to follow, but the scene was hardly intimidating, much less frightening.

Having bid my father "farewell" only the day before during an emotional memorial service still fresh in our minds, my mother and I had driven to southwest Missouri from Olathe, Kan., to attend Joplin High School's mid-afternoon commencement exercises since my 18-year-old niece was one of the 455 seniors in the Class of 2011.

We had left fairly early in the morning, allowing time to attend church in Foster and eat lunch in Lamar before we were expected to show up at my sister's house.

Waiting at the restaurant for us were my 11-year-old niece and my 19-year-old niece and her husband. We were soon joined by the guest of honor, her boyfriend, and my brother-in-law, a first-term state representative. Gone and headed for home in his new car was my 24-year-old nephew, having delivered the 11-year-old into the care of her older sister at the entrance.

After carefully studying the menu, I had my sights set on the item dubbed "Rise 'N Shine," a promising platter consisting of hash browns, bacon, eggs, and toast. My mother was leaning toward the Senior Sampler, a tempting offering featuring one buttermilk pancake, an egg, bacon, sausage, ham, and hash browns.

Decked out in the same outfit I had worn 24 hours earlier, which included Dad's 1950ish reporter's hat, a white shirt accented by Dad's favorite string tie, and a gray sport coat with a red, white, and blue sticker that simply said, "I Prayed," I placed my order when the waitress turned her head to politely gaze at me. I added a cup of hot tea to complement the meal.

At one point some of us overheard a young man at a nearby table, iPhone in hand, tell his companions that a tornado had touched down along Schifferdecker Avenue, a busy north-south thoroughfare on the western edge of the city. We were a bit concerned, of course, but we didn't panic and immediately start looking for a place to hide — just in case. After all, the general consensus among the weather forecasters was that the storm would probably bypass the historic mining town now inhabited by 50,000 people.

Less than a minute later the lights began to flicker off and on, and right after that the electricity went out for good, leaving us sitting there wondering if we would be seeing any food anytime soon. Not to worry, the dining staff reassured us, the cooks had another source of power they could rely on and would be able to finish preparing our dinner in 45 minutes.

Hastily locating his own iPhone, my brother-in-law went straight to a link that let him view a radar image of current weather conditions in the general area. And it wasn't a pretty picture — an ominous looking super-cell was fast encroaching on virtually the entire city. He quickly rose from his seat and headed for the exit to get a closer look at the ever-darkening sky.

When he returned to the table he told the rest of us in a calm yet firm voice that we ought to seriously think about moving to a safer area within the building — just in case. A similar message was communicated to the other customers in the north half of the restaurant, among them an older couple from Nevada who were about to receive a rude "welcome" to Missouri. By then they probably wished they'd stayed home and settled for a "staycation" because the odds were already much better in Vegas.

While we hurriedly scurried off toward the kitchen directly behind the stainless steel grill where the cooks were still hard at work, my broth-er-in-law stepped back outside long enough to take another peek at the sky. What he saw sent chills up and down his spine. High in the black bil-lowing clouds due west of Range Line Road, debris was clearly visible. A huge twister was squarely taking aim on the restaurant and everything else anywhere near it. We were rapidly running out of time.

Displaying a level of leadership truly typical of a former Marine, my brother-in-law assumed a key role in making sure everyone quickly found a place to "hunker down" before the full force of Nature's fury was brought to bear on the building. The restaurant manager and other employees also responded to the challenge admirably, thus increasing the chances, slim as they appeared to be, that no one would be lost.

My mother and I selected a spot near the back of the kitchen. I helped her to the floor and then positioned myself on top of her. My married niece and her husband were next to us, and beyond them my sister, her husband, and the 11-year-old. She was on the bottom of the pile, shielded primarily by her mother, a highly regarded neurosurgeon at Freeman Hospital, and to a slightly lesser extent by her father. Huddled together around the corner in a walk-in freezer were the graduate, still attached like glue to her diploma, and her boyfriend.

Informally "introduced" by the crisp command to "Watch out!" the much-dreaded moment of truth was not long in arriving as a loud roar, punctuated by the sound of breaking glass, immediately bombarded our ears. I kept saying "Dear Jesus," but still very much in a state of shock over what was happening, my abbreviated prayer never really went any further.

I was spiritually paralyzed, so to speak, despite my faith.

"Answer me when I call to you, O my righteous God. Give me relief from my distress; be merciful to me and hear my prayer." – Psalms 4:1 (NIV)

But at least I wasn't alone in petitioning the Almighty for a miracle, as the prayers of others could definitely be heard above the maddening din created by the convergence of strange noises coming from all directions.

For a solid two to three minutes, our International House of Pancakes became the "international house of prayer" as terrified customers and helpless employees alike pleaded with God to save them from the "monster" that was right on top of us.

"Turn, O Lord, and deliver me; save me because of your unfailing love. No one remembers you when he is dead. Who praises you from the grave?" – Psalms 6:4, 5 (NIV)

Familiar with the Bible story of the prophet Elijah and how he was transported to Heaven by way of a whirlwind, I wasn't exactly looking forward to experiencing a similar fate, and I'm quite sure neither was anyone else. But as swiftly as the storm had engulfed us, threatening to completely obliterate the restaurant with winds in excess of 200 miles per hour, it departed. An eerie silence ensued. Then came the call we'd desperately hoped to hear: "All clear!"

As I got up off the floor, helped my mother to her feet, and then emerged from what remained of the restaurant, I knew good and well what time it was — it was time to rise 'n shine! I had work to do. Because if God had chosen to spare my life and the lives of the 30 or so other people who had just had a close encounter with the "great beyond," I figure He must've had a different set of plans for all of us.

"'For I know the plans I have for you,' declares the Lord, 'plans to prosper you and not to harm you, plans to give you hope and a future." – Jeremiah 29:11 (NIV)

Happy just to be alive and grateful for the mercy God had shown us, I was eager to return to the "mission field" and took advantage of my first opportunity by comforting the hostess amid the rubble in the foyer. She had been slightly injured in the storm and was still visibly shaken and teary-eyed when I stepped over to reach her so I could give her a hug as she was talking to her mother on a cell phone.

Yes, like the menu at my new favorite pancake place says, "Rise 'N Shine." And while "Prayer" is officially not an option at this time, even as a side order, I strongly recommend it either at your table in the form of grace or, worst case scenario, down on your knees back in the kitchen.

"Be joyful always; pray continually; give thanks in all circumstances, for this is God's will for you in Christ Jesus." – 1 Thessalonians 5:16-18 (NIV)

Exactly one week later I watched and listened intently as President Barack Obama and Governor Jay Nixon, joined on stage by a few "prayer warriors" from the local faith community, paid tribute to the dead — well over 100 and counting — during a nationally televised memorial ceremony at Missouri Southern State University. But while the two leaders talked at length about loss and grief in an attempt to bring some comfort to those left behind, they also spoke of the need to rebuild the city, to pick up the pieces and move forward, to emerge stronger and even better than before, having persevered in the face of great adversity. I knew I had to do something to help — I couldn't stay on the sidelines forever, simply content to remain in my "comfort zone" while hundreds of other people were hard at work inside the disaster zone.

Five days earlier my mother and I had avoided Joplin altogether as we finally made our way back to Olathe from Springdale, Ark., where we had gone to see a dying relative, a day later than originally planned. We had no authority to be anywhere near Missouri's version of "ground zero," and I had seen more than enough of the ugly mess the previous day when I had driven to a house just a few blocks east of Range Line to take my niece's boyfriend home. The Home Depot. Walmart. Academy Sports. All three big-box stores lay in ruin, virtually unrecognizable.

I decided to "get my feet wet" while I was back in Joplin the middle of June to visit my sister's family and other relatives. Asked if she was aware of a specific situation where I might be of some assistance, my sister told me about a couple with nine children whose house had sustained enough damage to render it temporarily uninhabitable. She knew the family through the Joplin Stingrays, a swim team made up of a number of local youngsters including my 11-year-old niece.

Built in the early 1900s, the two-story house, located on Pearl Avenue near the former South Middle School, was going to be remodeled extensively on the lower level. I spent several hours there on a Friday, my primary accomplishment being the removal of a fair amount of the floor in the general vicinity of the back door. When I wasn't working on that, I stayed busy by sweeping and re-sweeping the rest of the floor and picking up debris in the yard. "Lunch" was a tasty snack and a cool drink provided by a Salvation Army truck that had rolled into the neighborhood in search of potential "customers."

Regular obligations in the Kansas City area prevented me from returning to Joplin, at least to work, the rest of the summer and on into fall. But I was heartened by something the pastor at my church shared with the congregation one Sunday during the course of his sermon. His older brother, a heavy equipment operator and a minimally religious man, had been involved in the ongoing clean-up effort, he reported, and the entire experience had a profound effect on him. Talk about your "good news!"

Given the "green light" to be in Joplin much of the week encompassing Thanksgiving, I made arrangements to again help with the rebuilding of the city, this time through the district office of the United Methodist Church (I am a Presbyterian). My first assignment took me to a one-story house on Byers Avenue relatively close to the old middle school that had suffered moderate damage. There I was asked to apply the second and third coats of lacquer to the hardwood floors in the living room, two bedrooms, and a short hallway. The goal was to get the owner, a single lady employed by Walmart who was at the store on Range Line when the tornado hit, back in her home by Christmas.

A day and a half later I found myself at a one-story house under construction in the 2700 block of Sergeant Avenue. The house that had been there was underinsured, prompting the owners, a couple roughly my age, to seek assistance from the church in the form of "free labor" to reduce the overall cost of the project. I spent half a day on odd jobs at that location, returning the day after Thanksgiving to leave a baby redbud tree just inside the front door on my way out of town. Now in a container filled with water, the tree had been offered to me following the ceremony three nights earlier at Cunningham Park, where scores of people had gathered to mark the six-month anniversary of the tornado. I, in turn, had offered the tree to the couple, who had already planted a few trees in their large yard but certainly had room for another.

In December I made two more trips to Joplin to work on the house on Sergeant, teaming up with members of Woods Chapel United Methodist Church in Lee's Summit, Mo., each time. They eagerly tolerated my limited skills as a carpenter and painter, as once again the goal was to have the home ready for occupancy by Christmas. And just as they were grateful for my help, they were equally grateful for my aunt and uncle's church, Byers Avenue United Methodist Church, which continued to provide overnight accommodations for volunteers from outside the immediate area.

My first visit to Joplin in the new year brought me to a two-story house on Wall Avenue near the former middle school, where I eventually went after the debris in the yard, then to a small house on 19th Street that was to be demolished the next day, where I helped with the installation of a "door" for an adjacent structure that was to be spared, then to a lot on Virginia Avenue, where we salvaged wood from a house that had been demolished three weeks earlier, and finally to a one-story house under construction in the 2400 block of Missouri Avenue. It was the tail end of January and yet the weather couldn't have been more agreeable, all things considered. There was even talk of record-setting temperatures!

The house on Missouri had an unobstructed view of what had been the home of the Eagles, Joplin High School, and was approximately a block away from the former site of my cousin's house. Fortunately for her, she, her daughter, her granddaughter, and her boyfriend had a basement they could go to as the twister approached, but the lady who will be living in this house didn't. She rode out the storm in her utility room and some-how survived. But other neighbors weren't so lucky — the homemade markers on some of the street corners attest to that. I toiled alongside members of two Methodist churches, one in Texas (Austin) and the other in Michigan (Midland), the week of Jan. 30-Feb. 3, assembling floor joists for a small addition to the house that Monday and manufacturing roof trusses that Thursday and Friday. I was back at the house within the first week of March, extending to five the number of months in a row I had managed to log at least some time "in the trenches" as a volunteer (just one of many!). I wish I could've put in more hours during this "streak," and yet I also realize that every little bit of help adds up to progress in the long run.

Board by board, brick by brick, house by house, and block by block, Joplin is slowly beginning to rise 'n shine, to emerge from the shadows and step with confidence into the light of a brand new day. Much was lost a year ago that can't be replaced period or, best case scenario, easily, but among the "survivors" that fateful day, three stand out — faith, hope and love. It is in this spirit, then, that the work must continue if the community is to at least partially recover from Nature's cruel blow. God's hand must be present in the process, His mighty presence sought daily in prayer.

"*Unless the Lord builds the house, its builders labor in vain. Unless the Lord watches over the city, the watchmen stand guard in vain.*" – Psalm 127:1

10. THE HOUSE OF BRICKS

BY RANDY TURNER

It was an odd thought, one that should probably have never crossed my mind as I looked at the shell that had once been an apartment complex behind the 15th Street Walmart.

I thought about the third little pig, the one who had been clever and resourceful and managed to thwart the Big Bad Wolf's plans to have him over for dinner as the main course.

Like hundreds of sightseers I snapped photos of the tornado-damaged apartments, listening to the sounds of people marching back and forth between their cars and the apartments, carrying anything that was salvageable. Only two days earlier, these had been homes.

These were not apartments made of straw or twigs; these had been brick apartments. Perhaps they were built to withstand a big, bad wolf huffing and puffing, but never managing to blow their houses down.

Not even bricks could stand against the force of an EF5 tornado.

I wasn't at the complex as a sightseer. I was serving as a guide to Terry Greene Sterling, a *Daily Beast* reporter. Earlier in the day, we had gone

The apartments behind the 15th Street Walmart.
PHOTO BY RANDY TURNER

through Joplin's neighboring community of Duquesne, which had also been ripped apart by the storm.

To avoid the long wait as traffic crawled along Duquesne Road, we asked a property owner for permission to park her car, and then walked to Duquesne. When we reached the roundabout in the center of the community, the damage was obvious.

The roundabout had been placed at 20th and Duquesne just before East Middle School, where I teach eighth grade communication arts, opened in the Fall of 2009. The businesses on either side of the street were gone, as far as the eye could see, and so were the homes to the east of the roundabout.

We headed east and stopped at what was left on the first home on the right hand side of the road. Ms. Sterling and I talked with Jodie and Christina Neil, who told us their story, which was featured in Ms. Sterling's article:

Jodie Neal and his wife, Christina, had no basement in their home.

They survived the fierce wind by rolling up in a green blanket, planting themselves in the hallway, and covering their two children with their bodies. Their house broke up around them. Jodie downplayed the red welts and scabs on his back, caused by flying shards of debris. "Some people died," he said. "This is nothing."

As we talked, a loud "meow" sound came and the excited children ran to their cat who had been missing since Sunday evening.

The joy was tempered by a somber pronouncement from Christina Neal. "We have two cats." I never found out if the other cat had been found.

After talking with the Neals, Ms. Sterling and I continued to East Middle School. We could not get into the building, but we were able to walk up to it. Had we been there a day earlier, we could have looked in the windows and seen the rooms. By this time on Tuesday morning, the windows were boarded up. I would have to wait another week to see how my room fared.

The auditorium, the heart and soul of our building, was gone and the walls of the gymnasium were also missing. The only thing that could be seen in the gymnasium was the giant Joplin Eagle.

After the visit to East, Ms. Sterling and I walked back to her car and managed to work our way to the apartment complex.

I had an ulterior motive for wanting to be with Ms. Sterling in this area. Since the tornado, I had been doing my best, as other teachers in the Joplin School District had, to make sure that my students were all right.

I had seen a Facebook message that indicated one of my students, a tall, gangly redheaded boy, had not been seen. As Ms. Sterling and I wound our way through the complex, I asked a number of people if they had seen him.

None of them even knew who he was.

Ms. Sterling and I came upon a woman and her father, who were removing belongings from a ground-level apartment. I asked about my student and the father also had no idea of who he was, but he had another tidbit of information that eased my mind. He said the apartment manager had said everyone was accounted for. Even as I breathed a sigh of relief, out of nowhere, he said, "But my son died."

And for the next several minutes, Ms. Sterling and I heard Terry Lucas and his daughter, Terri Bass, tell the story of Chris Lucas, who had been the manager of the Pizza Hut on Range Line.

Ms. Sterling wrote about the encounter in the *Daily Beast*:

But we did meet Terri Bass, the sister of Chris Lucas, a 27-year-old former Navy submariner and father of four who lived in this same complex and worked as manager of a nearby Pizza Hut.

When the storm hit, Lucas herded his employees into a sturdy cooler. Then he and another manager huddled into a more flimsy cooler, Bass told us.

Lucas was sucked into the storm. Rescue workers recovered his body several hundred yards from the cooler.

He died a hero, his sister said, risking his life for others. "He was a really good brother," Bass said.

What was not included in the story — Chris Lucas was the father of two small children with another on the way.

I watched Terry Lucas' anguished face as his daughter told Chris' story to Ms. Sterling and me. That haunted look, even more than the shell of the brick apartment complex, brought home the true devastation of the tornado.

11. A TALE OF SURVIVAL

BY ANDREA QUEEN

On May 22, 2011, our morning started out like any other. We woke up and went to church at Forest Park Baptist Church, with Pastor John Swadley. His message that morning was over Romans 5:6-8 and his message was "It's Not Fair" in reference to what happens in our lives may be unfair, but the mere fact that God had to send His own Son to Earth to die for our sins was unfair.

We went on about our day as usual and had settled in to watch the St. Louis Cardinals play the Kansas City Royals. In the bottom of the eighth inning, we began to hear rumblings about how bad the weather was supposed to get, so we grabbed a couple of backpacks and got prepared to stand outside and watch the weather coming in. About that time, my grandmother came by the house to bring me a beautiful red rose to plant. We stood outside talking about the clouds and how the weather was supposed to be getting more severe. I finally convinced her to go home, but she told me that she needed to run by Walmart first and then she was going straight home. I wish she had just gone home instead.

At about 5:30, the Cards and the Royals had just entered the 10th inning, tied at 7. Then, about 10 minutes later, the game ended with the Cards on top 8-7. Five minutes after that, we got the call that we needed to take shelter there was a possible tornado on the ground. I contacted both of my parents and begged them to take cover just in case. Five minutes after that, we got confirmation that a tornado was on the ground at St. John's and that we needed to take cover. The boys and I grabbed our backpacks that we had ready and we snatched up four blankets to lay down underneath us under the house in the crawl space. Then, as we had just gotten under the house, my husband and I looked at each other and we both knew what was coming. The four of us held hands and said a prayer of protection and faith. Something told me in the pit of my stomach that this was it — it was really happening, and we were right in the path of the monster.

Within two minutes, the wind ceased to blow, the air became green and we heard something that can only be described as evil come in our direction. After a couple of minutes, I saw the hatch get thrown off of the crawl space entry and the wind whip something that resembled a tree limb across the opening. That was the last thing I saw before I climbed on top of our youngest son Jackson, who is six. My husband, Franklin II, crawled on top of our oldest son Franklin III, who is 12, and held on to him for dear life. As the tornado got closer, the noise was deafening. Dirt, debris, and driving rains that were thrown under the house where we were taking shelter were pelting all four of us. The pressure forced our ears to pop repeatedly and all I could do was pray. When it hit, there was no screaming, like you would imagine. We were all calm, silent and determined to survive. Our youngest son Jackson, hollered at me, "Mommy, you're squishing me!!!" I replied, "I know baby, I know ..." To that he, hollered louder, "No, Mommy! Squish me harder!" What else could I do but oblige him and do my best to hold him to the ground, and pray that it would be enough to keep him safe.

When the tornado hit, I could hear the shattering of glass, the sound of screeching metal and the sound of shear destruction. In what seemed like an eternity later, but was maybe only two to three minutes, the storm finally passed.

Then I smelled the natural gas.

The gas meter was located about five feet from the entrance to the

PHOTO BY MIGUEL OLAVE

crawl space, and had literally been ripped apart. We had to get out from underneath that house quickly. We knew that we had a lot of damage but weren't quite prepared for what we all saw when we crawled out. A huge tree that was maybe seven feet around, that had sat about 15 feet from the house was on its side and maybe two feet away from the edge of the foundation where we had to crawl out. There was siding, a bedroom door, and other debris crowding our escape hatch, other than just the tree. Franklin was able to finally maneuver things around and get out first and lifted Jackson out and off to his right and Baby Franklin crawled out right behind his Daddy. I was on my way to crawl out and my husband began screaming to get back under the house quickly. The wind picked up again, almost to an intensity that we had just experienced, golf ball sized hail began raining down and Jackson's feet left the ground. He threw Jackson back down under the house to me and we scooted back just in time for Franklin III and his Dad to get under before we got hit by either a downdraft of sorts or another small spin-off tornado.

The natural gas was now completely overwhelming. We decided that we just had to get out before we couldn't breathe due to the fumes, so we crawled out and were still getting pelted by hail, driving rain and strong winds. We climbed up and stumbled over what used to be our master bedroom and jumped off the foundation and began to look around. All we could see was devastation.

Our entire house had been completely swept off of the foundation leaving nothing but the subflooring we had hidden under.

All we could do was stand in the street with the boys surveying the damage around us. Not thinking that the entire neighborhood was struck, we decided to walk west to get out of the destruction. As we walked and walked, we realized that there was virtually nothing standing. We crawled over downed power lines, felled trees, our neighbors' belongings, pieces of siding and roofing and breathed in the streaming natural gas.

Then the ammonia odor hit.

The General Mills factory about a mile away lost an ammonia tank and we were directly in the direction of the wind. My husband and I both remained completely calm as we led our children out of the destruction left behind. We walked for about a mile and a half until we found refuge in a house that still had a garage standing. After about 20 minutes, we decided to travel north on Duquesne Road towards my mother's house.

We walked another mile and a half to my mother's house to come in out of the rain. In all, we walked about 3 1/4 miles to get out of the path of the tornado.

Then it occurred to me that my 78-year-old grandmother had been in Walmart when the tornado struck. She had left my house about 30 minutes before the tornado hit Joplin. We didn't hear word from her or anything about her until around 2:30 in the morning. A nurse from St. John's Mercy in Springfield, Mo., contacted me to let me know she was in terrible shape, but still breathing. She had been carried out of Walmart on a door and transported to Memorial Hall in the back of someone's pick-up truck. She had been sitting behind a cinder block wall, which used to comprise one of the bathroom walls of the store. When the tornado hit Walmart, the cinder block wall came tumbling down on top of her.

My grandmother, Delores Rowan, stopped counting the blocks that hit her head after the sixth one fell. She suffered numerous contusions, lacerations, bruises, and a concussion, which included a serious brain bleed. When she tried to cover her head with her hands, a block ripped her hand from the impact, causing her hand to tear from in between her middle and ring fingers to the middle of her hand. Miraculously, she stayed in the hospital only 5 days and came home to us. She is still recovering, but lives for her great-grandbabies (her words, not mine).

The next morning, on May 23, 2011, we left my mother's house at 6 in the morning and went back to our "pile." When we reached our house, it became apparent that we received a direct hit and our car and truck had been thrown through the house at a direction to which, had we been hiding in the bathroom, we would not have survived. All that was still standing of our house was a section of siding about two feet long by 10 inches high. Also, upon closer inspection of the foundation we were hiding under, we found that the subflooring had started to rip up from the foundation. We figure that had the EF5 lasted for another 20-30 seconds, we would have lost our cover and been completely exposed.

While we were looking around at the "pile" it also became apparent that we were missing several appliances, such as a refrigerator, that should have been easily recognizable. However, even though we couldn't find one of the computers, we did find a thumb drive, which was plugged into it. Nothing around us made any sense. There was no rhyme or reason as to what we could and could not find from our house. It is still hard to comprehend so many weeks later.

It was so disheartening to look at all the destruction around us. And I felt guilty for being alive at that moment, because I knew that several of my neighbors had perished. Many of our other neighbors had been seriously injured. I had shielded the boys from one of the scenes of some person's ultimate demise on our way out of the rubble.

And then it occurred to me that our story was referenced the day before, by our pastor. It was unfair. There was nothing fair about anything that happened between 5:41 and 6 p.m. on May 22, 2011. Only by the grace of God did we escape the grasp of the tornado that evening with only minor bumps, scratches, and bruises. Only by the grace of God, did we live to tell our tale of survival. And, only by the grace of God, did so many come to our rescue in the coming days, weeks and months.

12. GROUND ZERO

By Jeff Wells

Hot and humid. I couldn't relax. I may have slept four hours. I felt uneasiness in the Joplin air late on Saturday, May 21, 2011. When the morning came, I asked my wife what she would think if we headed back to our home near Dallas a day early. She said that sounded like a good idea and we made plans to leave midday on Sunday, May 22. I never thought that restless night would be the last I would spend in the house where I grew up.

My parents purchased 2201 S. Illinois Ave. in June 1981. They bought it from the original owners — the Coffey family. The full-brick home was one of the oldest in the neighborhood. It was built in the early 1960s by Walt Ruestman (who built all the homes on that block of Illinois). The house's exterior bricks were old nineteenth-century bricks that were salvaged from the infamous House of Lords saloon and brothel that stood on Main Street during Joplin's rowdy mining days.

My mother is someone who has spent almost all of her life caring for other people before herself. My father, aunt, and grandfather all suffered long-term health problems and are all deceased. My mother helped care for them in addition to being a single parent and a working mom. In fact, my mother never stopped working after she graduated from Carl Junction High School. She even worked full time as she pursued her degrees from Joplin Junior College and Missouri Southern. She retired in 2010 after more than twenty-five years working at the corporate office of TAMKO Building Products. True to her character, my mother spent the first year of her retirement working rather than enjoying the fruits of her labor. She improved her home on Illinois, helped my 87-year-old grandmother maintain her independence, and volunteered at the Spiva Art Center. She didn't go on any trips or indulge in retirement. She saved for a year and was planning to install central air conditioning during the summer — the old house never had it. Of course, if the house had cool air then we might have not considered leaving Joplin a day earlier than we intended.

My wife and I left Joplin about 1 p.m. The skies were a gorgeous blue as we drove through Oklahoma. About an hour before the storm struck Joplin, John Hacker called to warn us of the approaching storm (not knowing we'd already left). I called my mother and she said she wasn't concerned. She said she had clothes on the line. I suggested she might want to bring them inside. As my wife drove through southern Oklahoma, I pulled up the local Joplin police scanner traffic on my telephone. I heard a chilling call from a storm spotter that a dangerous tornado was on the ground near 20th and Central City Road. I called my mom, told her to call my grandma and tell her to get in the bathtub and for her to then do the same. "Jeffrey, the storm sirens aren't even going," she protested. Just as soon as she said the words I could hear the siren next to her house activate. "I've got to go," she said. "Bye."

It was 5:37 p.m.

My mother called my grandmother with the warning. She then locked the doors to her house and put on her shoes — her normal routine during storms. She heard the tornado as she walked down the hallway and realized she didn't have time to retrieve her purse. She closed the bathroom door as the lights went out and the windows exploded. My mother and grandmother usually just sat in their bathrooms during storms. Getting in their bathtubs probably saved their lives. My mother laid down in her bathtub, as if soaking in a bath, and clutched two bed pillows. She heard the front wall of the house collapse then a tile wall fell on her. The wall stayed intact — mostly — and covered two-thirds of the tub like a lid. My mother was trapped in this sarcophagus, but it protected her on almost every side from the flying glass and debris that injured and killed so many people.

A friend told me that the security cameras at Joplin High School show the storm was over my mother's neighborhood for six minutes. The National Weather Service estimated the winds there reached 210 mph. My mother's home, her prized possession, crumbled around her. She says she heard the bricks grinding together and clanging against the side of the bathtub that protected her. She said she felt two distinct waves of the storm. She experienced the eye phenomenon. After surveying the debris, we're confident the storm's first round of fury destroyed the house. A telephone pole across the street snapped and acted as a wrecking ball crashing into the front of the house. The bathtub protecting her was dangerously exposed as the second wave crumbled what was left of the house at the top of the hill. My mother, understandably, suffered a heart attack.

After the storm passed, my mother decided to stay there in the tub until she heard someone near. She didn't have a clue how widespread the devastation. Then she smelled gas. She knew she had to find a way out. She didn't have the strength to lift the wall above her. She twisted and contorted her body until her head was at the foot of the bathtub. There was a small hole and a shaft through the debris. She could see the blue sky above. She removed one of the yellow pillowcases and waved it as high as she could. Neighbor Pete Box heard her cries for help and pulled her up and out of the rubble.

I can't imagine what she thought when she stood there atop of the ruins of her house. I climbed up there days later and it was a sickening vantage point. I could see everything from St. John's to Range Line — the neighborhoods gone, the churches gone, the high school gone, my mother's home — all gone. Standing there, her chest pounding with pain, she had to have been one of the first to realize the extent of the devastation. She said she worried about her mother who lived alone exactly one mile almost due east. She felt helpless because she knew there was no way she could help her.

My mother knew she needed help. Mr. Box helped Joanne Schenk from her house and my mother and Ms. Schenk left to find help. A minister from Neosho, Barrett Anderson, drove past them at 22nd and

Indiana. He was trying to get to a friend's house. He knew that it would be impossible to reach his destination and decided to help the two women. It took more than an hour, but he finally got them to Freeman Hospital.

I continued to listen to the police scanner and KZRG on my phone as we crossed into Texas. I was already getting panicked calls from friends and family. I too felt helpless. My mother was finally able to reach me on Mr. Anderson's phone. She managed to say, "Jeffrey, I have chest pains and I'm going to the hospital. The house is gone," before the call dropped. I wouldn't hear from her for another six hours.

I went to a Walmart in Sherman, Texas, and started buying everything I thought people would possibly need. My wife and I gathered cartloads of food, water, and supplies. My in-laws, who live in Fort Worth, saw Mike Bettes report on the horrible scene near Cunningham Park on the Weather Channel, jumped in their car, and headed in our direction. They met us in Sherman and we loaded their vehicle. I knew my mom was hurt and headed to the hospital. I assumed, given everything that I was hearing about her neighborhood, that my grandma was dead.

Evan Young, a friend of mine from Webb City, and his family fought their way to my grandma's house. Her neighbors told them that they had dug in the remains of her house and didn't hear or see anything. They assumed she wasn't home. They almost abandoned the search when Doug Adams, her neighbor's son, heard her weak cry for help. They pulled her from her bathtub and, in another miracle, she had only a small scratch. Another good Samaritan took her to the hospital. My friend called me with the good news just before we left the Walmart to begin our trip back to Joplin. My mom was able to get through to us as we passed though Muskogee just after midnight. She was at Freeman and Grandma was with her.

My mother had sat for hours in the crowded lobby of Freeman Hospital waiting for a chest x-ray and wondered if her mother was alive or dead. Did the storm somehow spare her house? Was my grandmother sitting there physically safe, but worried about my mom. Was she trapped? There were thousands of people crowded into that building. My mom heard a woman cough. She told Ms. Schenk, "That sounds like my mother's cough." Unable to stand, my mother looked around and didn't see her. The woman coughed again. Ms. Schenk stood and said, "Barbara, it's your mother." She was sitting several rows away.

The reunion of my mother and grandmother was brief. My grandma was taken downstairs and examined. They put my mother in the emergency room with the more serious cases. We arrived at the hospital at 2 a.m., but weren't able to see them or even get confirmation that they were still there. Freeman was out of power and overwhelmed. We heard that the hospital staff and volunteers performed admirably in the hours immediately after the disaster, but by the time we arrived everyone was starting to wear down. Two hours passed and we had no information. A woman slept under a pile of blankets across the room. When she woke up and sat up, I saw it was Ms. Schenk. Her wounds were minor so the hospital didn't treat her. I was glad that I was able to use one of the first aid kits I bought to help my mother's neighbor of 30 years and one of her closest friends. Two hours later, someone wheeled my grandma into the lobby. "Is the family of Syble David here? Will someone claim her?" The man was going to place her on the bus to the shelter at MSSU. "I'll claim her," I cried. That was one of the happiest moments of my life.

The hospital staff finally confirmed that my mother was in the ER, but wouldn't let me go back there. I heard horror stories from families that discovered their loved ones had been evacuated to Tulsa, Springfield, or further away hours earlier and that they weren't notified until hours later. I couldn't sit and wait any longer. I went outside and started looking inside every window and down every corridor. I peered inside every ambulance. I saw people in the worst condition. It was like a war or horror movie. Men and women lie covered in blood with severed limbs, head wounds, and broken bones. Some people looked like they'd been in a blender filled with glass — they had been. I cringed about what my mother would look like when I found her.

Finally, after hours of persistence, the staff allowed me into the ER to see my mother. Just in time. They were preparing to load her on an ambulance. She was ashen, but looked physically OK. She was clearly in a lot of pain. I went back to the lobby and asked my wife and father-in-law to take care of my grandmother. The crew allowed me to ride in the front of the ambulance as they transported my mom to Mercy Hospital in Rogers, Ark. I knew my mother would be fine when I heard her joke with the emergency medical technician that she was going down to Arkansas "to call those Hogs." My parents used to attend Razorbacks' games years ago.

My mother was hospitalized until the Wednesday following the storm.

My grandmother stayed at my cousin's house while my wife and father-in-law tried to salvage what they could of my mother's possessions. They had a lot of help. A group of U.S. Marine Corps recruiters were among the first volunteers to assist — a thrill for my father-in-law who is a retired Marine officer. Then, in my father-in-law's words, "the cavalry arrived." TAMKO provided crews and trucks to help employees, retirees, and their families. The TAMKO team labored for days at my mother and grandmother's houses. Unfortunately, there wasn't much worth salvaging, but they sure tried.

My wife secured my mother and grandmother a room at the Days Inn. Because my mother was in the hospital for the first few days after the storm, we weren't in a position to find her and grandma an apartment, a rental house, or another temporary place to live until later that week. By the time we started looking, all of the rental units in Joplin were gone and the real estate market was becoming a feeding frenzy.

On Wednesday, the doctors told my mother to go home — where exactly was that she asked — and rest, but my mother, almost immediately upon returning to Joplin from the hospital, said she was going to rebuild on Illinois. She asked me to call Mike Landis, a homebuilder and friend, to schedule a meeting and get started. As we continued to try to salvage family photos and heirlooms, my mother and grandmother filed insurance paperwork and, following the advice of city officials, registered with FEMA.

Things seemed to be going as well as possible. We felt extremely blessed. The death toll continued to climb and it seemed an even bigger miracle that my mother, grandmother, and uncle, who lived down the street from my mother, all survived. Then the second disaster struck.

My grandmother was unable to get her blood pressure medicine for several days following the storm. About a week after the tornado, we had just concluded a meeting with an insurance adjuster when my grandma slumped over in the hotel room. My grandfather had suffered two strokes so we knew the signs. An ambulance arrived quickly and she was to the hospital in less than 15 minutes after the onset of symptoms.

My grandmother's condition forced my mother to temporarily postpone her plans for rebuilding on Illinois. She knew she had to find a place before my grandmother was discharged. We couldn't find an apartment and the housing market was crazy. My mother wanted to find a house near the hospital with no steps and suitable for someone in a wheelchair. She made a bid on one house, but was outbid by someone who paid significantly more than the asking price.

My grandmother was hospitalized for almost three weeks. In that time, Jennifer Reaves from Keller Williams worked miracles for us. In the midst of the craziest real estate market Joplin has ever seen, she helped us find them a house, make an offer, get an inspection, and close in less than a week. Amazing. My mother closed on her new home 30 years to the day after her and my father bought 2201 S. Illinois Ave. She told us at closing that when she retired that she never imagined she would ever buy another home.

Back on Illinois Avenue, Samaritan's Purse helped remove the debris from my mother's property. After the debris was removed, friends and a group from the First Presbyterian Church of Colorado Springs, Colo., toiled with me in the sun for hours cleaning and sorting bricks. We salvaged approximately 2,000 of the House of Lords bricks. A contractor told me that should be enough to build at least a partial façade across part of a new house. My mother hired a crew to demolish the foundation. More volunteers came and raked and bagged loose debris. Unfortunately, several times over the next several months, contractors hired by the city and utility crews would drive across the lot leaving ruts and trash or dig trenches and leave rocks and piles of dirt.

The intersection of 22nd and Illinois is no longer my mother's address. It's ground zero. It still amazes me that my mother and her immediate neighbors survived considering the intensity of the storm at that point and because many people died within a few hundred yards of her house. A photo of the neighborhood immediately after the storm is featured on the cover of the book *5:41: Stories from the Joplin Tornado*, co-written by my friend John Hacker. That intersection witnessed the worst of the storm's fury and, fittingly, provides an excellent view of Joplin's recovery. New churches, homes, and the new Joplin High School are being built nearby. I hope my mother is able to rebuild there soon.

Jeff Wells is the former editor of Joplin Tri-State Business Journal.

13. WILL THERE BE A CHRISTMAS TREE?

By Marty Oetting

Debris and rubble tell stories. They give clues to what used to be and reasons to ponder what might again be in the future. I had occasion to think long and hard about these things over the Thanksgiving holiday weekend when I made my first trip back to the Joplin area following the May 22, 2011, tornado. I may live four hours away in Columbia, but a big part of my soul was deeply disturbed by the disaster, and I felt the pain and struggle from afar. I have been in Joplin, in spirit. I sensed the pain, even if I didn't feel it physically like so many who were there.

I lived in Joplin in the 1980s, graduating from Parkwood High School in 1982 and worked at Red Baron Pizza on 20th Street. (It was only there a couple of years.) I also was familiar with St. James United Methodist Church on 20th Street as my father was a district superintendent for the Methodist churches in southwest Missouri. We lived on the corner of 28th and Illinois. More importantly, I drove up and down 20th Street every day for many years. It is an important part of my memories of growing up. Shopping at Dillon's; watching trains at the 20th Street crossing of the Kansas City Southern Railroad; watching little league games; filling up at the Sinclair at 20th and Range Line; and just driving up and down that road every day.

I have always had a fascination with tornadoes and severe weather. When skies would threaten, my friends and I would hop in the car and chase severe storms, hoping to get a glimpse of a funnel cloud. While a student at Missouri Southern, we even did a special series on the anniversary of the tornado that hit Joplin in the early 1970s for *The Chart* newspaper. We never saw a tornado while I lived in Joplin.

But that was not the case on May 22, 2011. I had been visiting my parents in nearby Carthage that very weekend, and brought them back to Columbia to celebrate my son's high school graduation. But this isn't about my story of the storm and how I survived it. I was two hours away when it hit, and believe me, many of your stories in Joplin are so compelling that I feel my heart race and my hair stand on end when I read your accounts of survival.

And so it was — Thanksgiving weekend 2011 I found myself in the parking lot of what was left of the shopping center on 20th and Rhode Island that used to house Red Baron Pizza. It was leveled by the center of the tornado, most of the debris hauled away long ago. I walked around and looked at the foundation and rubble. Soon I realized it told a story. I began to see things begging for further inspection. I found a large piece of the instrument panel from a car. I found a CD billfold that held several homemade compact discs. I found a windshield wiper. I found a woman's shoe. And not too far away, another woman's shoe.

But then I saw two things that really hit me. The first was a child's knitted glove. It was just lying on the pavement near the foundation. I wondered where the other glove was, and more importantly, where was the little girl who wore those gloves? I wanted to believe she was celebrating Thanksgiving with her family in a new location. But I also knew there was the possibility she and her family were not all still here.

The second thing I saw was a string of Christmas tree lights. They were knotted up in a tight, tangled wad. I wasn't sure if they were left that way from the last holiday celebration, or if they were tangled in the winds of the tornado. But I knew this — they would not be decorating a

Christmas tree this year. Where did they come from? How far did they fly in the wind? Would that family have a Christmas tree this year?

I will always remember the Joplin tornado, and how it destroyed the physical location of so much of my childhood. There was Cunningham Park, where I went swimming and played tennis. And Main Street, where I visited different restaurants while riding around with friends on Friday nights. I think of my high school, which was so sad to see in a pile of rubble and twisted beams. My old house survived but looked forlorn, stripped of all trees and in need of roof repair. And then there was that old pizza restaurant with the salad bar that looked like a biplane cowling, now nothing but a flat foundation.

So I decided I wanted to keep some things found in the rubble, to remind me and others of the awesome power of Mother Nature and the struggle to overcome the disaster. I found an old brick in the rubble from Red Baron Pizza. I found a small shard of split wood framing. I found a shredded and twisted piece of siding. And I found a piece of metal flashing that was twisted in an odd shape from the wind. They all went in the back of my car and came to Columbia with me. I will arrange them in a display that will serve as a tribute to memories of the Joplin I once knew and the resilience of a community after tragedy.

And each Christmas, when I am getting out the lights to decorate, I will always think about my chance discovery of a string of lights in Joplin after the 2011 tornado. And I will wonder, will they have a Christmas tree?

Former Joplin resident Marty Oetting works for the University of Missouri.

14. WE WERE ALL AFFECTED

By Rebecca Williams

One hundred sixty-one people lost their lives. Nearly 10,000 had their homes damaged or destroyed. These people were affected in a way that can't be understood except first hand but there is another way the tornado affected people. Everyone in our region was affected. We all knew someone or know someone who knew someone that was killed. In this area none of us is more than one degree of separation from someone who lost their life May 22, 2011. This is a story of people who were not in the path of storm..

For locals the assassination of President Kennedy, 9/11 and the May 22 tornado are similar mental benchmarks. Our much anticipated Sunday dinner was just ready to take out of the oven when the sirens went off in Neosho. We did what the NOAA study said many in the area did, we sat down to eat our dinner. We were watching KSN coverage carefully while we ate but we sat down to dinner instead of taking shelter all the same. Tornado warnings are routine in the Ozarks and like so many we were complacent.

Sometime during dinner Joplin was hit. We have had tornadoes nearby before. The May 2008 tornado tore through three states and 50 miles of Newton County, killing 14. In our minds, the tornado that was hitting Joplin would be similar. Our Wi-Fi went down as did our local TV. We wondered how bad it was in Joplin.

My daughter got on her iPhone and created a Facebook page, Joplin Tornado Info (JTI). One of her other Facebook pages, The Real Spooklight, had over 2,000 fans so I posted on it asking for people to fan JTI.

That is the first word we had that St. John's had been hit ... (Spooklight post). This was confirmed shortly by Kristen Stremmel, a St. John's nurse. After posting on The Real Spooklight page, JTI began to go viral.

Almost 10 months later, JTI retains nearly 48,000 of those 49,000 viral fans. My daughter and I have just published *The Use of Social Media for Disaster Recovery* — a field guide with David Burton - University of Missouri Extension, published and released through the University of Missouri. We are all in hope that in some small way this will help "pay it forward" for all that has been done for Joplin out of the kindness of others.

JTI remains active nearly a year after the tornado but it could have accomplished very little without smaller Facebook groups and the people of the JTI community. I could not tell the story of how I was affected by the tornado or the use of social media for disaster recovery without including some of the stories from our Joplin Tornado Info Community

THE TEACHER LOUISE RUSK

You know, I am one of those people who wasn't "in" the tornado, but was definitely "affected" by the tornado. My son Galen and I both struggled with survivor guilt as well as compassion fatigue over the weeks that passed after the tornado and couldn't go through the tornado zone without a visceral response for months. My husband went to St John's that night to help the evacuation. He wasn't working that night. I don't think we realize how much social media has connected us and supported us, in so many ways, through this nightmare. I sincerely hope people in other areas have the same experience with it.

I live in Carthage, but teach in Joplin and have lived in Joplin. One of my sons graduated from MSSU on May 21, 2011, went to Joplin High, and has been very involved at College Heights church and with the International Studies and Foreign Languages program at Missouri Southern. We had family in from St. Louis for my son's graduation at MSSU that weekend. Some of them stayed in hotels in Joplin, some stayed with us. On Sunday afternoon, one of my daughters who lived in Joplin and worked in Joplin for several years, was going to drive back into Joplin, with her husband, to visit some friends. They would have headed over to Range Line, around 24th Street. The weather reports, by about 5 p.m. had them concerned enough that they decided to head back to St. Louis, instead. They literally saw the storm behind them as they drove up I-44.

As word of what happened in Joplin reached my daughter, she cried and cried over the devastation and loss of a town she had come to love. She felt guilty for having left for home when she did. I am just so grateful they didn't head into Joplin that afternoon. My other daughter, her husband and baby were still in Carthage, at our house, when the storm came through Joplin. There were eight of us in that small, interior half bath in our Carthage home, that evening. Five were adults. Three were children, one of them was 11 months old, my grandson. As I have read and watched the loss and suffering of so many in Joplin, my mind goes back to hunching down in that small room with so many of the people I love best in all the world, listening to the hand crank radio. The storm calmed down and went south about 10 miles south of where our home sits. We were just fortunate that day. I can't bear to think about what could have happened to us. We took shelter in an interior bathroom during the storm, not knowing where it would hit or end, using a hand crank radio to listen to KZRG as the storm was grinding through Joplin.

My husband is a MedFlight nurse for St. John's and, of course, we were devastated when he heard that the hospital had been hit, and then the high school. My son and I were on Facebook as soon as the storm danger had passed to contact people we knew in Joplin, to find out who was OK and who needed help. One of my son's instructors from Southern was able to post to Facebook that she was stuck in her basement and we posted, asking for someone to check on her at that address. Neighbors were able to get her out. We got Facebook updates asking for help at Memorial Hall (my son is a Spanish translator) that night, and he went. We got updates from the Joplin Family Y (one of my son's friends heads up the

PHOTO BY MIGUEL OLAVE

kids program). They needed help for the free childcare they were offering right after the tornado. My son and I both went for several weeks to help out. I put out the word, through Facebook, that teachers were needed to volunteer at the Y, having background checks in place, already. We kept track of the number of people missing and accounted for through Facebook. Facebook became a lifeline for the Joplin School District, as Dr. Huff raced to get all of our staff and families accounted for, which he did by the Friday after the tornado. Phone lines were not working or reliable, so we couldn't call in information to the school district, as requested. School district families and staff posted to the Joplin Schools page or the Tornado info page. I shared many, many updates about the need for volunteers, donations, money, homes for abandoned pets, through Facebook, to my friends all over the country. I am from St. Louis and the St Louis crew came down a number of times, along with people from the church I used to attend in St. Louis. We kept track of the death toll and the names of those deceased as we tried to figure out who we lost among our friends, colleagues and co-workers. The links were invaluable — Red Cross,

Humane Society, *Joplin Globe*, the school district, the collection and distribution centers, the emergency shelters. There has been SO much valuable information that I have been able to find and pass on since May 22. I follow Aunt Tracey's walk (aunt of the late Will Norton) on Facebook. She is so full of encouragement and inspiration, in all that family has been through. I am sure I am leaving out a bunch of stuff that just eludes my memory right now. All the pages that have had post-tornado info have been lifelines for all of us. I, along with many other teachers, am teaching in a temporary facility (a FEMA trailer) as a result of the tornado. Many of us taught summer school for seven weeks this summer to give our kids a place to go and something positive and constructive to do in June and July. Many of my students and their families were in the tornado. None of them that I knew personally lost their lives. Thank you, Joplin Tornado Info page, for being a lifeline, and to all the other sites that have given us the info, the support, the connections we have needed to get through this time.

THE NURSE:
CATE LOCH / SCRUBS FOR JOPLIN

My story began on my trip home from Kansas City the afternoon of May 22, 2011. Noticing the sky looked strange, instead of stopping for lunch in Ft. Scott I decided to head on home. It was at this time I switched over to the radio to listen for weather updates. Between Ft. Scott and Pittsburg, hail had begun to fall, I pulled under an overpass for a few minutes to wait it out. As I drove on through Pittsburg, I was actually in the storm that would, from that location, take a right turn towards Joplin. I've driven through heavy rains before but nothing that black. Upon reaching Highway 171, I was able to drive east out of the storm, but remember looking from one side of the road to the other to determine where best to head if a tornado was to develop.

As I neared the intersection of North Main Street Road and Highway 171, the weather report continued to state the storm would be hitting north of Joplin. I took a picture of the skies to the north; to me they weren't that impressive. As I headed down North Main, in the vicinity of the Joplin Humane Society, I noticed a very strange cloud formation to the southwest. It wasn't until a couple of days later that I realized I had actually taken a picture of the storm as it approached Joplin. Living just 10 blocks south of 32nd Street, and near Freeman Hospital, I was very lucky to have made my way down Main Street to our home when I did. Had I actually stopped to eat in Fort Scott, my story could have been much different, one possibly of being on Main Street as the tornado struck.

My husband was out of the country; our kids live in the Los Angeles area. They weren't able to reach me by phone until after midnight, and it wasn't until their phone calls that I realized how devastating the tornado had been. Although, I could tell by the sound of the tornado and the pressure I felt on my body that it had to have been massive.

The following day there were many phone calls and emails from friends and family checking up on how we were doing and the conditions in Joplin. One of the emails came from a former co-worker of mine at Anne Arundel Medical Center (AAMC) in Annapolis, Maryland. Mary first asked if we were OK. Her follow up email asked, "What can we do to help". At that time I told her I didn't have a clue!

May 23 was to have been the May Monthly Luncheon for the Joplin Area Welcome Club, of which I'm the current club president. Since we canceled the luncheon I felt it was important to get as many of our club members together the following week to see exactly how things stood for everyone, what their needs might be (we did have one club member die who lived close to St. Mary's, others that lost their homes), so I invited everyone to our house the following Wednesday. The first person to arrive worked as a pediatric nurse at Freeman Hospital and answered the call to help that night. She mentioned how many in the medical community had lost their homes. My thought was, they will need something to wear for work. I emailed Mary back in Annapolis with my idea, that's how "Scrubs for Joplin" was born.

Within three weeks of the tornado I had received my first shipment of scrubs from Annapolis and was driving around to offices and homes of doctors I knew handing out scrubs. I was also able to get some of the scrubs dropped off at Memorial Hall where St. John's had set up a temporary location. Many had lost everything while others had their homes but were still in need of scrubs due to theirs being either left in medical buildings that were destroyed or haven been ruined while working in the debris field.

In an attempt to reach more people I started a "Scrubs for Joplin"

Facebook page. Without others knowing it existed, it was hard to get the word out about my program. Then I thought of Joplin Tornado Information and some of the other Facebook pages that were created after May 22, 2011. It seemed everyone had heard of Joplin Tornado Info, it was through them and KZRG that we were able to stay updated during those first few days and weeks after the tornado struck. They were the lifeline for our community. Once I explained what I was doing they were more than happy to "Like" my page and spread the word. Each of the groups seemed willing to help the others; it was as if we had become this big extended family. Although in most cases we had never met in person, we became friends. Once others got the word out for me, my Facebook page became a useful tool.

As weeks went by, more and more hospitals, nursing homes, and individuals, started up their own local scrub drives and were shipping them to me. To date I've received somewhere between 3,000 and 4,000 scrubs from several different states. It became impossible to keep track of numbers after deliveries started arriving while "Scrubbies" (what I call people who have received scrubs from me) were at our house. They would want to see what scrubs the new delivery might contain. The FedEx man finally asked me one day what exactly was in all the boxes I kept receiving.

Although scrubs were made available to anyone in need, St. John's Hospital really jumped on board, including my information in the weekly electronic newsletter that goes out to their employees. One department head even came over to pick up scrubs making it easier on their employees; so many had lost their cars. Once they closed down their Hammons location they sent all the scrubs they had to my house with the thought that it would be easier for their employees to have just the one location to go to for scrubs.

I had people calling to set up appointments from as early as 7:10 a.m. to as late as 9:30 p.m. It was important that I work around what best fit their schedules. Many had to move to locations out of town, many were carpooling with others. As much as I thought this was something I was doing to help others, I soon learned I would be the one receiving the greatest blessings. Those needing scrubs would maybe spend 15 minutes looking through what I had and then another 45 minutes sharing their experiences. I felt honored to be there for them, in many cases hearing of losses that were unimaginable. I always tried to ask how they were doing and if there was anything we could do to help. To hear people say, "We're doing OK, we only lost our house and cars," "We're doing OK, I lost my home, car, job, was buried in debris for three hours, but only suffered four broken bones," or hear someone say, "We lost two family members" ... it's almost impossible to wrap your mind around something like that, our new reality.

One story that will stick with me happened just two days after the tornado. I was driving around handing out flashlights, work gloves, and water. I noticed a young father walking away from what once was his home. When I got out of the car to see if there was anything I could do his response was, "My wife and kids are fine, and I've found my son's basketball. We're OK." It came down to being that basic, their home was gone but he would be a hero in his son's eyes for having found the basketball.

I never felt like one to take things for granted, but these men and women certainly made we realize how fortunate and blessed so many of us truly are, and in turn made me want to do all the more to help others. To hear a young mother say how every day her daughter cries, wanting to know what happened to her dolls; how could I not go upstairs and give her some of the dolls I had saved from when my daughter was young? There were many other "things" I had in my house that were non-essentials, that is, unless you've lost everything. To some those same items become a part of putting their lives back together. Being able to go on Facebook every day and find a way in which I can volunteer to help with the recovery effort has been such a blessing. So many want to help but just don't know where or how. I'm fortunate to have the freedom to be able help, and have met some wonderful people along the way. I've worked with Relief Spark, Rebuild Joplin, Habitat for Humanity, Extreme Makeover Home Edition, Misti's Mission, Homes of Hope, Hope for Joplin, Joplin School District, Joplin Humane Society, at food tents, we've housed volunteers ... the list of organizations out there that need our help is long, it's up to us to lend a hand.

I think back over the hundreds of men and women I've welcomed into my home since creating "Scrubs for Joplin" and wonder how many of them I would not have been able to reach without having some sort of social media at work. It was my honor to help out so many that I consider true heroes. Maybe they all weren't out there saving lives, but the fact that they are able to recover from the horrors that many of them dealt with that day makes them all heroes in my eyes. That takes a great deal of inner strength.

With the future of Joplin in the hands of so many wonderful people I have no doubt that we'll recover. However, I do have a concern for some of those still trying to cope with what they went through. It seems to me that the majority simply want a chance to sit down with others that had similar experiences and share their stories, gain some comfort in knowing they are not the only ones feeling "this way." Some of the recent Facebook pages seem to be ones allowing survivors an avenue through which to share their stories. I do think that will help. But, we can all help our neighbors by simply asking, "How are you doing? Is there anything I can do to help?"

I know what you mean about telling our stories, and at times it doesn't feel like we even have the right to have a story of our own with not being directly impacted by the tornado. But we all are emotionally impacted just the same. Some of those with material damage I think are finding it easier to move on than those of us without. In rebuilding they are moving on with their lives. For us it's like we're left in limbo. Plus, I'm to the point of what do I do when the scrubs program is no longer needed? That gave me a purpose for so many months.

KRISTEN TRENARY-STREMMEL
THE NURSE

Until the night of May 22, 2011, my use of social networking was mainly to connect with friends, sharing pictures, planning events and sharing our daily joys and sorrows. That night, it became much more than social. It became life-saving and the thread that kept us all connected. As an ICU RN at St. John's, I was not working that day, but had traveled to St. Louis. The tornado hit as we were on I-44 headed home to Joplin. Stories of the damage were coming in from the radio, texts, phone calls as we were frantically trying to get home safe so that I could go in and help take care of the injured. I found that as helpless as I felt in the car, I could at least help by utilizing Facebook to tell those who needed information what I was learning from various Joplin sources. I was extremely fearful for what I would see when we arrived home.

My family's home being safe but only about a mile from the devastation, I quickly changed into my scrubs and went in to work in the ICU at Freeman Hospital. Nurses were needed and they came from everywhere to help. I jumped into action in the ICU and worked all night taking care of patients and despondent families.

Every day, I reflect on what I saw that night and the weeks following May 22. My greatest comfort lies in knowing that even having left the hands-on patient care part of the disaster, my journey did not end. I was able to connect with people from all over the world and give information about the needs of Joplin and Duquesne residents to complete strangers, now friends, that found me randomly on Facebook.

The storm has forever changed me and my town. My family lost a member and people have moved on and rebuilt. I have had new experiences, friends and new opportunities. I still rely heavily on my Facebook profile to keep in touch with everyone. We all need each other. We were there for each other.

The tornado changed not only the landscape of Joplin but the hearts of the people of the region.

We have come to realize that while we feel guilty about it those of us who weren't "affected" by the tornado have a need to tell our stories, too.

15. THIS TOWN IS MY HOME

By Laela Zaidi

In the hours before the May 22, 2011, tornado, I remember the afternoon being filled with laughter. The beautiful day was a reminder to my friends and I that summer was around the corner, just two weeks away. I anticipated it not only because of the freedom, but it was the summer after my first year in high school. My plans were to spend it with old friends and new and to play tennis for my upcoming fall season. It seemed as if nothing could bring me down; I was content with life.

Of course, nothing could prepare me for what would happen hours later. The beautiful afternoon turned ugly as a massive EF5 tornado tore the town apart and destroyed countless homes and businesses — including my home, three of my family's homes, my dad's office and the hospital which he worked at. My high school, which I also lived across the street from, was torn to pieces. A few days after the tornado, I climbed to the top of what was left of my home. Standing on a gray slab (what used to be my room) I looked over the damage. There was nothing in sight except endless debris, chewed up homes, and, in the distance, the shell of St. Johns.

A realization came upon me; the unchanged life I had known for fifteen years in this town would never be the same.

With nowhere left to go, 20 members of my family to look after, and the possibility of more tornadoes, my parents decided to move everyone to the MSSU Red Cross Shelter for a week. My sister, who lives in Chicago, came down and stayed with me at a friend's. However, this situation couldn't last forever. A quick decision was made that we would move to Monett, Mo. This small town, just under an hour outside of Joplin, is where my mom commutes to work three times a week. With my dad out of work in town, it seemed like the only choice. My aunt and her three kids followed us there.

Despite what had happened in Joplin on May 22, it never crossed my mind to actually leave. My house may have been gone, but this town has been my home for fifteen years. Once moving what little we had to Monett, this dawned on my parents as well. My dad signed up with Mercy St. John's and we found a new house in Joplin. By August, we moved back in town. Nothing felt better than being reunited with my friends, seeing familiar faces, and being home. Of course, our new house still didn't feel right, but at least I was back in a familiar place. The uncertainty of living in Monett made me feel homeless, lonely, and depressed. Despite the genuine sympathy from those I met there, nobody could relate or understand the emotional roller coaster of losing your home, high school, and neighborhood in a natural disaster. After a summer spent in misery, I felt so much joy to be back where I should be. The support of friends, family, and familiarity of the town helped in getting back to some sense of normalcy, and it has been encouraging to watch businesses and homes spring up from the rubble.

One aspect of life forever changed, one both individually affecting citizens of Joplin and collectively, is school. For two thousand students, the loss of our only public high school has changed the way most of us think of school spirit forever. The first home football game clearly proved this. Luckily, our off-campus football stadium was spared in the tornado's path. The filled stands were vibrant in our school colors and nothing could bring the energy of the crowds down.

Because of the loss of our building, the high school was split into two campuses. One for 9/10th graders, at a building recently used as a middle school, and a modern, newly built campus in our mall for 11/12th graders.

While both are "Joplin High School," everyone can agree the high school experience in Joplin is definitely far from normal. In order to make up for the hundreds of textbooks lost, JHS has adopted "21st-Century Learning." Every student has his or her own MacBook laptop, and most work is done electronically. Classroom projects are done through video editing, presentations, and various other technology outlets. To most people, this seems like a unique way to learn. In reality, the ability to focus on work and be productive has become near impossible. The quality of education hasn't increased, and there is nothing healthy about spending seven hours a day on a computer screen. Being a lover of books, paper, and pens myself may leave me biased, but many students feel just as frustrated at times as I do.

Like any change, especially dramatic ones this year has seen, time and patience are needed for them to be broken in. The new learning strategy Joplin schools has adopted has much room for improvement, and without older kids to look up to in the hallways (in a place where many of them recently went to middle school) the chance for freshmen to grow up and mature proves much more difficult. Despite all this, the chance to continue our education, on time, has been the greatest blessing. High school life is far from normal, but knowing our teachers and administrators are doing everything they can to make it the best it can be is the greatest comfort.

While the May 22 tornado robbed me of a summer and "normal" high school year, it also gave a once in a lifetime opportunity. During the summer, Tom Fey, director of tennis at Indian Wells Tennis Garden in Indian Wells, California, came down and saw the damage of the storm. After keeping close contact with the JHS Tennis Team's head coach, Sean McWilliams, he made it possible for three boys and girls to attend and be ball kids at the BNP Paribas Open — the fifth largest professional tennis tournament in the world. The top 100 players from various countries are required to participate, giving us a chance to watch world-class tennis, and even be on court with top players such as Andy Murray, Juan Martin Del Potro, Maria Sharapova, Caroline Wozniacki, and more. What made the trip special was the fact all expenses were paid by donations and efforts of Tom Fey, Indian Wells Tennis Garden community, and the BNP Paribas Bank. Even celebrities are reaching out to our school. David Cook, American Idol winner and Missouri native, performed at our football homecoming (also giving me a chance to rush the stage and high five him!), and pop star Katy Perry is donating money, decorations, and dresses for the JHS Senior Prom. Opportunities such as these are reminders that the world still cares about what happened here on May 22, even months after the disaster.

Throughout the year, the skeleton of JHS stood as a reminder of comforting memories; My history teacher's closet where his students hung out and did homework, the classrooms, the teachers I said hello to everyday (some whom I don't see anymore) are all things I still miss. Often, I revisit those places in my mind. One last time I walk the hallways, sit in the classrooms, and say my goodbyes. I venture across the street and one lay in the backyard of my beautiful three-story home. Sometimes I even drive past those places and envision those buildings still standing as they once did. Years from now, the old Joplin High School and the red brick, green mansard roof home of mine will be forgotten. But hopefully, there will be something bigger and better in their place. The land where my house once was will be a part of something that provides young adults an education and opportunities for generations to come. While these places leave me finding myself heartbroken today, one day I hope to look at them with pride in what my community has rebuilt in their place. Until then, the story of what took place on May 22 will be told as one of resilience, human spirit, and what it truly means to not have a house, but rather a home shared with an entire community.

Laela Zaidi will be a junior at Joplin High School during the 2012-2013 school year.

16. PEACE IN THE MIDST OF THE STORM

By Chris Robinson

May 22, 2011, started out as an ordinary day. I went with my friend Becky, to Joplin to the 15th Street Walmart and as was my custom, I took my dog Dusty as well. He loves to go for car rides and he likes to be included. We took my friend's car and headed to town. We started our shopping and Dusty hung out in the car. After 15-20 minutes of shopping, the Walmart employees told us that a tornado warning had been issued and the sirens had sounded. They wanted us all to go to the back of the store and wait until it was "all clear." My friend went to the back of the store and I headed out to check on Dusty. My friend asked if I could bring Dusty into the store for safety and they said "no." So, I called my daughter and asked her to check the weather on TV and she said that she didn't see anything.

I sat there for a while and the sky got darker. (The sun was shining when I went out.) I called my daughter again and she said there was a tornado and it was on Seventh Street, and it was going north. I decided the wind was picking up and I got Dusty and we headed up by the pop machines just outside Walmart's door. We prayed that not one hair on Dusty would be injured and that we would remain unharmed.

When I looked up, it was very windy and I saw the biggest, brownish, spinning rotation I've ever seen. I saw cars and houses and metal things spinning and flying around in the air. There was rain spinning with it. I knew then I was going into Walmart with the dog.

As I approached the door, it opened and the man inside let me in and said, "Run for your life." We ran in and by then, the lights were busted and all over the floor. There wasn't any power and all the electric lines were all over the floor. The sprinkler system had already gone off and there was water everywhere. Dusty and I were running through about two inches of water. I had come in through the food entrance. I was being pulled by my dog and I was on the end of a 26-inch leash. Imagine that! I'd never run so fast in my entire life.

My dog, Dusty, who is not a Walmart shopper, did really well. He ran us straight to the back of the store, turned right, went past lay away, and then turned left into some doorway. I crouched down in the doorway and within a minute, Dusty was sucked out of my arms. I was sucked out of the doorway and shot out into the store, like a human cannon ball. Then, all kinds of shelves and debris kept falling on me. It made a little lean-to and that kept most of the debris off my chest. I had a small air hole and I could see the roof spin away and beams fall and debris of everything flying everywhere. The noise was horrible. It sounded like driving down a flooded road at a high speed. That was the sound of the storm, but magnify it about 50 times. I was buried under about 10 feet of rubble. I had one of the roof beams fall very close to me, and I thought I was going to die. I actually heard GOD speak to me and HE said, "There is a peace in the midst of the storm." So, I knew then that I would be OK! I had watched the roof spin away and the whole store was like an open arena. No part of the roof was left at all. That was my experience, and something I won't forget.

After the tornado, the two people on top of me had to dig me out. These were the only two people I saw that were alive, and I thought everyone else was dead. It took us about 20 minutes after the wind died down to dig out and get to the front of the store. We didn't see others until we got to the front of the store. So, I called my daughter and told her I was OK and then I found my friend. We attempted to find Dusty, but couldn't figure out where I had been during the storm. My friend and I were told to leave the store, as there was a gas leak so we headed to the parking lot. I was freezing and my clothes were wet and shredded. A man came by and handed us dry shirts and we walked over to a tractor-trailer truck to change shirts. About that time, a lady came over and told us to get away from her truck. I responded, "Man, I've just climbed out of all that rubble and I'm just changing my shirt." The lady stated, "That's my truck and it has a gas leak!" So, we took our wet clothes and went and sat in the parking lot to wait.

A couple of hours later, I ran into a guy from my church and he had seen a dog that looked like Dusty. Becky went searching for the dog and while she was gone, I saw a vision that my dog was going to come running across the parking lot. I didn't know if my mind was playing tricks on me, so I prayed and asked God, "Are you the same God that told me that there's a peace in the midst of the storm while I was in the tornado?" He said, "I AM." About that time, Dusty came running across the parking lot, dragging Becky behind! My dog, Dusty, was completely dry, had no glass in his hair, in his feet, or anywhere on him, no insulation, or any other debris anywhere on him. He was completely unharmed, just like I had prayed for. He looked like he had just come back from the groomers, but I think God or the angels had him. So we knelt down and thanked God in the middle of Walmart parking lot that he had saved Dusty and us. We waited a little longer and about 8:30 p.m. we got a ride home with a friend from church. We are miracles and we give God all the praise! This is a one hundred percent true story and I hope it touches your heart about how great our God is and HE still performs miracles.

I have shared this story with others and really never understood exactly where Dusty was for those 2 1/2 hours until I saw him again. I prayed about it many times and asked God where Dusty had been and how he had stayed so clean and dry. One day, a month ago, God told me where Dusty was. He reminded me of the story of the three Hebrew boys, who were bound and thrown into the fiery furnace. The king stated he saw four men in the furnace and one looked like the son of man. So, they came out of the furnace unharmed and not even singed and didn't smell like smoke. God told me that He had Dusty, just like He had protected those three men. That is what I prayed for, by the Coke machine outside Walmart, before it hit and that had been my prayer that not a hair on Dusty would be hurt and that is exactly what I received. I thank God for my miracle and I am a miracle too. Thank God that He still performs miracles today. I hope that this inspires and encourages you with your relationship with God.

17. MIRACLES AT WALMART

By Becky Kropf

On May 22, 2011, it started out like any ordinary Sunday. I got up and went to church and my friend Chris, who usually goes with me, stayed at home. After church, at my house, my friend and her daughter were there, having a quiet afternoon. Nicole was planning her wedding, and Chris and I decided to go to town and pick up some items. We took her dog Dusty with us as, if the weather permits, he loves to go for a car ride. We stopped at Lowe's, Kohl's, and Harbor Freight and picked up some items at several places. We ended up at Walmart at 15th and Range Line about 4:45 p.m. We started off with the cart and got 40 pounds of dog food first and then started adding in the rest of my groceries. Chris went to the sporting goods department and purchased some bullets, a couple of water bottles and a shirt. A little after 5 p.m., they announced that the tornado sirens had sounded in Joplin and asked all customers to proceed to their safe area, back in electronics. Chris stated she was going to check out the weather and Dusty and proceeded out to the car. I took the cart and headed to electronics with the rest of the shoppers.

In the store, we chatted with each other and kept asking when we could return to shopping. I had picked up milk and other "cold" items and didn't want to have it sit there a long time. We all got out our phones and pulled up the weather maps and alerts and all the weather reports indicated that the "bad weather" was heading across the north part of Joplin. There were alerts for Airport Drive, Webb City, etc. We never imagined what was going to happen over the next 20 minutes. People chatted about where they were going next and what else they needed to pick up and kept asking when we could resume our shopping. The Walmart employees were very serious about keeping us together and "rounded" us up and kept us in the back of the store. No one was allowed to check out and everyone was encouraged to stay together. I visited with those standing around in the back with me and also with Chris who was in the car.

She called me at first and said the weather outside was fine and the sun was shining. She also said she was trying to call her daughter so she could check the weather out on the TV. A few minutes later, she called and said there was information on TV stating there was a tornado heading for the north side of Joplin. She also said it was getting darker outside and the wind was picking up. The last time I talked to her before the tornado, she said she was looking for the dog leash and could she bring the dog in the store. The answer was "no." I told her they said she could come in, but not the dog. That was the last I heard from her before the tornado. I became more frantic as the wind picked up and the sky got darker. I went from the back of the store to the front several times to see if I could see her or call her. The cell phone wasn't working in the back now. I asked the man at the front of the store how it was and he said, "It's looking bad." The last time I went to the front of the store, the sky and outside were black and the man at the door, screamed that we were going to get hit and to "Run!" We all turned and ran to the back of the store and I grabbed some towels off an end cap. I threw them at the lady by my cart who had a 2-year-old girl. I told her to wrap her in it and we put her under the cart where you stack extras. Then, I knelt down and put my head under the cart, too, and the lady and man with the 2-year-old girl did, also. The next thing I knew, the lights went out and the roof ripped off. It was the loudest roar I've ever heard. Then, the sucking sensation started, and the cart lifted off the floor and dropped back down. We held on with all our might. People were screaming and you've never heard more people calling out for God in one place at one time. The only name coming out was "Jesus Save Me!!!!" and "God Save Me!!!!" I do believe God heard from more people that afternoon than He had heard from in a long time! We had five to six minutes of the cart being sucked up off the floor and us pulling it back down. We were all praying out loud and the name heard above the winds was Jesus. I knew in my heart that if I was going through this, that Chris and Dusty in the car were worse off. I prayed for them too and just asked God to spare us all. I also prayed with the people at my cart for everyone's safety. We were pelted by huge hail and the rain was intense. We were also being hit with flying debris and glass and metal. Our only protection was the dog food in the cart.

When the wind finally died down and the hail was noticeably smaller we started standing up and checking out the store. Unbelievable! It was gone!! There was no roof, no walls, just debris everywhere. Then we started seeing others stand up and started trying to crawl out from under the shelves and debris.

When I stood up, I could see the apartments behind Walmart and the top floor of the three-story apartments was missing for most of them. We started helping each other up, and started trying to get people that could walk out of the store.

Once again, the Walmart employees jumped in and took over and led an orderly line out of the store. They helped carry those that couldn't walk, and providing first aid for those that needed it. They identified those too injured to move and had an employee stand by that person so they wouldn't be alone. They ripped blankets and comforters out and covered people up that were injured and tried to keep them warm. I helped lead some people to the front who were too shaky to walk by themselves and came back and walked more out. I found the gentleman I had met before the storm and we exchanged "so glad you made it" statements. It was like we had an immediate bond that we had all survived something so horrific. I was still looking for my friend Chris, and the dog, but I couldn't seem to find her. I went to the parking lot and my car had been picked up and dropped three rows over, and was destroyed. Most of my purchases that day had been sucked out and even my front license plate had been ripped off. I felt a little sick as I realized if Chris and Dusty had been in the car, that they were gone. On my third trip to the front of the store with helping people out, a Walmart employee, asked me what my friend looked like and the dog's description. He told me that he had let them in, right before the tornado hit. I started my trip back with renewed hope of finding Chris and Dusty.

Again, I helped another lady walk to the front of the store, and this time when I made it to the front, my friend Chris was there! My first prayer had been answered. GOD had saved my friend. The car no longer mattered, my friend was alive!!! I asked about Dusty, and she told me that right after the roof got ripped off, the dog had gotten sucked out of her arms and into the air. I was so sad, but again realized we were alive, and I told her we could look for Dusty and if he hadn't made it, we could find a different dog. She thought she was in shoes, so we went back again to the back of the store to help out and look for any sign of the dog. We arrived at the back, and the Walmart employees paused in helping people out so they could call out for people trapped and rescue them. The Walmart employees were the search and rescue. No one had made it to help us, and they did an amazing job. They broke open first aid kits and administered first aid, wrapped up bleeding arms, hands, legs, etc. and identified those with serious injuries who could not be moved. They did it in such a calm and practiced manner, that they passed that onto the rest of us and that helped keep everyone as calm as possible. I know that some people weren't as lucky as my friend Chris and I and the others that walked out of there, but every person that left that store alive received a miracle that day. If it wasn't for the Grace of GOD, all should have perished. There is no way you can look at what was left of that store and believe that hundreds lived.

Finally, they told everyone that we should all leave the store as the smell of gas was getting stronger. The employees were still there, but the rest of us were told to leave. Then, we were left with the task of trying to find a way home. Chris and I still didn't have Dusty and we were sad, but still happy to be alive ourselves. We tried to call people to come and get us, but no one could get through. Then, we heard the hospital had been hit as well as a large part of Joplin. Everywhere we looked, there was devastation.

A young man with dry T-shirts approached us and we each took one. We went over to a tractor-trailer truck to change our shirts as our clothes were wet and "shredded". About that time, a lady came up and told us to get away. We were surprised and Chris said, "Man, I've just climbed out of all that rubble and I'm just changing my shirt."

The lady responded with, "That's my truck and it has a gas leak. It could explode!" We heard it was carrying dynamite and quickly left the truck! We sat down in the parking lot and finally got hold of Chris' daughter. She was unable to come and get us as traffic wasn't being let into Joplin. She got hold of a friend from church and they started planning how we would get home.

By now it was like 7:30, two hours after the tornado. I had heard from my daughters and they were in Arkansas with their dad. Sarah's fiancé also tried to get to us, but again couldn't drive and so ended up having to start walking. The destruction was extensive and horrible. A little before 8 p.m., I felt led by God to walk around to the back of the store and look for Dusty. I asked everyone I saw, and finally at the back of the store, I ran into two guys who told me they had just seen a golden lab, running down the street. I couldn't believe it, but I ran to look for the dog they'd just seen. I ran up to the first house that was only minimally damaged and a young girl there told me that she had just seen a dog like Dusty run into the woods by the base of the water tower. I ran over, and called his name, and Dusty came running into my arms!

My second prayer was answered too! I first couldn't believe it and the young girl said, "Is it yours?"

I cried out yes and just hugged him and cried over him and thanked God for saving Dusty, too. Then, I had to get him back to Chris. He had no collar, no leash, they had both been sucked off. The amazing thing was the dog was dry and had no debris on him. He had no glass, no insulation, and no dirt on him. The young girl went and got a leash from her grandmother and helped me put it on Dusty and I walked him back to Chris. Once he caught sight of her, I could hardly keep up with him as he ran to his mom. It was a joyous reunion and we both thanked God again and again. He's now known as the "miracle dog."

About 8:45 p.m., we finally got a ride from a gentleman from our church and Aaron, Sarah's fiancé also walked to help us. We arrived home two hours later, because all the main roads were blocked. We both know that God was with us today and we will never stop thanking Him or praising Him for saving us and Dusty.

18. MY TORNADO STORY: A STORY ABOUT THE HEART OF AMERICA

BY JENNIFER NGUYEN

"Happy Birthday!"

Everyone knows that these words are meant to be said out of happiness and celebration. But when they are expressed on a day of total destruction, devastation, and depression, are they really that effective? A birthday, a day of joy targeted at the passing of age, is usually a whole day filled with presents, smiles, and cake. Lots and lots of cake! Well, that's at least what my family thought birthdays were supposed to be like. That was, until the day came. The day that was life changing and will be forever marked in the history books of our nation. The day that caused souls to be ripped apart from their families and thrown out into a jungle of madness. The day that my city lost, what seemed at the time, everything.

I woke up that Sunday morning to a bright, dazzling sun. As I went through my daily morning routine, I checked my iPod to discover the weather conditions for this particular Sunday. What it seemed like to me, was that Joplin would be experiencing rain showers and maybe a few bolts of lightning. This was not unusual for this time of the year, which was late spring, in our Southern Missouri region. So, my family and I attended our regular 11:15 mass at St. Peter's Apostle Church. By that time, the sky had developed a grayish color and was covered with poufy, dark clouds scattered into bunches, piling up into the air. What was ironic was that during church that day, my parish prayed for the unfortunate people in the paths of the latest natural disasters, without a single clue about what was heading our way…

My cousin had her birthday party held at about noon that same day, so, as you can imagine, we rushed out of our church right after mass finished. Actually, she was having two birthday parties! One with her friends and one with her family, and I was invited to both! Her birthday party with her other five-year-old friends was at the Maccaroo Gym, the most wonderful place a five-year-old could dream of. Who wouldn't want to spend three hours jumping on blown up, bouncy devices? I think I was there to help the little kids have fun, but considering the fact that I wasn't allowed in quite a few bouncy houses, I don't know if I was any help. Anyway, when her first party was over, around two to three o'clock, the sky was at a dark, cloudy phase. But at that time, no one was really worried. It was just another heavy rainstorm, wasn't it?

After that party, she had another party that started around 4-5:30. You would think that a little five-year-old would be partied out, but apparently, she wasn't. So, at that time, the sky was still pretty dark. And when I say "dark," I mean a deep gray. But halfway through the party, right after we finished dinner, it really started pouring outside, hard. We didn't think much of it.

But as the weather started to get worse, we decided to click on the weather channel and take a look at the news reports. We weren't really scared, yet; we just wanted to make sure. Hey, it's better to be safe than sorry. There was only one problem. In the path of my aunt and the remote control was a very difficult obstacle. My dad. These things happened to us all the time (the storm, I meant), and my dad wasn't going to easily let go of the remote and the heated show of "Cops" that was on the television screen. In his mind, in everyone's mind, this was just the same crazy Missouri weather that always circled our region. In fact, my aunt had to practically wrestle the remote from my dad! It was not an easy battle. But in the end, everyone was laughing ... until the news flashed on. At that point, there was no more laughing and merry faces, just serious expressions and gasps from the silent, but alert audience.

We had a lot of people at the birthday party who were not only family, but also close friends, so we decided to take precautions. All the kids were shoveled into the center of the house, which was the living room, away from the windows. I'm pretty sure the panic mode kicked in when the first tornado siren went off and a power outage engulfed the entire neighborhood. That was when the crying started. The crying, whimpering, and outbursts of sudden prayers. Right then, my uncle, who works at the Granby Fire Department as fire chief, left the party to alert his town about the forming twister. When I heard he was leaving, I almost started crying, myself. Everything was going wrong. It was a horrible nightmare.

By the time the second siren went off, total chaos was already loose among our party and its attendants, especially the children. We had kids that ranged from the age of 16 months to 12 years old. We totaled to a headcount of about 10 remaining kids and 11 adults. When I used the term, "remaining," I meant that stayed at the party. The hosts of the party, my aunt and uncle, tried to calm everyone down enough to escort them to their underground crawlspace. Actually, they didn't really escort; they rushed. By the time most of the population of the party was safe underground, the sirens were blaring in our eardrums. All I could do was sit there and stare. Stare into sudden space. Stare into the midst of the dusty underground lantern. Stare, while clasping my hands together in a firm grip and muttering silent prayers.

We stayed down there in the musty underground shelter for what seemed like hours. My dad, along with the other "brave," but ignorant, men of the family, stayed outside to watch the skies. But soon enough, a low rumble grew louder and louder until it produced the sound that could very well be compared to the coming of a train. The sky held a vision of death, itself. By then, my dad, as well as the others, gained their senses and bolted toward the shelter. They quickly jumped/sprang into the safety of the haven with sighs of clear relief.

Terror filled the eyes of many as the raging storm continued on. Silent prayers of plea and help were whispered through a heavy flow of tears. Mother clutched son; son clutched father; father clutched wife. Parents soothed their young children in the panic of the night. All sat there, awaiting possible death. Then, a sudden silence filled the walls of the heavily guarded shelter, and all was still. Those moments were filled with astonishment, with joy. We had survived. We survived the storm that surely caused damage in our beloved town.

We came out of the shelter to a neighborhood trashed entirely with debris. Everywhere, and I mean everywhere, there were pieces of paper, parts of furniture, and even precious family heirlooms. We knew that the area we were in was pretty lucky; we didn't get hit that badly. The worst of the disastrous tornado was yet to be discovered. The way it seemed, at the time, over the radio, was that our town had encountered some serious damage, deadly damage. The only transportation of information was over the treasured MP3 player my little sister had brought along with her to the party. We listened intently to the faithful radio speakers as they delivered updates, news, and messages from distraught loved ones. Our eyes swelled with tears as we discovered that many of our friends were hit. Did they survive? We didn't know. At the time, the cell phone signals were weak, and everybody was having the same idea, to call their friends, families, and neighbors. Actually, everybody they knew! Enemies called enemies, friends called foes, kids called kids they hardly knew. There was a concern for everybody and everyone around. Some calls were sent through, but most were, sadly, unsuccessful.

As the search for lost ones continued on, the traffic in town became heavier and heavier. Due to the fallen power lines, trees, and buildings, many streets were closed. You just couldn't get through them! Destruction was everywhere! And to make matters worse, the direct routes everyone took to get through town were blocked by police officers because of certain disastrous matters.

So when people finally got through to see the aftermath of our town, they were shocked, astonished even. I was shocked. Restaurants, grocery stores, banks, clothing stores, they were all gone! Well, some of them were not completely gone, but they were pretty close. Buildings were shred to pieces, with foundation and cushioning flung everywhere. You couldn't even recognize where you were or what street you were on. Tidbits of debris gave hints and clues about what buildings might have been where, but other than that, citizens walking up and down the destruction path were completely clueless. What hit me the most, though, was that St. John's Regional

Medical Center was a direct hit during the lasting minutes of the deadly tornado. This was the same hospital my sister, my cousin, and I were all born at. To drive by the once tall standing building was absolutely heartbreaking. I felt my insides shatter as I saw the charred edges of the once smooth, glistening skyscraper. I felt a pang of pain go through my chest as I realized that while an image of remembrance for the hospital, before the damage, was still around, that one day, it would eventually disappear. And all that would remain would be a memory of what unfortunate fate was put upon the hospital and how that fate came to be.

We drove countless roads discovering the same horrid things over and over again. Neighborhoods held corrupted streets. Some even contained lifeless bodies. Searches for signs of life in heavily damaged areas were organized every day. With the help of volunteers from Joplin, and many other cities, tons of lives were spared. Still, families were on the streets with nothing left but a few salvageable items. Tear-stained faces were seen about every minute of every day. Our city wasn't crying because we felt pity for ourselves; we were crying because we felt pity for others.

Yes, we cried, mourned, and sorrowed, but that's not all we did. We did these things while we worked, while we worked to rebuild. Yes, when the tornado came by, we were, in a sense, crushed and devastated by what had been put upon our town. But did we give up? Did we sit around on our butts thinking about our losses and everything that went wrong? No. We looked at the future, at what the rebirth of Joplin would bring. We had hope, faith, and love in our eyes and hearts, and we accepted the challenge that awaited us with an air of determination. Everyone and I mean EVERYONE felt an urgent need to get up, to do something. Hundreds of policemen and special forces came to our rescue. We might have been struck down, but in the process of getting back up, we had not only the help of our local citizens, but also the help of our nation.

Volunteers from all around the states came to distribute food, water, clothing, and supplies. Shelters were set up in the town's Memorial Hall, and many local townspeople opened up their homes for the homeless and for the many volunteers that came. One volunteer even traveled the sea for Joplin. He came all the way from Japan just days after the tragic incident. When asked why he chose to come help our town, he simply replied that our nation had done the same for his when the cruel tsunami raged through Japan last March. With so much help and support from our nation, from our world even, Joplin was starting to brighten.

With all the work efforts, Joplin was starting to look like itself again. Streets were cleared up a bit, and trash was starting to be picked up and disposed of. The tornado might have crushed our town, but it didn't touch our spirits. And it certainly didn't touch a sign of hope. Through the rubble of East 26th Street, the cross of St. Mary's Catholic Church stood proudly above all the destruction. It was like a sign of hope, a sign telling our community that Joplin will heal; we will rebuild.

Over the days, weeks, and months, Joplin did recover. Most of the trash, if not all of it, was either taken to the dump or recycled. Homes were on the verge of rebuilding, and businesses were signing construction contracts. The roads were reopened, and flowers even started growing on the sides of the highway again. The Extreme Home Makeover team even came to our town to rebuild a few houses and replenish Cunningham Park. Things almost seemed to be on a normal flow, like before. Sadly, that wasn't the case. When the storm came by, it changed Joplin. I can't say with a definite expression that Joplin will ever be the same. We lost so many precious lives in that tornado. We lost our homes, our jobs, our families, our friends. We lost so much, but in our time of need, we were not forgotten. We had the support of not only our nation, but also many other nations that aided us after the terrible windstorm.

We had the care and love of other communities as our community tried to pick itself up. Weirdly enough, disaster really does bring a community together. It makes you appreciate what you have rather than what you want. It makes you realize the difference between what's important and what's not. Some people refer to our Joplin, Mo., community as the heart of America, and when we were hit, they said that the heart was cracked, that there was no hope. That was on the day of the tornado. Now, those same people look at us and say otherwise. The heart is healing. It might have a few rough patches and bumps along the way, but it is healing. Why do they say this? Because we have the strength and love to prove them wrong. We have the integrity, effort, and persistence to show them that we can rebuild, even if we are starting from the scratch. We have and truly are the wings to the eagle.

Jennifer Nguyen is an eighth grader at East Middle School. She will attend Joplin High School during the 2012-2013 school year.

19. BIG BUILDS

BY JOHN HACKER

In October and November of 2011, two groups put together a massive effort to build a total of 17 homes in just a few weeks.

The famed television show Extreme Makeover Home Edition came to Joplin with the intention of completing the show's largest build and its 200th episode. The show's producers decided they had to help more than one family in a catastrophe the size of the Joplin tornado so they made plans to build seven homes for seven families in seven days.

This 200th episode, which aired on Jan. 13, 2012, turned out to be the final episode of the series.

The week after that, Habitat for Humanity-Tulsa, Okla., teamed up with Habitat for Humanity-Joplin and a number of corporate sponsors to build 10 houses in two weeks.

Those homes were concentrated in an area west of the former Joplin High School location.

The Extreme Makeover build team donated leftover building materials to the Habitat build.

Sam Clifton, owner of Millstone Custom Homes in Springfield, is the lead builder on the project to build seven homes in seven days for Joplin tornado victims.

PHOTO BY JOHN HACKER

Carrie Cook and her children Zachary, 8, and Alden, 7, look out the window of the wall they had just help raise at the wall-raising ceremony at Habitat for Humanity's Ten for Joplin build on Oct. 29.

PHOTO BY JOHN HACKER

Michael Maloney, one of the designers with the television show Extreme Makeover: Home Edition, poses for photos and signs construction helmets for fans at the build site on Connor Avenue in Joplin last week.

PHOTO BY JOHN HACKER

These efforts are just a drop in the massive bucket of need in Joplin, but they are a much-needed shot in the arm for a city that has been through so much.

They represented the concentrated effort of thousands of volunteers, and those efforts continue through groups such as Samaritan's Purse, Convoy of Hope and the continued efforts of Habitat for Humanity to continue to build homes for Joplin residents.

Keith Stammer, Joplin's Emergency Management Director, talks about the Joplin Tornado at the National Weather Service's Severe Weather Workshop March 2, 2012.
PHOTO BY JOHN HACKER

20. PUSHED TO THE BREAKING POINT

By John Hacker

"It is my opinion that weaknesses are generally just strengths that are pushed too hard."

In Joplin, on May 22, 2011, many, many strengths were pushed to the breaking point. One of the people pushing those strengths as hard as possible was Keith Stammer, Joplin's Emergency Management Director.

Stammer talked about that day with people who know and feel his struggle, emergency managers and meteorologists at the National Weather Service's Severe Weather Workshop on March 2, 2012, in Norman, Okla.

An interesting thing about Stammer's presentation is he spoke for more than an hour to a crowd of more than 100 that hung on his every word, but he used no notes; only a slideshow.

Each image evoking memories of a specific place, or event, or casualty, or triumph on May 22 and in the days that followed.

Each memory burned into his brain by an event that emergency management directors try to prepare for, but hope they never have to work — a major catastrophe in their town.

And how do you prepare for something like what happened to Joplin on May 22, 2011? It's hard to practice for something that seems impossible to imagine.

"If I had walked into that exercise design committee meeting with this scenario in my back pocket, I would have been laughed out of the room. They would have said let's do something we know," Stammer said. "Well, not now."

PRELUDE TO DISASTER

Stammer gave the crowd a mental picture of Joplin before the storm.

"We sleep 50,000 more or less. On a given workday, population swells by 5 with almost 250,000 people.

"You can watch the headlights come into town in the morning. You can watch the taillights go out of town at night. The thing that makes that significant as far as May 22 was May 22 was a Sunday evening; it was not a Monday evening. So Sunday evening at 5:41 was a lot different than a Monday evening at 5:41 and for that, we are most grateful, it made a big difference in terms of the number of people in town.

"Joplin does not own its own utilities; gas, water, electric are owned by for-profit companies which makes it a very interesting situation when you are running an emergency operations center and trying to coordinate all of the utility activities that happen."

He also talked about what he was doing on May 22 prior to 5:41 p.m.

"We were under tornado watch as of about noon that day. I was sitting at home watching the Cardinals play, had my iPad on watching the radar and also I was on NWS chat with the Springfield office talking about what was going on. At about 4:30 p.m. we, being Kathy and I, decided it was time to go down to the EOC (Emergency Operations Center). She goes with me, she brings her knitting and sits in the EOC and we visit.

"Things started getting crazy, turned on sirens at approximately 11 minutes after (5:11 p.m.), then decided to turn them on again about 20 minutes after that (5:31 p.m.)."

THE STORM

At 5:41 p.m. something happened that shocked meteorologists.

Steve Runnels, warning coordination meteorologist, attended the conference in Norman and described for his peers how this storm was different from any other he had seen.

"An EF5 tornado, capable of producing 200-mile-per-hour-plus winds, only occurs one out of a thousand tornadoes. Even at that, the type of storm that produces such a tornado, called a supercell, is a relatively rare event. We get maybe 10 days or two weeks out of the year when we see supercells and maybe three or four of those produce tornadoes.

Was Joplin rare in terms of intensity? Yes.

"But even on top of that, supercells like to form in an environment where they are the only storm in the region. They require a strong inflow into a rotating updraft to survive. What was really strange about the Joplin event is that we had supercells that were forming and then merging within other cells. It was an event that normally the environment does not produce the types of storms that we saw that day.

"The other thing that perhaps was a little bit strange from a supercell's perspective was that the tornado itself was masked in rain. So you had three-quarters to one-mile wide tornado with lots of debris, but on top of that you had rain further blocking visibility.

"These factors together really went into the fact of making this an odd event. Like the Picher Tornado that occurred back on Mother's Day, 2008, this event does show that there are times when the National Weather Service can forecast tornado outbreaks a week in advance, a.k.a. the storm system that came through in 2003, but there will be other times where the day before or even the morning of the tornado, our forecasts are being further refined."

THE STORM HITS

Joplin's Emergency Operations Center, or EOC, is located at the Donald E. Clark Safety and Justice Center at 303 E. Third St. about 20 blocks north of what was to become the path of the most destructive storm in recent memory.

It's where Keith Stammer goes to coordinate services when disaster

ST. JOHN'S HOSPITAL DESTROYED

The crowd at the banquet at the National Weather Service's Severe Weather Workshop March 2, 2012, listens to Keith Stammer.

PHOTO BY JOHN HACKER

strikes. Stammer had set off the sirens twice on the evening of May 22, once for a tornado warning sounded in the north end of Joplin and a second time for a warning the Weather Service issued further south shortly after 5:30 p.m.

Stammer was talking to one of the local radio stations when the tornado struck.

"KZRG was talking to me on the cell phone and they said, 'Why are the sirens going off,' and I was explaining why the sirens were going off, we had a report of a touchdown and they said, 'Thank you very ...' I looked at my cell phone and said, 'Why did you hang up on me?' Then I realized the cell phones were down and I looked over and our phones were down and the cable was out and the Internet was down. We had backups for all of that, but the tornado just ripped all of that out of there so we did not have access to all of our phone lines."

Stammer said he had some communication and reports of damage were starting to trickle in.

"We did have cell text messaging. It was kind of spotty, but we used that quite a bit. We do have a robust radio system on 800 megahertz; we have towers on the north and south sides of Joplin. None of that was affected. A big thing for us as opposed to Tuscaloosa, Ala., was that they lost their police station; they lost their EOC all through the path of that tornado, none of that was true with us. It went through a residential area. We lost two fire stations. Ninety-five percent of primary and secondary streets were impassable. We lost the street signs, street lights, traffic signals. . ."

EVACUATING A HOSPITAL

Stammer talked about the incredible events transpiring at Joplin's largest hospital. St. John's Regional Medical Center, located at 26th Street and McClelland Boulevard, took a direct hit from a tornado that had rapidly spun up to incredible strength.

Security camera video, shot on May 22 and not released until May 2012, show winds sweeping through the hospital's emergency room waiting area, rendering it to a shambles in seconds.

"Five years ago, I attended evacuation exercises at St. John's, where we practiced taking people from upper floors to lower floors, practiced surging from the building to the parking lot. That was in all of our plans, if the hospitals needed to surge, they needed to expand someplace, they would just go to the parking lot because all their equipment is there, doctors are there why go to a different location? We evacuated something like 50 pretend patients in something in the neighborhood of two to three hours and were quite pleased with ourselves.

"St. John's had 180 patients that night plus the doctors and staff that were there. That entire building was evacuated in 90 minutes flat. They did an outstanding job, it's amazing what you can do when you have to."

Stammer talked about the damage the nine-story, 40-year-old hospital sustained.

"The hospital itself, you may have heard various stories about it being moved off its foundation. What actually happened was the top three floors of the hospital twisted about four inches. Those of you know the engineering understand concrete and steel do fine job up and down. Left and right, not so much, so when that happened, the building was done.

"They are in the process this year of starting to take it down by jackhammer and by backhoe and balls. We wanted them to blow it up, I thought that might be kind of fun, but the problem with Joplin is that it is totally undermined with old lead and zinc mines and the engineers said we really don't want to lower streets for a mile around. (Laughter) You think that's funny, but I can tell you that two years ago, St. John's, on one side, had a three story parking garage and that parking garage sank three inches, so they had to take it down. So that's a very real concern in that area.

"It's coming down, St. John's Hospital is rebuilding, they have a temporary building, they've put up semi-permanent buildings, they are going to be in the process of putting up a permanent building on I-44. Sisters of Mercy and St. John's, which is now called Mercy, are now going to spend $1 billion in erecting a new medical facility. It's going to be very nice, it's going to be state of the art, and they did a fine job."

TEMPORARY MEDICAL FACILITIES

Stammer talked about the temporary medical facilities, set up to support Freeman West Hospital, which had suddenly become Joplin's only operating hospital and emergency room at exactly the time when the city needed all the medical help it could get.

"The state of Missouri has what is known as a Medical Mobile Unit (MMU).

"I know Dottie Brinkle, she's the director of nursing for St. John's Hospital. Our elder daughter used to baby-sit her daughters. She called me up and said, 'Keith, I want the MMU,' and hung up. I said, 'Yes ma'am.' I called the state and they brought in the whole unit, it's a MASH-type hospital that will handle 60 beds and the national guard set that up, they're known locally as the MONG, the Missouri National Guard, they helped set that up.

"Memorial Hall is owned by Joplin. In 2007 we had an ice storm come through. Lost power for a week, and we set up a shelter there in Memorial Hall. We had a nursing home or two and several residents who had no power, and we ran a shelter there for an entire seven days.

"We said well, that worked out very well. What we're going to do is incorporate that into our Local Emergency Operations Plan, part of our after-action review, so the next time we have a disaster, we know we go to that shelter. Apparently the medical review committee was also in on that because as soon as this happened, the doctors at St. John's marched themselves down the street to Memorial Hall, walked in the door and said we're here to take over, this is now our building.

"In a matter of an hour or two, they were doing surgery on the basketball court. Most impressive. We ran there for quite a while until they could get quarters set up in other places. Doctors set up offices there for practice. That's not how we exactly envisioned it, but you do what you have to based on your past experience and the situation you find yourself in at the moment. Again, our hats off to our medical community and the work that they did."

INFRASTRUCTURE

Stammer described the massive damage to the utility infrastructure of the city. He also showed pictures of the damage to the Empire District Electric Company substation on 26th Street and Wall Avenue.

"We had widespread electrical outages, damaged or missing distribution points, you can see the top right hand, that is an Empire District Electric Company substation that was totally gone just from the wind, fires around the area and that didn't do us a whole lot of good because there was no water for a three-mile area.

"When the houses were destroyed, we refer to that as smoothing, when the houses were smoothed all the utilities were still there but it broke off all the access. So it broke off the gas, broke off the water, broke off the meters. They had to go around and turn off every individual water line to every house in that entire area, the same thing for all the gas lines. It took about three days to get the water pressure back up."

He also described the response from 110 outside municipal public works departments that sent people and equipment to help.

"Within 36 hours after the storm, 100 percent of the primary and 70 percent of the secondary streets were cleared. I remember Sunday night, the city manager, Mark Rohr, came into the EOC, all the department heads had come in and, in one conversation, I remember he turned to the director of public works and said, 'Job one is to clear the streets. Why are you still standing here? Go clear the streets.' So that's what we did all Sunday night. SEMA, the State Emergency Management Agency, was there on Sunday night, FEMA came in on Monday morning, actually they started coming in the middle of the night and as soon as dawn broke they were out. They said they really could not believe that you could get to the locations. We needed that done."

'HUNDREDS DEAD'

Stammer talked about the shock in the reports from his first responders as they fanned out in Joplin that first night.

"Honestly folks, our first responders said, when they went out in the field, we have hundreds dead. Just looking at everything out there. The police department and ambulance people, they were discussing how to set up a triage. We practiced triage before; we had gone through that kind of thing, but always on a smaller scale. They figured out all you had to do was pull an ambulance into a residential area that had been hit and turn on their lights. When you turned on your lights, they literally came out of the woodwork."

He said the residents of Joplin themselves became first responders that day.

"A man and his two dogs came in and bought the house in my neighborhood after the storm, I think the dogs were cosigners. He said they rode out the storm in an interior room, multiple walls and between him and the exterior in a closet holding on to the door of the closet to keep the wind from pulling it open. When it was done, he kicked the closet door open; all that was left was a closet. He looked over to one side and he sees some debris move, so he went over and helped his neighbor dig out. The two of them looked over on the other side and saw a hand waving from the debris so they went over and dug a woman out and that's kind of how they survived. As far as triage was concerned, people were trying to help each other all the way around.

"We had 5,000 emergency personnel from 435 agencies come to Joplin. Our city manager was extremely straightforward about this, he said we will not stop looking until there is no one to look for, so that's what we did. We started search and rescue that night, we brought in dog teams, we brought in search and rescue teams. Urban Search and Rescue teams out of Arkansas, Oklahoma, Kansas, Kansas City and St. Louis, Mo. These are teams that have all the equipment, the hard hats, the ropes, they know how to do all this stuff. And they can just go through a big box store in literally 45 minutes; it was quite amazing.

"We had a lot of dogs, some 80 different search and rescue dog teams, we made six passes across the city from east to west and from west to east going back and forth. We found our last live person on Tuesday afternoon. Physicians were telling on Wednesday, people had a 50 percent chance survival if they were trapped, Friday it's like about 10 percent. Wanted to make sure we hadn't missed anyone.

"Another thing was from the air. People brought in helicopters and we flew every treetop, every building, every roof that we could. They brought in search and rescue teams as far as CERT, Community Emergency Response Teams, put them on the ground in the path going down to Newton County. Dive teams, we dove every pond, every swimming pool, every golf course hazard from one end to the other just to make sure we didn't miss anything."

FEEDING VOLUNTEERS AND VICTIMS

One big problem was feeding the victims that were coming out of the rubble and the massive army of volunteers that was going in to search and clean up.

"Feeding stations were set up everywhere. Tyson Chicken came in and set up right outside the EOC and it was really nice, chicken for breakfast, chicken for lunch, chicken for dinner and sometimes they put eggs with it. (Laughter) I went to see them and said I only have one requirement; you don't turn anybody away. The first several days, anyone that wanted to eat could come up and do that.

"The health department was pulling their hair out. They're used to doing inspections of food services and talking about cleanliness. Yeah, 40 feeding stations opened up simultaneously, that doesn't count everyone who owned a grill. Because the volunteers came in and people just took their grills out of the garage and started cooking hamburgers and hot dogs and handing out cokes. The health department went by and said I'm going to pretend this didn't happen and went down the street to something else."

FAITH-BASED RESPONSE

Stammer talked about the role of churches in Joplin's response.

"I'm going to tell you right now, those, from an emergency management standpoint, this job cannot be done without the faith-based organizations. Every major denomination of which I am aware of in the United States has a division for emergency response; they all know each other. They all work together on these and they specialize in different things, not the least of which is, God bless 'em, those Southern Baptist women who know how to cook. They came in one time with a trailer and said we're here for two weeks. I said OK, great, they said we need a location; we have our own people, all of our own food. I asked how many can you do, she said we can do 1,200 meals a day. That's what they do.

"The Latter Day Saints called and said we can put 600 boots on the ground over the weekend, where do you need them. The Presbyterian Church specializes in the housing of volunteers later on, the Mennonites, they have people who pull off their jobs, they give up their vacations and they come in and work with people who have no money, but they get their roof put back on, their carports repaired that type of things. They work with their own NGOS, non-governmental organizations. They work with our NGO liaison out of the EOC.

"Here's the key in all of this operation, how things went. For seven years I've been there and we've done this before, we do exercises, we do drills, we do after-action reviews and for me the one key thing was this, there was not one major player who walked into the EOC that I did not already know. Any faith-based, any governmental organization, any business that came in to talk, we'd all seen each other. The statement is the disaster scene is not the place to exchange business cards. We want to know who you are, that's how things worked and it worked very well when we did it."

VOLUNTEERS COME IN

Stammer praised the response of Americorps, the federal office coordinating volunteers that come into the city to help.

"Anyone familiar with Americorps?" he said. "They're good kids aren't they? They march to a little different drummer. In the EOC on Sunday night, one of my people could not remember the name but they remembered them from 2007, they said where are the hippies?

"Oh, you mean Americorps, Bruce is already coming, they are authorized to respond, they were in St. Louis, he called and said we're en route, we'll be there at about 3 o'clock in the morning. They helped out a lot, we had to divide out the debris into five different piles, white goods over here, metals over here, vegetation debris that's hauled off separately.

"The other thing they did is ran our volunteer registration area, which was a godsend because it helped us get people's names and addresses and who are you and when you come in and when you leave. That gives us volunteer hours.

"Another rule worthy of repeating: all disasters are local, they start locally, they end locally. They may rise to national prominence as ours did somewhere in between, but at some point, with all due respect to all of you who have come, all you foreigners are going to go away at some point and we are going to be left here to handle it ourselves so we're not giving up local control.

"The volunteers did a wonderful job. Missouri Southern State University, they're a nice college, a drive-in sort of place, and only 950 dorm rooms. There is no alcohol, no smoking, it's kind of like come in, get your education, leave, thank you very much. It's a great college.

"They had just signed a memorandum of understanding with the

American Red Cross two weeks before to act as a shelter. When this happened, they stepped up. We filled up their dorm rooms, we filled up their gymnasium, FEMA came in a few days after the tornado and said how many people, how many structures, we didn't know, we were guessing. They said how many shelters; we said one. They said one? I said it holds 1,000 people. If it fills up we'll go get another one. The most we ever had were 650. It's kind of interesting; people take care of themselves around here. That was our first question, where did everybody go? They went with family and friends, the churches were grabbing people off the street, calling parishioners and asking can you take three, yes, here's six thank you very much. It was amazing and it worked real well for the first three weeks."

"THE FISH"

One of the most important contributions from the federal government, in the early days of the disaster, was helping to map out the tornado's path.

"If you don't get anything else out of this evening, please get this. This is our map of the destruction of the tornado running from west to east through Joplin. Basically, it fired up on the west side, it gained its strength, you can see that outlined against the white, that's the damage path itself, then it went over to the east side of Joplin, approximately six miles, began to spool down a little bit, made a right hand turn and went on down into Newton County down toward Diamond, Mo., approximately 13.8 miles in all.

"Our first responders refer to this particular map as the fish, because of its shape, so they came into the EOC and said do you have anymore maps of the fish? Initially our fire chief got into a helicopter and sketched out the damage area. This particular map was brought to us by benefit of FEMA and the U.S. Geological Survey and their satellites. This has been of multiple uses for us.

"One thing that has been rather nice is that we've had multiple communities ask us for copies of this as an overlay and they then took that overlay to their communities and said this is what happened to Joplin, coming through a residential area, what would happen to us if the same thing happened?"

"Let me just say right up front, I'm going to sound like a PSA for FEMA and that's fine. We saw the stories of Katrina; the FEMA of today is not the FEMA of back then. They are very collaborative, they were very cooperative, they helped us in any way, shape or form that they could, not the least of which is they brought in this satellite data map and so we could do some grid work on this for search and rescue and for rebuild.

"They zoomed in from a satellite to each individual property and identified it as destroyed, majorly destroyed, partially destroyed, lightly destroyed, by looking at them. For many of you in the industry, you know this is true, for the rest of you who are not in the industry, those stories about the government being able to look down from the sky and read your license plate — they are true. And I know that's true because I asked for an electronic copy of this, they say no. Why not, because you can zoom in on these places as well. They gave us printouts all we wanted, but we never did get an electronic copy of it.

"We used this in our discussions we've had on after-action reviews since then. That map pretty much is the story, you can see where it started out small and got wider and then went across the city from west to east."

STATE AND FEDERAL RESPONSE

Stammer said the state and federal agencies that responded were generally very helpful and respectful of the local control he and the city sought to maintain.

"The state emergency response and the federal emergency response to us was outstanding. Again, we have worked with the Missouri Emergency Response agencies for years, they know us by name, they've been to our EOC, I have most of those people on my speed dial on my phone, I have 420 names on my phone, which is just a work phone, so if you called me and your name did not show up, you went to voice mail.

"FEMA came in and did some rather innovative things for us. Number one, I told you about the map. Another thing that was interesting that they did was they provided us with a full time administrative assistant. She knew everybody and their emails and their super-secret phone numbers, so when the city manager came by and said I need to talk to that one gal who came by and handed out the stuff that had to do with the housing, she said oh yeah, that's so and so, I'll get her for you. She was wonderful.

"The weather service brought in an embedded meteorologist, Kevin Hoover, we love Kevin, he got along with everyone real well, he has that southern drawl that just kind of makes everyone melt. He likes to eat; we had lots of chicken. (Laughter)"

Stammer talked about coordinating all the different agencies in town at the height of the response.

"We would do a briefing at 7 a.m. and 7 p.m. every day. We had what was called an Incident Action Plan (IAP). It was a bible for us. It listed what our objectives were for that day, who was in charge of the objectives, when we wanted those done, what equipment and supplies were required.

"Everyone that was out in the field their position, their cell phone numbers, the day's weather report, any other materials that we needed, hazardous materials reports, anything like that was all part and parcel of that IAP, and very quickly word spread amongst all of the other organizations that we need one of those IAPs, we said fine, there's a price, you have to come to our 7 a.m. meeting and Kelly would give us the weather report at 7 a.m. and 7 p.m., every day.

"Probably one of those lessons learned, one of the things we didn't do well there, we should, instead of printing 50 copies of the IAP for department heads, we should have printed like 300 and handed them out to every cop, every firefighter, everybody in the health department so they would know exactly what our plans were for that particular day."

THE EOC

The nerve center of Joplin's response to the catastrophe was the Emergency Operations Center, a Cold-War-era bunker in the basement of the Donald E. Clark Safety and Justice Center in the north part of town.

"It is a very nice place," Stammer said. "It has full power, electricity, in a basement. My standing joke is when we have storms, I can stand there; watch the radar, drink a latte and a tornado goes over the top and we say what was that? I have no idea; we are under two feet of stressed-reinforced concrete. We had quite a few crews set up there."

The help from the state came in the form of more than rescue crews in the debris area. The state sent teams to help with the reams of reports and paperwork that comes with keeping track of the living and dead, those evacuated and those searching for survivors. He said as trivial as it might seem to worry about paperwork, those reports and documents were important to keeping track of the search, keeping people safe and wasting as little time as possible.

"Incident Support Teams, they were a godsend to us. An incident support team, if you've been through the National Incident Management System, I'm trying hard not to say NIMS and ICS and all that, if you've been through the Incident Command training through the National Incident Management System, you'll know you have a standardized method of arranging yourself. You have an incident commander, you have a public information officer, a safety officer, a liaison officer, then you have four department heads for operations, planning, logistics and finance and admin.

"We had all those people. Some of them weren't in town; some of them were victims. My police department PIO, it took him 30 minutes to get out of his basement. He radioed in and said 'I'm out of service.' A week later we saw him. One of my primary backups as incident commander, the same story on him. We have, in the state of Missouri, Incident Support Teams that are trained to come into a city or a town, an area, to help support in this particular situation.

"I called Ryan Nichols, emergency management director in Springfield, about 7 p.m. that night, I'd been calling him all night because I needed this and that. I finally called him and said I need an IST, they were there in two hours."

Stammer said the terrorist attacks on Sept. 11, 2001 changed everything when it came to emergency management in America.

He said it freed up money for preparing for disasters as well as terrorist attacks.

"Now thanks to the funding that was available after 9/11, when you call for a fire department you get a truck, maybe two, they have radios that can be tuned to different frequencies, they will bring a mass casualty trailer, they will bring a hazmat trailer, and often times they will bring a communications trailer. The incident support team out of Springfield brought all their own stuff in terms of forms and everything they needed to run an office and they brought their own communications trailer, which was a microwave relay truck. We didn't have phones so they just set it up, pointed it back toward Springfield and for the next 11 days we ran off of Springfield's phone system."

21. LOCAL RADIO'S
FINEST HOUR

THE FOLLOWING SPEECH WAS PRESENTED BY GOV. JAY NIXON TO THE MISSOURI
BROADCASTERS CONVENTION SATURDAY, JUNE 5, 2011.

I want to thank all of you in the Missouri Broadcasters Association - especially those of who are here today from Joplin, Sedalia and the surrounding areas.

Some of you may have been personally affected by the tornado; you may have lost friends, neighbors, colleagues, homes and possessions.

But you kept going.

On behalf of all the people in the state of Missouri, I salute your courage, your professionalism and your dedication to serving your community throughout this catastrophe.

Courage.

Professionalism.

Service to others.

These are the hallmarks of broadcast journalism at its finest.

And in the last two weeks in Missouri, in the aftermath of one of the most destructive tornadoes in history, I have seen broadcast journalism in its finest hour. You play a critical role in getting accurate information to the public when time is of the essence: warning folks of the coming dangers, helping them prepare and get to safety, and finding help after the immediate crisis is past.

We've had more than our fair share of crises this year: the historic blizzard that required us to close I-70; the flooding of 130,000 acres in the Bootheel; the New Year's and Good Friday tornadoes; and, of course, the devastating EF5 tornado in Joplin.

Unfortunately, it doesn't look like Mother Nature is ready to give us a break. Yesterday I was in St. Joe, where we are trying to help communities along the Missouri River prepare for imminent flooding. The river's already up, and it's only going to keep getting higher.

So you'd better keep some boots in the trunk of your car.

In times of crisis, things are chaotic.

People are scared.

People hear rumors.

People don't know what to do or where to go for help.

And in times like those we've witnessed in Missouri in the last six months, what you do — or don't do — can literally make the difference between life and death.

Unlike the national media, you are in it for the long haul.

Unlike the national media, you've got skin in the game because you live here.

When you get it right, your community gets the benefit.

When you get it wrong, your community suffers.

The point is that what you do matters. Not sometimes; all the time. Not in theory; in the real world.

In the first few days after the Joplin tornado, my office received hundreds of calls from the national and international media asking for interviews and updates, body counts and damage estimates.

Everyone from the BBC to Al Jazeera wanted to know what was happening in Joplin, and what we were going to do next.

I was interviewed on Fox, CNN, NBC, CBS, NPR and many others. It was an exceptional opportunity to share Joplin's story with a global audience, and hopefully it will help in Joplin's recovery.

But if the national broadcast media get it wrong, they don't have to live with the consequences the way you do.

National media don't run the risk of bumping into the city manager or the police chief in the checkout lane at the grocery store, or in the next pew on Sunday.

They're one and done.

All of you are part of your communities; you're in it for the long haul, for better or for worse.

And that brings me to a remarkable story I'd like to share with you today, about some of your colleagues down in Joplin.

At about 4 p.m. on May 22, Radio station KZRG in Joplin began getting reports that severe weather in Kansas was sweeping in from the West - headed right toward Joplin.

They crashed their normal schedule, and went to live, wall-to-wall coverage of the impending storm.

As he watched the rain blowing sideways and chunks of debris flying through the air, News Director Josh Marsh was on the phone with emergency responders on the scene, as the tornado touched down, chewing its way through the heart of Joplin.

At exactly 5:41 p.m., the line went dead.

The tornado had knocked out cell phone towers and 20,000 people were without electricity.

But the radio signal was still strong.

Once their back-up generators kicked on, KZRG broke the "Golden Rule" of radio, and began taking live, unscreened calls on the air.

The first caller was a woman, pregnant with twins, frantically looking for her husband.

Hearing her voice on the radio, he called the station to let her know he was at work and OK.

Then a call came in from Duquesne, where the tornado had knocked out police radios; they wanted help dispatching officers where they were needed most.

Two KZRG reporters, Chad Elliot and Rob Meyer, hit the streets, describing a scene that looked like hell had exploded: mangled cars, houses and business in ruins, people screaming and running.

The calls kept coming: Can you find my daughter? Can you help me get a doctor? I have food, where can I take it?

It was chaos.

But in the eye of the chaos, the folks at KZRG had a moment of clarity.

Joplin needed a lifeline; so that's what they would be.

"You have to step into that role, so that's what you do," Marsh said.

Miles away, station owner James Zimmer had a similar moment of clarity. He was on vacation with his family; they had gathered to observe the one-year anniversary of the death of James's oldest son, Michael, 25. Michael had just graduated from St. Louis University law school. On Mother's Day of last year, he was in an accident. Two weeks later he was gone. He died on May 22, 2010.

When the call came in from Joplin, James answered.

He got off the phone and his surviving son looked at him and said, "Dad, you need to go." And James said "I know. That's what we do."

Like his five brothers — three of whom are here today — James Zimmer grew up in the radio business started by their dad, Jerome. James started working at radio stations when he was 12, emptying trash cans and cleaning bathrooms.

And so, just minutes after the tornado struck, James put his grief on hold, drove to Joplin and went back to his old job — emptying trash cans and cleaning bathrooms. At age 52.

Things snowballed from there. Everyone at Zimmer pitched in, including eight employees - a quarter of the station's workforce - left homeless by the tornado. Sales manager Chris Bullard got a relief effort going in the parking lot.

Others brought barbecue pits and started cooking for anybody who was hungry. For days, so many people came to the station to give and get help, it looked like a street party, 24/7.

And 24/7, KZRG was on the air with the latest news and information, holding that lifeline taut between victims and volunteers, shelters and the homeless, state services and those in need, the lost and the found.

They helped spread the word about the memorial service held last Sunday at Missouri Southern State University, where President Obama and I were present. Their coverage was interrupted only once, at precisely 5:41 p.m. last Sunday, when the city of Joplin observed a moment of silence.

By Wednesday of this week, the mood of Joplin had started to shift.

After talking with community and business leaders and taking their pulse, James felt it was time to move on.

The wall-to-wall disaster coverage was getting folks down. They were ready for a little music… a little laughter… ready to reconnect through broadcast news to the rest of the universe.

This weekend, James and his wife are going to get out of town and take some time off. They need to grieve a while, James said, and then they'll be ready to move on.

I offer their story to remind all of us here of the great power, and the great responsibility, of broadcast media, not just to inform and entertain us, but to connect and protect us, to unite and uplift us.

The role of the free press is sacred in our democracy. In fact, it was so important to the framers, Thomas Jefferson in particular, that the press is the only economic enterprise mentioned specifically in the Constitution.

In the course of more than five decades as a public figure, Jefferson took his share of lumps from the press, and it left him a little sensitive to criticism.

But because the press both reflects and affects public opinion, Jefferson considered it essential in holding government accountable to the people.

There's a lot of responsibility on both ends of that transaction.

It's your responsibility to hold government - to hold your Governor - accountable.

It's also your responsibility to hold yourselves to the highest standards of accuracy, fairness and balance in order to serve the public.

When the next crisis comes, I hope you will seize the opportunity to serve the public the way no other entity can.

It could very well be your finest hour.

22. MIRACLE OF THE HUMAN SPIRIT

THE FOLLOWING SPEECH WAS GIVEN BY JOPLIN CITY MANAGER MARK ROHR MAY 29, 2011, ONE WEEK AFTER THE JOPLIN TORNADO, DURING A CEREMONY AT LANDRETH PARK.

Being the Joplin city manager, typically, if you've been watching during the week, I prepare statements to read to the press. Beneath the monotone, there's a turbulent sea and that is my way, in terms of planning and dealing with things, to try and be as structured as possible. Today I speak from the heart. I do have some notes, I do have an outline to help me if I lose my way, but the message comes from the heart.

If I have trouble getting through this, I apologize to the citizens in advance.

Approximately a week ago, the city of Joplin suffered an unspeakable tragedy. We lost family members, loved ones, friends, neighbors and fellow citizens. We suffered inestimable losses in terms of property within the city of Joplin. But I have always been of the opinion that out of something bad, something good can happen if you have the right perspective.

And what I've witnessed here in the last week is the miracle of the human spirit. It has reaffirmed my belief in mankind. The people behind me, my department heads, have worked in excess of 100 hours this week to recover from this tragedy. We have had innumerable volunteers come into Joplin from literally all over the country. We have had help from other government agencies throughout the region, state and nation come to Joplin to help our citizens.

We have received countless emails and messages from throughout the world extending their condolences to the city of Joplin and pledging their help to enable us to recover. We have had excellent assistance from our state and federal government and if you heard the messages today, they pledge to stay with us throughout. In my past experiences in life, when someone close to me has passed away or some other tragedy has occurred, I always talk to other people and say, man that really slows you down, that really requires you to sit and put things into perspective and try to determine what is important and what isn't important. But like most people, that wears off in a few days and you get caught up in the pace of your everyday life and, in the circumstance that surrounds you, slowing down and gathering perspective wanes.

I tried to think of a way to commemorate those people who lost their lives in this unspeakable tragedy and what I came up with is a request that I am making of you here today: that we capture and invoke the miracle of the human spirit that we have seen here in Joplin and we utilize it and we channel it.

And if I forget, you remind me, and if you forget, I'm going to remind you. We direct that spirit toward rebuilding Joplin better than it was before the storm and we return our lives to a state of peace, love and prosperity as soon as possible.

23. SOMETIMES, LOVE IS ALL YOU HAVE

By Amy Gilbert

We recently had been through a terrible EF5 tornado that took all of our material belongings, but luckily we were spared. The few days after the tornado were a blur, don't really recall a whole lot that happened, just having to deal with all the things that were most important. Getting our children somewhere safe and other things such as disconnecting utilities, dealing with housing issues, insurance issues, trying to be proactive and finding a place to live was most important. Our girls were staying with family members and getting them back home to us was the first and foremost thought that entered our minds every day!

The Wednesday after the tornado, we had found a cute little house that would be our new home, sadly, we weren't able to take possession until June 24th which meant our girls would have to continue to stay with family, but then we could focus on replacing our vehicles and trying to salvage what we could and with the burden of where we were going to live being taken care of — we did just that, found two cars quickly and things seemed to be falling into place - as best they could with all the emotions that came along with our lives that had forever been changed.

Then Thursday, June 2, we received a call from a dear family friend who worked for MTV that she had submitted our story to CMT; Sugarland was planning on doing a relief effort for the victims of the recent tornadoes in Tuscaloosa and Joplin. Our friend told them what our situation was, along with submitted pictures and CMT wanted our girls to be a part of the show. We had very little time to prepare, our girls were in Columbia with their aunt and uncle and there was a lot to do before we could go to Nashville and be a part of the CMT Music Awards. We needed to be down there the following Tuesday for rehearsal for the show. The girls were driven to Kansas City by their aunt and uncle; Eric and I drove up by ourselves. And we were just beyond thrilled to see our girls, we hadn't seen them since May 23, and it was a very emotional time for us all. And we were all so very excited, but still reeling from what had happened to get us there.

On the airplane to Nashville, the seats were unassigned and we had to sit separately. Tiffani was visiting with a couple sitting next to her, when a gentleman asked me if Lexi and I were with her and if he heard correctly that we were going to be a part of the show with Sugarland. I told him that we were, and he introduced himself as Joseph Loyd, the stage manager for Sugarland. Needless to say, we talked throughout the flight and he learned that Lexi went by Lou most of the time and he was just so nice and genuine. After the flight, in baggage claim, Joseph had started introducing Lou and Tiff to other members of the crew, we met Whitney Pastorek (PR for Sugarland), and just a whole slew of people who were part of the Sugarland family. The ice was broken and our nervousness was turning into excitement and anticipation of what to expect next.

We left the airport and drove to the hotel. There was a CMT care package for us down at the front desk. It was filled with all sorts of wonderful things, tickets to the four-day Country Music Festival, t-shirts, hats, coupons for various attractions, it was truly amazing. Rehearsal was at 7 p.m. and we drove to the arena. Inside the arena, our "Talent Escort" Laura greeted us and she was assigned to us until the show was over. Along with Laura, came a "security guard" named Dave for Lexi, because she was a minor, she had to have a security guard with her at all times. We then started to go into the arena and Joseph saw us and called out to us by name, it was incredible. The Sugarland family was so nice and just took us under their wings to help us with all that we needed to do and explain what was happening and what to expect along the way.

We were then introduced to Jennifer Nettles and Kristian Bush of Sugarland. Talk about compassionate, caring people, they were absolutely amazing. The girls started doing what they needed to do with the song that Jennifer and Kristian were going to do during the award show the next night. The song was called "Stand Up," and people could call in and donate money to the relief efforts to the Red Cross for the victims of the tornadoes. The girls were going to be flying the LOVE flag that Jennifer painted at the beginning of the song. They walked throughout the crowd, and waved it proudly for our community in hopes that everyone would donate to help the victims of this horrible tornado.

During the practice runs, we got to see Zac Brown Band and Toby Keith perform as well as Sugarland. It was truly amazing. The girls practiced twice, and then it was over. We were interviewed by Billboard.com, The Weather Channel, and then by Sugarland's media crew. We had to have fittings with our wardrobe people; we all received outfits provided by CMT, and the girls received outfits to take home with them as well. Words can never express how much of a dream this was for our family, we just were so overwhelmed with everything that it felt just like that - a dream.

The day of the show, we went to the arena around noon, even though the show didn't start until 7. We were so starstruck as soon as we walked in the back door, greeted by Laura and Dave and then we were taken to our dressing room. They put the minor performers in the same dressing room. The minors at the show were none other than Justin Bieber, Lauren Alaina, and Scotty McCreary. We were all so excited but we never did actually stay in the same dressing room. But we did get the pleasure of meeting all three of them, as well as pictures with Scotty and Lauren and JB autographed a CD and DVD for Lexi, as well as pictures with him. It truly was a dream come true for her! Every eight-year-old girl in America loved Justin Bieber. It is something we all will never, ever forget.

The day of the show was a complete whirlwind. We were all over the place with doing another practice run, getting our attire situated, and just watching all these superstars who were starting to show up. We saw Ludacris, Shania Twain, Lady Antebellum, Luke Bryan, Naomi Judd, Gary

Busey, John Rich (Big and Rich), Thompson Square, Keith Urban, Nicole Kidman, The Band Perry, Rascal Flatts, Martina McBride, Jason Aldean, Kid Rock and Sheryl Crow, just to name a few. We also got to meet Kiefer Thompson of Thompson Square, he wanted to meet with us because he is from the area, found out in speaking with him that he had both worked in Joplin and went to college at Missouri Southern. Such a small, small world.

This never would have been a possibility for our family if our community had not been ravaged by this horrible tornado. It was just an unreal experience and helped us to heal to the extent that something good can come from something bad. It gave us an opportunity to spend some time with our girls and it allowed us to leave the reality of what had happened to us personally and Joplin for just a week, but in the next breath, we were still trying to deal with what was going on back home, our hearts were heavy at the same time because we wanted to be there.

When Sugarland finally took the stage and the girls were waving the LOVE flag throughout the crowd, the tears were flowing, both because the song was so beautiful and fitting for what we were going through and also because our girls made us so proud. This memory will forever be in our hearts, that even through the hard times "love" can get you through anything. That you have to stand up and make a difference and that you can help just by opening your hearts.

We are forever grateful for these memories, because sometimes, love is all you have.

24. I'LL NEVER FORGET

BY AMY HERRON

It has been two months since the day I'll never forget.

Never forget the roar of the tornado, the prayers rolling off my lips, the silence of a family member's dropped call in the midst of the storm. I'll never forget the tears that we cried when we emerged from the basement. I'll never forget the relief of hearing my Dad's voice. I'll never forget the embrace of the unfamiliar volunteer who drove 16 hours to ensure we had food in our stomachs and love in our hearts.

I'll never forget the night I shared the bed with my little sister because we didn't want to be alone. I'll never forget falling asleep to the sound of sirens and the smell of gasoline. I'll never forget going to sleep, knowing that people were still buried, under the rubble. I'll never forget the night I felt God's embrace. I'll never forget the weeks that I saw angels, doing unthinkable acts of kindness. I'll never forget not knowing if my friends and family survived. I'll never forget those who didn't.

I'll never forget. We will never forget. Joplin will never forget.

Amy Herron is a student at Pittsburg State University

25. COMING TOGETHER

BY JOHN HACKER

The tempest of May 22, 2011, set off a wave of change in health care in Joplin, and in Carthage, that no one could possibly have imagined on May 21, 2011.

For nearly 20 years, since Freeman Hospital bought Oak Hill Hospital and became Freeman Health Systems, Joplin has been a two-hospital town.

Freeman Health Systems and St. John's Regional Medical Center faced their shares of challenges while struggling to meet the demand for services in an increasingly complex medical world.

Like they had since the 1970s, the two medical giants of Southwest Missouri eyed each other from either side of the county line, Freeman in Newton County and St. John's in Jasper County. The two hospitals cooperated in many ways to avoid duplication of services, but they were competitors as well, battling for a share of the medical dollars Missouri, Kansas, Oklahoma and to a lesser extent, Arkansas.

In Carthage, McCune-Brooks Regional Hospital, a 26-bed city-owned hospital, had been in its new building on Russell Smith Way just off U.S.

Highway 71 for a little more than three years.

Like many community hospitals, McCune-Brooks had its share of struggles. Money was tight enough that the hospital had to plan carefully and make changes to meet the covenants it needed to avoid defaulting on the bonds it sold to finance the $50 million building. Federal health care reform loomed in the near future, bringing uncertainty to many aspects of medical care.

WHIRLWIND OF CHANGE

Everything changed for all three hospitals in less than half an hour.

The change at St. John's was immediate. The winds tore through the iconic, nine-story hospital that had stood on the south Joplin skyline for more than 40 years, rendering it useless in minutes. St. John's doctors immediately started treating patients in the parking lot and evacuating their own hospital while looking for a place to set up shop and continue treating the wounded. They eventually headed downtown to Joplin's Memorial Hall and set up an emergency room there before moving into a MASH-like set of tents in the shadow of their shattered building.

It was almost as immediate at Freeman. Wounded from St. John's and the area around both hospitals started streaming into Freeman West almost instantly, leaving little time to adjust to the new reality that half of Joplin's hospital beds and one entire emergency room had been wiped out.

It took less than an hour for the magnitude of the disaster to register in Carthage. McCune-Brooks doctors, nurses and staff would treat more than 300 patients, some with severe injuries rarely seen away from a battlefield, in one night.

What happened that night has already been recorded. What happened in the next few months is almost as dramatic as the medical community in two towns changed forever.

COOPERATION AND EXPANSION

Within days of the tornado, officials with Sisters of Mercy Health System announced that St. John's would be rebuilt under a new name, Mercy Joplin.

Freeman was adding beds and would eventually announce that it

Mike McCurry, Chief Operating Officer for Mercy Health System, speaks to a crowd at the April 11, 2012, ribbon cutting for the new Mercy Joplin component hospital.
PHOTO BY JOHN HACKER

would complete the two top floors of the Gary and Donna Hall tower, adding more than 100 beds to its capacity.

McCune-Brooks also announced an expansion. Carthage's community hospital had been built with an extra wing left empty for future expansion. McCune-Brooks officials announced that they would double its bed capacity from 25 to 52.

McCune-Brooks CEO Bob Copeland said he didn't know if the increase would be permanent, but it would likely last at least until a new St. John's Regional Medical Center is built in Joplin.

"We're definitely planning on this for the next two and a half years because it's going to take them that long to rebuild," Copeland said. "In addition to the nursing personnel, we need additional physical therapists, we need respiratory therapists, lab workers, x-ray techs. Most clinical departments will be expanding including the support departments like housekeeping, food service and etc.

"Also a part of this will be additional physicians and we're working with St. John's to get some of their physicians over here to begin working."

And that was just the beginning.

Copeland said McCune-Brooks is "leasing" these 70 employees from St. John's to help staff the expanded hospital. The employees will still be employed by Mercy St. John's and Mercy St. John's will bill McCune-Brooks for their services.

Copeland said McCune-Brooks plans to use space that was built for future expansion and turn that space into patient rooms and other service locations now. The hospital will go from 25 to 52 patient rooms, activate and equip a third surgery suite, expand the birthing center, and expand other services.

Copeland estimated the cost to buy all the beds and equipment to expand to this new level at about $1.5 million.

"It's going to bust the budget from an expense standpoint but hopefully at the end of the day we'll have higher revenue to pay for it," Copeland said. "We're working with St. John's on some of those expenditures. They know that we're taking care of their patients and the growth has occurred with them so at the end of the day I think St. John's will help us with some of those expenditures. We're in the process of working on those details at the present time."

It was the beginning of a relationship between Mercy and McCune-

Brooks that would grow.

On June 30, 2011, McCune-Brooks announced that Mercy would give the Carthage hospital $1.8 million to buy the equipment so McCune-Brooks could bring those rooms, and an additional surgical suite, online.

"On behalf of the co-workers there at Mercy, the physicians, board members and all of the Sisters of Mercy Health Systems, we want to express our gratitude for this opportunity to work closely together," said Mercy Joplin President Gary Pulsipher. "Many of our co-workers are here already. And you guys have welcomed them just very, very well, but the important thing for us, as Bob noted so well, this will give us a chance for our physicians and our staff to come and work to keep their skills strong while we work on rebuilding in Joplin so we're so grateful for this opportunity."

RELATIONSHIP GROWS

Rumors of a deeper relationship between Mercy and McCune-Brooks began to flourish as the weeks progressed.

The two hospital leaders, Pulsipher in Joplin and Copeland in Carthage, talked in September 2011 about what was developing in open, but somewhat cryptic and guarded terms.

From Copeland:

"I have excess capacity here, we had the empty 1800 wing and we had a third operating room that we were not using, so Mercy desires to take advantage of the excess capacity we have primarily because they want their general surgeons and other surgeons to work and in addition to the services they already have over in Joplin, they can also work here. They're using our 1800 pod and our third operating room and for that Mercy gave us an unrestricted gift of $1.8 million and we've used that money to buy the equipment needed to outfit those two rooms. Plus we've purchased other equipment in other departments necessary to increase the load that we've experienced. We've essentially doubled the size of our hospital.

"A very important part of the assistance agreement is that Mercy is providing to is anesthesiologists and hospitalists. This hospital has never had anesthesiologists on our staff. We've been very blessed to have wonderful nurse anesthetists that work for us, but to have that physician supervision piece in the operating room for anesthesia purposes really sets up to the standard of care that already exists at St. John's and Freeman. We're really very happy to have that.

"Secondly, with the hospitalists, we've never had those kinds of physicians here either. Those kinds of physicians provide patient care. If there is a direct admission from the medical unit from St. John's, they can accept those direct admissions, plus they will accept any unassigned patients out of our emergency room."

From Pulsipher:

"Mercy's whole focus is what's best for the community. No one came in to Bob and said here, take it or leave it, here's the deal. We've got any number of relationships across Mercy; we're across the four states here. In fact, even with Freeman, for example, because Freeman and St. John's have been hardy competitors, but they utilize our courier and delivery services. They were spending a lot of money couriering stuff back and forth and we found a way they could use our guys because our guys were making the trips anyway. It could be something as simple as that.

"We're looking at all the things that we can potentially do and if there are ways we can help this community and this hospital, then we may just work on some of those things. It's still very early in the process but it's been such a relief to have McCune-Brooks here. Bob and his board really reached out and said we're here to help; we can put your people to work. We started getting after it the first few days to see how we can get some of our surgeons to work. Our family practice physicians that work with us in town are about 30 percent busier than they've been, but our specialists, because they don't have a place to work, are about 50 percent as busy as they were, so for Bob to have an operating room is huge."

Copeland talked about how the relationship between the small community hospital and the eighth-largest Catholic medical system in the country developed.

"It goes without saying that, right after the tornado, I reached out to Gary and we also reached out to the corporate office in St. Louis. I just wanted someone to know, within Mercy, that we had excess capacity and that we will do anything we can to help. To me, that's the right thing to do in health care. We're all in this business to help other people and we wanted to help, because I would expect, if the same thing were to happen to me, Freeman and St. John's would help our hospital so it was my turn to help them. It was just a few days later that a couple of senior executives from

Mercy, and Gary, toured our hospital, and they saw the excess capacity we had.

"They saw our beautiful private rooms, they saw the fact that we bring nature into the building, they learned of our plans for growth, the fact that both wings, the 1800 pod and the 1700 pod have a firm foundation that if in the future we want to go up, we can. They heard about our plans for horizontal expansion, then finally we concluded the tour in our hospital chapel, and they heard and saw first hand that our chapel is located in the direct center of our hospital, just as in us, our heart lies within the center of us, it represents who we are. They saw the steel crossbeams that make the cross inside the chapel. So I think when the senior executives of Mercy saw these things, they thought what a wonderful place for our patients to go and then we entered into these two agreements."

At that time, Pulsipher and Copeland would not say how far this relationship would go, but it was clear it was going somewhere.

"I'd say it's still very early," Pulsipher said. "We're still working to make sure the assistance agreements work out, the things that we're already doing. Then we're just looking at the options that are there that would make sense."

Copeland said, as tragic as it was, the tornado was bringing positive change to his community hospital.

When asked how McCune-Brooks had been doing as far as paying off its construction debts, Copeland said: "We were not setting the world on fire financially. We have three big bond covenants, the operating ratio, the day's cash on hand and the debt service coverage ratio are the three big covenants that we have to meet. Since we've moved out here, we've missed two of the three or one of the three every year.

"This past year, we missed the debt service coverage ratio, and that has a penalty that if I miss that two years in a row, then we could be in default of our bonds. This fiscal year, 2012, is critical to our hospital from a financial perspective. We had to be able to hit that ratio and we had a good plan in place, we got our expenses under control, we renegotiated some managed care contracts, we worked with our physicians and we had a really good plan. In fact, on May 22, we had 18 or 19 patients in here that day, so we were starting the month out really well. Then May 22 happened and with the increased volume that we've had, we are well above the mark on two of those three. The day's cash on hand takes a long time to rebuild, so we're well below the mark on that, but we're making good strides toward making that."

Mercy stepped in to help McCune-Brooks by buying most of the outstanding bonds, putting the big Catholic ministry in charge of setting the rules for McCune-Brooks' debt.

"I do not know specifically how many bonds have been purchased, but it is a true statement," Copeland said. "But bondholders have no control over this hospital. The only way the bondholders have control of this hospital is in the event of a default. Again, the way we're going, that's just not going to happen."

"This action actually ensures that it won't," Pulsipher added. "If Mercy can hold the majority of those, bondholders who don't know hospital operations can require Bob to do some goofy things."

MORE BEDS

As Mercy and McCune-Brooks moved closer together, Freeman Health Systems was doing what it had to do to meet the sudden shortage of bed space in Joplin.

At the time of the tornado, Freeman had 287 beds compared to St. John's with more than 320 beds. After the tornado, St. John's quickly set up a 60-bed hospital in a system of tents, while McCune-Brooks added more than 25 beds to its hospital, but it wasn't enough to make up for the lost capacity.

In September, Freeman announced it was completing the top two-floors of its new Gary and Donna Hall tower. This space, like the 1800 wing at McCune-Brooks, had been completed with the intention of using it for future expansion, but the future came much more quickly than the hospitals could have imagined.

The work added 58 beds to Freeman's capacity, bringing it to 345 beds.

"When we built the west tower campus, we completed that project in the fall of 2007, we actually shelled out the fifth and sixth floor so they are concrete slabs ready for future expansion," said Jeffrey Carrier, chief nursing officer at Freeman Health Systems. "Fast forward four years later, we are taking advantage of that wisdom and vision our board had in building out that fifth and sixth floor and we're going to build these 50 brand new, high-end, acuity-adaptable rooms.

"Acuity adaptable bed or a universal bed is one a patient can occupy from admission to discharge even if the patient's condition changes. Obviously there is a lot of benefit when you have that kind of system."

Carrier said in September 2011, the project to complete the rooms would cost Freeman a total of $15 million. The fifth floor was ready to occupy in April 2012 and the sixth floor was finished in July 2012.

Carrier said the hospital hopes to not only increase bed capacity, but also improve the patient's experience at the hospital at the same time.

"We're going to have an improvement in patient progression, or 'through-put,' in our hospital as well," Carrier said. "This is a big one, a decrease in wait times and delays in care. Right now when you come to several hospitals in this area, you have a lengthy wait time and we hope to decrease that with this expansion. We also hope to improve the patient experience and perception of care because these rooms are really beautiful, nice warm colors, wood floors, comfortable furniture, state-of-the-art beds, high definition, flat screen televisions on the walls, wireless capability for family members if they want to surf the internet, a couch in the room, if they want to sleep in the room, a really nice pullout couch."

Christen Stark, spokeswoman for Freeman, said the hospital hired an additional 80-100 clinical and non-clinical staff to operate the new rooms.

MERCY REBUILDS

The Sisters of Mercy, in the meantime, continued to plan for reconstruction of the former St. John's hospital, now to be known as Mercy Joplin.

Construction started on what was called a modular hospital immediately south of the tent facility on St. John's Boulevard in Joplin.

The modular hospital was made up of components that were assembled by a company in California, and then shipped to Joplin.

Mercy was also looking for a new place to build the final replacement for the old St. John's. The company decided not to rebuild on the existing lot at 26th and McClelland Boulevard, citing mines under part of the land that made it unusable for expansion.

Instead it decided to donate that land to the city, school district and other entities and announced in August 2011 plans to build a nearly $1 billion campus on 50th Street near the intersection of I-44 and Hearnes

Boulevard (South Main Street).

"We are making this commitment because it's the right thing to do for Joplin," Lynn Britton, president/CEO of Mercy which includes 28 hospitals and more than 200 outpatient facilities in a seven-state area, said in a media release. "The May 22 tornado devastated our community here in Joplin and destroyed our hospital, but we've promised all along we would rebuild. We plan to break ground January 2012 and open the new hospital, as well as a secondary northeast campus, in 2014 and 2015." The new 327-bed hospital will be built about three miles from the destroyed St. John's Hospital. The new hospital will include medical, surgical, critical care, women's/children's (labor, delivery, recovery and postpartum rooms), behavioral health and rehab, with planned expansion up to 424 beds as needed. The new hospital is slated for completion in 2015.

The decision went against the suggestion of some in Joplin that the hospital rebuild along the U.S. Highway 249 corridor in the northeast part of town but Mercy's plans to rebuild, made clear by the ministry since the days immediately following the storm, were a relief to Joplin city officials.

"St. John's was the largest employer in Joplin and it was important that those health care providers not leave this community," said Kim Day, president of Mercy's Central Region of hospitals, in September 2011. "Often times when that kind of tragedy hits a town, people do leave, and it was important that they stay. The city manager in Joplin has told us over and over that that commitment that we made has really helped us retain people in Joplin. We've had very few of our co-workers leave. We have about 2,200 co-workers and our salary runs about $2.5 million every two weeks so we're continuing to make sure that happens. We've had very few of our doctors leave which was extremely important."

In all, Mercy committed nearly $1 billion to the rebuilding effort in Joplin, including more than $100 million for the 110-bed component hospital that will serve until the new hospital is finished in 2015, and more than $800 million for the 50th Street campus and the proposed northeast campus.

Plans for that northeast campus became clear in October 2011 when Mercy announced plans to lease McCune-Brooks Regional Hospital in Carthage from the city of Carthage, with an option to buy that $50 million hospital in five years, pending approval by voters in Carthage.

Day said the pressure on Mercy to build the replacement for St. John's near the intersection of Missouri 249 and Zora Street in northeast Joplin was big, but Mercy decided to go with the 50th Street location and use McCune-Brooks as that northeast facility.

"We did have a lot of community members and a lot of people helping us do a site selection," Day said. "They made it very clear that the growth corridor in this area was on the northeast side and that's where we needed to put this facility. We got a lot of pressure to make that happen and we did push back and said we don't think that's right, if we build our main facility at 249 and Zora, it's going to have a significant impact on McCune-Brooks.

"We made the decision to put our facility at I-44 and Main, but what we do know is that the northeast corridor is extremely important to us. We do know there will be growth up here. We believe strongly that McCune-Brooks gives us the opportunity to have a significant presence in that northeast corridor so what we want to do is we want to build a stronger relationship with McCune-Brooks and actually expand and build services here in this community that will allow us to serve this entire growth corridor that we think is going to grow significantly in the future."

Day talked about the opportunity Mercy had to move forward with the new campus on 50th street. He compared them to the financial troubles McCune-Brooks CEO Bob Copeland described at the Carthage hospital.

"We were struggling at St. John's," Day said. "Bob talked about the financial troubles we were having at McCune-Brooks. St. John's in Joplin, we were struggling financially. Even more difficult than that, the hospital there was built on significant mines and we had significant facility issues. About six months ago, prior to that storm, we had to tear down our parking garage because it was sinking. We didn't have managed care contracts prior to Mercy taking over. We're trying very hard to resolve that particular issue. But as we look forward right now, we have the opportunity to completely start over and to completely reposition ourselves in the marketplace."

In November, the Carthage City Council approved Mercy's lease of McCune-Brooks, to take affect on Jan. 1, 2012, when that hospital became Mercy McCune-Brooks Hospital.

Ron Petersen Sr., chairman of the McCune-Brooks Board of Trustees, told the Carthage City Council there were four reasons the lease was in the

While initially designed to be a temporary hospital for use only until the perma-nent hospital on 50th Street is finished, Mercy officials now say they are consid-ering keeping this building and using it after the permanent hospital is finished.
PHOTO BY JOHN HACKER

best interest of McCune-Brooks and Carthage residents.

• It prepares us for health care reform, and it is coming.

• Financially, this is in our best interest.

• Our community will have the additional services and Mercy's com-mitment of capital to grow.

• McCune-Brooks Regional Hospital can help Mercy.

26. AUTISTIC CHILDREN BENEFIT FROM OZARK CENTER

By John Hacker

Melissa Smith and her family probably would have moved away from the Joplin area to get help for their son, Braylon, if it hadn't been for the Ozark Center for Autism.

Daniel Grizzel's family believes Daniel, who has autism, could have benefited if the Ozark Center had been around when he was much younger.

All these people gathered last month to help bring awareness to a cause they believe in and help raise money for a center they believe is helping children across the region.

"I just want to support the cause and help him," said Daniel Grizzel's mom, Yolonda Grizzel, Carthage, at last month's Walk for Autism Awareness, an event that benefited the Freeman Health Systems' Ozark Center for Autism.

"If we can raise awareness for it, that's good," Yolonda Grizzel said.

Justyce Gardner celebrates after reading a thank you card during a Dec. 9, 2011, ceremony in which his grandparents, Rex and Judy Gardner of Grove, presented Ozark Center for Autism with a $20,000 gift in honor of Joe Knowles, a long-time member of Vintage Car Rally Association.

PHOTO BY JOHN HACKER

"People don't really know a whole lot about autism. I don't know a whole lot about it, I just know what I've experienced with Daniel. People need to know in case it ever happens to anyone they know or in their family."

New statistics, released by the Centers for Disease Control and Prevention in March, show that the number of children with conditions on the autism spectrum of disorders is much larger than previously thought.

Melissa Smith, whose son, Braylon, also has autism, knows the statistics all too well.

"There were 1 in 110 kids with some kind of autism and now its 1 in 88 so any opportunity we have to spread education and get everyone involved we want to be a part of that," Melissa Smith said as she held Braylon prior to the April 21 Walk for Autism Awareness at the Northpark Mall. "It means a lot for us. We would have probably moved to some other state had it not been for the Ozark Center for Autism. It's the best treatment option, it is the ideal place for Braylon to be so he can have the quality of life that we hope for and have these choices in life and opportunities that other kids can have."

The Ozark Center School of Autism has been around since 2007 and serves about 50 children in a number of different programs.

Jennifer Kirby, director of the Ozark Center, said the school is recovering quickly from the May 22, 2011, tornado, which destroyed its original facility at 2411 S. Jackson Ave.

The Center was back up and running a week after the tornado in temporary facilities at The Bridge in south Joplin and has since moved to offices at 3230 S. Wisconsin Ave.

But even these are temporary quarters. The Center received a donation from the Leffen Family of $3 million, which will be used to build a specialized, state-of-the-art facility on Picher Avenue.

"We found through the storm that we really can't do what we do without a place to do it," Kirby said. "That was a big revelation. I don't think we ever really thought about it before. We realized even more after the storm that that place has to be a specialized place for exactly what they need. We're relocating on Picher Avenue. We don't have a timetable but we're hoping to move on that soon."

In the meantime, with the help of more than $25,000 raised at last month's Walk for Autism Awareness, the center will continue working with children like, Braylon Smith, and adults from its current facility.

"Treatment at 18 months all the way through, has been our key piece to what has allowed him to advance," Melissa Smith said. "The Ozark Center for Autism has been such a support system for me and they have a support group that I can attend to talk and vent and get ideas from other individuals. That has been a real blessing in our lives."

27. MERCY JOPLIN OPENS COMPONENT HOSPITAL

BY JOHN HACKER

An unknown Mercy employee said it best as she was walking into the ribbon cutting for the new Mercy Joplin Hospital on April 11; "It's the most permanent-looking temporary building I've ever seen."

The startling thing in first seeing the new Mercy Hospital Joplin – the factory built, trucked-in replacement for the building destroyed by the May 22, 2011, tornado – is how attractive and permanent it looks.

Joplin has a new hospital as of mid-April, and this one isn't tents or trailers.

"This facility is a concrete and steel structure that will serve as our last temporary home until the opening of the new Mercy Joplin in 2015." Said John Farnen, executive director for planning, design and construction for Mercy Health System. "With additional services and conveniences for our patients and guests, the facility will have Labor and Delivery, a Pediatric Unit, an expanded Emergency and ICU department and up to 120 beds.

An aerial photo of the component hospital in February 2012 before completion.
PHOTO BY JOHN HACKER

Mercy is proud to be able to bring back these important services to Joplin."

The new facility will offer patients all the comforts and most services they would expect from a Mercy hospital. With steel construction that is sturdier than the old St. John's Regional Medical Center, the new Mercy building is a testament to modern technology and overtime workers coming together to build a complete hospital in eight months.

The new facility includes a full-scale emergency department. Surgeons can again conduct complex, open-heart procedures. Mercy doctors can deliver babies again. Patients can rest in rooms with monitoring features, communication capabilities and private

From the beginning of the day on May 22, 2011, to April 15, 2012, this will be the fourth new facility opened and operated by Mercy doctors, nurses and staff. That includes the old St. John's Regional Medical Center that was destroyed in the tornado, the temporary hospital that was opened at Joplin's Memorial Hall for a few weeks immediately after the storm, the tents installed to the east of the old St. John's that served for the past seven

Bob Copeland, CEO of Mercy McCune-Brooks Hospital in Carthage, attended the April 11 tour and ribbon cutting of the new Mercy Joplin Hospital.

PHOTO BY JOHN HACKER

months, and this 110-bed component hospital, assembled in a record eight months.

Farnen said the company took lessons learned from May 22 and incorporated them into this building.

"There will be flashlights, new communication systems, new battery lights not just emergency power," Farnen said. "It includes a protected emergency supply area, additional safe areas and training for future events and safer egress paths.

"The new design will incorporate a hardened structure for the utilities. The generators and all power switches will be housed in a reinforced concrete and brick structure. All utility lines will be buried in a tunnel from the plant to the Hospital. Fuel tanks will also be underground. The old hospital had outside, above ground fuel tanks and generators exposed to the elements. This reinforced plant will also have storage area for emergency supplies that can be accessed through the tunnel to the hospital or a loading dock for off-site facilities. We will also have a covered dock area for storing an emergency trailer to protect it from weather."

Mike McCurry, Chief Operating Officer for Mercy Health System, paid tribute to the staff and co-workers that have had to adapt to these new facilities every few months since their original beloved building was destroyed.

"Imagine that your entire work environment and the tools that you use and the process that you follow, the building that you are in, the people that you are around, it all just up and changes every few months," McCurry said. "All of it, every bit of it, so nothing is the same, the building is not the same, the tools are not the same, the beds are not the same, the docs are not the same. It's everything imaginable that we're asking them to adapt to and change, and the magnitude of change is immense."

McCurry said the change has been unprecedented, and that same staff will go through an even larger change in 2015 when the massive new Mercy Joplin campus, under construction on 50th Street, opens.

But Mercy had a choice.

"The choice was to just simply be out of business for three years," McCurry said. "We were so concerned that if we let that happen, valuable talents would atrophy or leave the community. We knew we could get the hospital opened back up, but if there's nobody there with the talent and the know-how and, frankly, the compassion of the community to run it, then it's little good."

The modular hospital is stronger even than the old St. John's building, with glass windows and walls built to withstand 200 mile-per-hour winds.

The speed in which this building was assembled and erected is also unprecedented.

"No one has ever built a hospital of this size in eight months," McCurry said.

28. AN END AND A BEGINNING

BY JOHN HACKER

Crystal Harvey spent 16 years working at the St. John's Regional Medical Center building at 26th and McClelland Boulevard, but that building was so much more than just a place to work.

"My grandma passed away there, I've had two uncles pass away there," Harvey said on Jan. 29. "I met my husband there and he was born there."

Even though the May 22 tornado made that building unusable, it was still hard for people like Harvey to watch as a wrecking ball took the first of the thousands of swings that it will eventually take to bring down the massive building.

Fortunately for Harvey and her co-workers, Jan. 29 was not only the beginning of the end for their old workplace, it was the beginning of the beginning for their new workplace as Mercy and its employees and city leaders turned the dirt at a groundbreaking at the future home of Mercy Joplin on 50th Street.

Justin Gilstrap, an employee of Mercy St. John's, brought his son, Jackson Gilstrap, 6, to the groundbreaking for the new Mercy Joplin Hospital on Jan. 29.
PHOTO BY JOHN HACKER

Mercy

A wrecking ball takes a ceremonial strike on the side of the tornado-ravaged St. John's Regional Medical Center at a ceremony marking the start of the demolition of the damaged shell.

PHOTO BY JOHN HACKER

"It was very tough to see that wrecking ball hit the building," Harvey said. "It is closure to the end of one era and we came directly here to the beginning of a new era. And it's good to close it and begin it all in the same day."

Harvey was one of hundreds who attended the dual ceremonies on Jan. 29.

Under a tent in the parking lot on the east side of the tornado ravaged former hospital, co-workers and Mercy leaders joined Joplin leaders to watch the beginning of the process of tearing down the building.

In the ceremony, co-workers described the history of St. John's through the eyes of the founders, Sister Mary Francis Sullivan, who led the effort to build the first St. John's hospital in the late 1800s, and Sister Mary Austin O'Donahue, who led the hospital as it moved to the 26th and McClelland area in the 1960s.

They also heard from Bishop James Van Johnston, leader of the Springfield-Cape Girardeau Diocese, Sister Mary Roch Rocklage of the Sisters of Mercy, Mercy CEO Lynn Britton and Mercy Joplin CEO Gary Pulsipher, among others.

After watching the wrecking ball take the first whacks at the side of the building, the crowd drove to the new site on the old Messenger College property east of Hearnes Boulevard on 50th Street, led by a wooden cross that once hung in the old St. John's and will spend the rest of its days in the Mercy McCune-Brooks Hospital in Carthage.

Here they heard from the same leaders about the new, $950 million hospital that will be built there before grabbing shovels of their own and joining hospital officials and dignitaries in breaking the ground for the hospital.

"It was nice to have closure for the old building," said Justin Gilstrap, who works in radiology for Mercy Joplin. "My wife was born there, both my sons were born there, my grandmother passed away there, my mother had bypass surgery almost 21 years ago there and she's still alive. This was also important to acknowledge that something new was coming. We've been looking forward to that."

Joplin Superintendent C.J. Huff speaks to the media with other school superin-
tendents and members of the Joplin Board of Education behind him on May 23,
2011, at North Middle School. Two days later, Huff would tell the world that
Joplin schools would be open for business on time for the 2012-2013 school year.
PHOTO BY JOHN HACKER

29. WE WILL HAVE SCHOOL

BY RANDY TURNER

"Which one is the superintendent?" a photographer for one of the cable networks asked the middle-aged woman standing a few feet from him.

She pointed at the man standing a few feet away from the makeshift podium that had been set up in front of the shattered remnants of what only two weeks before had been Joplin High School.

At first, the photographer didn't believe her. School superintendents were older, distinguished gentlemen, wearing suits and fighting the effects that too many chicken dinners at too many educational seminars can create for the waistline.

These, however, were not ordinary times in Joplin, Missouri, and C. J.

Huff was not an ordinary superintendent. Maybe he had been a couple of weeks before, in those blissful days before a tornado destroyed one-third of the city and damaged or destroyed 10 of his schools, including the one a few feet behind him. Normalcy was a thing of the past for Huff and it would be a long time before it would ever return.

A brisk wind whipped through the gathering crowd as it waited for the superintendent to speak. This was the first meeting of school district personnel since the tornado — a family reunion of sorts, and the audience was filled with the same dreadful fears that had taken hold of their lives since 5:41 p.m. on May 22.

Had their colleagues survived? Were the students who had sat in the classrooms a few days before ever going to have a chance to move on to the next grade, or to grow to adulthood?

They also had to worry about their jobs. It was almost a certainty that there would be fewer students whenever school started again. Would there be the need for as many teachers, as many secretarial staff, as many custodians? Was there a possibility that this gathering might be the last time they would ever see each other as co-workers and colleagues?

As the photographer took a closer look at C. J. Huff, his earlier doubts had been erased. Though he had cast aside the suit and tie in favor of a maroon baseball cap with a proud "J" for Joplin and looked more like a Sunday golfer than a community leader, it was clear that this was the man in charge.

The face was boyish, something that had concerned some Joplin School District patrons when Huff had been hired. Ironically, the May 2008 board meeting when Huff had first been introduced to the public had been interrupted by the sounding of a tornado siren. Outwardly, the superintendent looked the same, but a closer examination showed the stress of having to deal with a crisis few school administrators had ever faced, the slight redness in eyes that had not been closed many times since the tornado.

Huff and his staff had been at the biggest event of the 2010-2011 school year, the culmination of 13 years of schooling, the high school graduation, held at Missouri Southern State University, when the tornado sirens sounded.

It seemed like an eternity had passed. In the days since, school officials and teachers had mounted an unceasing effort to locate every employee and every student in the school district.

It was no easy task. Phone service was down in many areas. Those whose homes had been hit by the tornado were staying in hotels or with relatives, some out of state.

It was a task made easier due to the advent of social networking. Through Facebook, teachers were able to locate many students.

But even with that technological marvel, district employees who had reported to work the day after the tornado, did much of the work by going door-to-door in the devastated areas of the city, marking as many names off the list as they could.

And there were other concerns. The administrative office building had been hit by the tornado. The team had to spread to different buildings and somehow manage to coordinate its duties. After some trial and error, the team had established a working rhythm.

Its ability to do so was aided by the members of the Board of Education. In a meeting, two days after the tornado, Huff told them, "We are going to start school on time."

Their reaction to that seemingly impossible goal did not surprise the superintendent. "They didn't question the decision. They got out in front and took care of business," Huff said.

"These folks on a normal day work long, hard hours at the job and deal with patron calls about everything from overcooked chicken nuggets to angry cheerleader moms."

The board also included a board member who had lost her home. "They were all affected by the tornado."

Despite all of this, the board never hesitated to do what needed to be done. "They knew getting our kids back to school and out of the rubble was the best thing we could do for our community," Huff said.

The first order of business was to give Huff and his staff the ability to do what needed to be done without having to call a school board meeting for approval every day. They approved a Missouri School Boards Association policy granting authority to Huff to make emergency purchasing decisions without board approval.

At the same time as the hunt for staff and students continued, Huff and his team were making arrangements for temporary buildings that could house the students when the 2011-2012 school year began, a task made all that much more daunting by the fact that school was scheduled to start just 87 days after the tornado.

And now on Memorial Day, May 30, 2011, just eight days after the tornado, Huff prepared to address the "family gathering."

The crowd quieted as a man stepped to the microphone and said, "How about a great hand for our superintendent of schools, C. J. Huff?"

As the crowd applauded, Huff adjusted the microphone and wiped sweat from his forehead.

"First of all, it's good to see the family here. I miss you guys. I want to thank you for making the time to join your Joplin Schools family today as we celebrate life in the midst of destruction."

"Memorial Day is set aside to honor those who have given their lives to defend those principles we hold most dear. I was thinking about this last night and the parallels to our situation are striking. Our soldiers don't choose the battles they fight. They suit up, show up, and do their jobs. We didn't sign up for this war either. But true to form, in the past week you have pulled together as a family, supporting one another through prayer, words of encouragement, volunteerism, and action. No task was more daunting than our primary mission following the tornado last Sunday evening — the mission — locate and account for all of our family members."

At that point, Huff's voice began to falter and tears streaked down his face. He took a few seconds to collect himself as he prepared to deliver the most difficult portion of the most difficult speech of his life.

"At 3:16 last Friday, I received a text message," he stopped again, took a deep breath.

"Are you all right?" someone asked, the question picked up by the microphone.

Huff nodded and continued his sentence, "That indicated that mission was complete. As a result of your diligence and unwavering fortitude in the face of insurmountable challenges, 100 percent of our family are accounted for."

The hoops, hollers, and applause began, but the news was not as positive as Huff's words indicated. All of the family members had been accounted for, but not all of them had survived the tornado.

"I personally believe that all things happen for a reason," Huff continued. "I believe in God and I believe 3:16 last Friday had significance for all of us. It was a great moment of relief for our family, but more significantly, I believe there were biblical implications, as well.

"John 3:16 says this, 'For God so loved the world that He gave his only begotten son that whosoever believe him shall not perish, but shall have eternal life.'"

Huff paused, took a deep breath and collected himself once more. Many in the crowd, understanding the words that would come next, were also fighting tears, some unsuccessfully.

"Today, we grieve the loss of eight members of our family. We lost seven children and one educator. Today, we celebrate that we are all together again in body and in eternal spirit. Please join me in a moment of silence to honor the family members who are no longer with us."

After the moment of silence, Huff began what he knew would be the most important part of his speech. With all of the death and destruction that had hit Joplin eight days earlier, with all of the school buildings that were damaged and destroyed, Huff had to point his family toward the goal that would pull them all together; the goal that became a rallying cry for the community that sounded across the nation.

It would have been easy to use the tornado as an excuse for canceling summer school and delaying the beginning of the 2011-2012 school year. Not one person would have questioned that decision had it been made.

Huff, his team, and the Joplin Board of Education never considered any option other than full speed ahead.

"Schools are at the heart of every community," Huff continued. "It's where we go to learn, to be inspired and discover and cultivate those qualities that eventually evolve into our careers, so it is only fitting that our schools are not only an essential part of our recovery, but are helping to lead the charge, working in concert with city, state, and federal officials and we will recover and come back stronger than ever.

"One week and one day ago, we were celebrating graduation and preparing for a flurry of parties and other activities. Today, we find ourselves on the back end of a natural disaster that brought more chaos and havoc than we have ever seen before in our lives.

"Our loss has been great. We must never forget those who died in this battle. And today, we celebrate their lives, and their hopes and dreams. We honor their memories by moving forward, rebuilding, and continuing to take care of one another as a family.

"Taking care of family means being your advocate and helping you make it through this crisis. Several of you have inquired if you still have jobs. Let me assure you, we need you now more than ever. It may seem chaotic until we get all of our buildings rebuilt and restored and you might find classes meeting in locations you haven't expected ... but we will have school," Huff said, emphasizing each of those last four words.

The news, even though Huff had already made the comment shortly after the tornado, was unexpected to many in the crowd, that somehow, despite all odds, the goal was to start school on time, without a single day of delay, was greeted with thunderous applause.

Thanks to the cameras from the local television stations, as well as those from the networks, and those videoing it to place it on YouTube, C. J. Huff's words became a rallying cry, not only for the school, but for the city of Joplin. The work that went into making those words a reality made the city and the school district the symbol for a nation.

30. WILL NORTON IS WITH US IN SPIRIT

By Randy Turner

Will Norton was light years ahead of his classmates (and most other people) when it came to effective use of social media.

The Joplin, Mo., High School senior had built a nationwide YouTube following and was also a master at Facebook, Twitter, and Tumblr.

His mastery of 21st century communication made it that much more ironic when, for days on end, the most important message Will was waiting to receive was coming his way in an old fashioned envelope courtesy of the U. S. Postal Service.

The message that Will wanted to receive more than anything was an acceptance letter to Chapman University.

"He loved the campus, the town of Orange, and the excitement," his father, Mark Norton, said. "He just felt so comfortable there and he had heard so many good things about the university and the friendliness of students and faculty."

After his visit, Will waited for word. "The day he received the acceptance letter, his mom and I were watching him reach into the mailbox. He had this huge smile and he hadn't even opened the packet. I asked him why he was smiling."

"Of course, I was accepted, Dad," Will replied. "They don't have to send you an entire packet to turn you down, just a letter."

"He was so excited to be accepted," Mark Norton said.

Will was so enthused that he joined the Chapman Class of 2015 Facebook site and immediately began making friends with his future classmates.

On Friday, May 20, Linda Zhou, a Chapman freshman from Anaheim Hills, noticed "someone had reblogged one of my blog posts of a picture of Chapman University on Tumblr.com. I recognized his username, will-norton, from the Chapman 2015 page. I looked him up on Facebook and requested him as a friend so I could share my excitement for finding a fellow soon-to-be Chapman freshman on Tumblr as well as Facebook.'

Their friendship started the next day. "We talked via Facebook messages and discussed our majors, our excitement, and he shared his YouTube account with me. That day was my prom day so I did not get a chance to have a thorough, continuous conversation with him and I didn't get to check out his YouTube videos until the next day.

"I sent him a message on Sunday about how I enjoyed watching his videos and how honored I was to be talking to such a star. He never got a chance to see that message."

Sunday, May 22, was the day Will Norton graduated from Joplin High School — and it was also the day he died.

The day was scheduled to be a complete celebration of Will's passage into adulthood, with his graduation to be followed by a party at his home.

With bad weather approaching, the methodical droning roll call of seniors' names was quickened as the ceremony continued. When the final name was called, Will's friend and classmate Becky Cooper said, "We turned our tassels together, then we threw our hats in the air, and it was all over."

The students had to go into another room to pick up their diplomas. "I went and took pictures with my family and people were filing out. I remember my aunt saying, 'Becky, there's sirens going off,' but I told her to ignore it. The sirens go off all the time."

Will Norton at graduation on May 22, 2011.
PHOTO COURTESY 'HELP FIND WILL NORTON'

With rain approaching and the winds picking up, Mark Norton told his wife Trish, daughter Sara and niece Whitney to go on. He told them he would wait for Will and ride home with him.

Shortly after they left, Will emerged from the building. "I hugged him and congratulated him." As they walked to Will's Hummer, the tornado siren sounded.

"We got nervous, but they stopped." As Will drove home, his father received a call from daughter Sara. "She said they were home, but the power was out and the storm was bad."

As Mark Norton talked to his daughter, something hit the hood and the window on Will's side blew out.

"Will asked me what to do and I told him to turn into Summit Ridge Subdivision. He began reciting Bible verses and praying."

The tornado, which had winds in excess of 200 miles per hour, picked up the Hummer and flipped it over. "All of the windows blew out. I put my left hand on Will and held on, but somehow he must have flown out of the sun roof.

"Once the H3 stopped flipping, I looked over and Will was gone."

Mark Norton shouted for his son, but there was no answer. When rescue workers arrived, he told them to look for Will.

"They couldn't find him."

For the next few days, the smiling face of Will Norton became the face of the Joplin tornado, thanks to the Help Find Will Norton Facebook page started by his family.

The search for Will Norton went national, as the media told the story of a young man who had built a sizable following on his Willdabeest YouTube videos, which showed his potential as a comic filmmaker, a talent he planned to hone at Chapman University.

One of those who followed the coverage was Chapman President James L. Doti, who began researching Will Norton as the search continued.

"I have to tell you, this young man in every way, shape, and form, was a superstar," Doti said. In addition to his filmmaking prowess, Will Norton has a nearly perfect GPA and "some of the highest ACT scores I have ever seen."

For the next few days, the hunt continued, and one of those following with interest was incoming Chapman freshman Linda Zhou. "I couldn't believe — I didn't want to believe — that he had gone missing."

It was the same emotion that another Chapman freshman, Allie Reidy of Palos Verde, had. "It was a strange thing for me. Even though I had only spoken to him once, it completely turned my world around. I was so devastated and I never thought I would cry for someone that I barely knew, but he had shown me so much kindness. And by reading what everyone else was saying about him, I knew he had affected many other people's lives.

"I followed all of the updates in their search for him and I prayed every day that God kept a firm hand on him, and I guess he did, just in an unexpected way."

Five days after the tornado, Will's body was discovered.

***

Two weeks after the last time she saw Will Norton's luminous smile, his classmate Becky Cooper saw it once again, only in a way she had never expected.

When she entered Christ's Church of Oronogo, Mo., for what was termed "a celebration of Will Norton's life," the first thing Becky saw, on a large screen television, was that smile, over and over, in a loop as Will's life was replayed for the hundreds who gathered to pay tribute.

Some of the photos were taken from the good times with his family, some with his friends at school, and others from his celebrated YouTube videos.

"Will loved watching YouTube videos and made his first video about his pet sugar gliders (an Australian flying squirrel)," his father recalled. "It was such a hit; he was instantly hooked. His views skyrocketed (some of his videos have been viewed more than 50,000 times) and he was encouraged to keep filming. Eventually, YouTube asked him to be part of their partner program so he could share advertising revenue. He loved that because it let him purchase better filming equipment. He just loved creating videos that people got joy from watching."

The eulogy for Will was presented by Rev. Aaron Brown, whose church was also a victim of the tornado that had taken Will's life. Just a week earlier, Rev. Brown had spoken before a nationwide audience at the Joplin Tornado Memorial Service at Missouri Southern State University.

When it comes to Will Norton, Rev. Brown said, "Death doesn't get the last word."

And for those who came to mourn for the teenager, the tears were mixed with smiles and often with heartfelt laughter.

Will himself provided the highlights of the celebration, in one of his Willdabeest YouTube videos.

Stories were told about a young man who had celebrated life every day, through videos, through social networking, through flying (he already had a pilot's license) and through building a large network of friends.

"Will was an All-American kid," his classmate Savanah Sweeton recalled. "I had two classes with Will this year, one of which I sat quite close to him, so close I could reach out and touch him. Small things like reaching out and touching someone seem miniscule living an everyday life until that person is no longer a part of this life."

As the celebration of Will's life continued, Becky Cooper found herself laughing several times, sometimes at Will's videos, and often as others told stories about her friend. "I laughed because someone mentioned how his dad always made lunch for him every day. Well, I used to eat part of that lunch every day.

"Will always put others first and he always took the time to ask me how I was doing and what my plans for the Fall were."

"I'm going to miss him."

One of the speakers at the service, Joplin High School Principal Kerry Sachetta, spoke about the graduation, something that had only taken place two weeks before, but now seemed an eternity. "I was able to shake Will's hand for the last time." The principal presented Mark and Trish Norton with a replacement diploma for their son.

Rev. Brown concluded the ceremony by saying, "Will would not want to be remembered as a young man killed in the Joplin tornado. He would want to be remembered for how he lived.

"Will knew how to enjoy life, didn't he?"

***

Though Will Norton never attended a class at Chapman University, officials say his presence will be felt.

Part of that, advertising/marketing Professor Cory O'Connor says, is due to Will's innovative use of social networking.

"Will was a very talented young man. He brought people together through his community, through his Twitter and YouTube videos, you get a sense of who he was, and how excited he was about coming to Chapman.

"I am convinced that Will's life was meant to teach us all something. He left for us a biography of who he was through his two Twitter feeds and his YouTube videos."

Chapman University will also pay tribute to Will Norton when freshmen arrive in August, according to Nancy Brink, director of church relations. "Our tradition has been to honor students who have died and we are going to do that for Will."

Will's name will be added to the Memorial Wall in the Fish Interfaith Center, Ms. Brink said.

It will be the first time that such an honor has been given to someone who had yet to attend a class at Chapman, she added.

"We were looking forward to Will being a part of our freshman class," Dean of Students Jerry Price said. "Will wanted a career in TV and film. It was his desire to come out here to pursue this passion that really resonated with us."

Before Will was found, Price said, "We talked with his family and found out how much Chapman meant to him."

That included a bedroom full of Chapman posters, University President James Doti said.

Doti hopes that Will Norton's short life will serve as an inspiration for Chapman students. "He lived a whole life. It is a tragedy to lose such an incredible young man.

"When I tell students about Will Norton, hopefully, they will be inspired by his life and take these years at Chapman with more seriousness and dedication.

"This was a great tragedy. We are always going to consider Will to be a member of Chapman's family.

"He is with us in spirit."

31. I WILL KEEP THE SPOTLIGHT ON JOPLIN, MISSOURI

SYNDICATED TALK SHOW HOST RUSH LIMBAUGH GAVE THE FOLLOWING SPEECH JULY 4, 2011, AT LANDRETH PARK IN JOPLIN.

Thank you all very much. Thank you so much. But I can't hear you. I am a little bit hard of hearing. I have got to tell you, folks, thank you so much for allowing me to be a part of this tonight. It's a thrill and it's an honor for me to be here among all of you. It's the 4th of July. Do you know what we are celebrating today? We are celebrating a revolution. We are celebrating the most unique revolution in the history of humanity. Most revolutions install dictatorships. No, I am not going there tonight folks. Um. Our revolution.

Have you ever thought. I ask myself frequently as I have gotten older. The country I have gotten more and more in awe of. I have asked myself, "We are 235 years old today. There are countries, civilizations, thousands of years older than we are. In 235 years, we have become the most powerful, the most benevolent, the most productive, the richest society in the history of the world. How did this happen?" And realize that even to this day, the United States today produces 25 percent of all of the world's economic output. Twenty-five percent, how did it happen? My friends seriously, we are no different DNA-wise than any other human being anywhere in the planet. There is nothing special about us genetically. So what is it about us as Americans <"Freedom" from crowd> that is special? I heard a key word from the crowd. <crowd shout> The word is freedom. But I want you to stop and to think about something very seriously. This country has produced opportunity and prosperity unlike the world has ever seen before. The first reason is that our founders, this country is a miracle, our founders believed in the power of the freedom of the individual. Not the power of a lead government to dictate for people. The individual. They knew that people using their God given gifts, their own ambitions and desires could exceed their own expectations. Could-could-could realize their dreams and in so doing could create the best and most prosperous country in the history of civilization. But there is one other element to American exceptionalism.

This is a term that when people bandied about, we say, "We are better than everyone else. We are exceptional. "That is not what it means. The history of the world is oppression, tyranny, and dungeons. Not here. We are an exception to the way human beings have always lived on this planet. This is a nation blessed by God. It is our exceptionalism. <cheers> This is not a country chosen by God. We are blessed by God because our founders, it is all in our declaration folks, we are all endowed by our creator, there it is, with certain inalienable rights, among them, life, liberty, and pursuit of happiness. That's all up to us. This country turns Americans loose. It turns individuals loose. And look what has happened in 235 years. We, even to this day, we run the world but we do it benevolently. We liberate people from tyranny when there is a disaster anywhere in this world. We are the first to arrive. Now you, those of you here from Joplin, Mo., you may not know it yet, but you are the essence of what the founding fathers had in mind. You are the epitome. You are the people who make this country work. What happened here is something that you are going to erase. You will never forget it from your memories. You are going to build back. This is going to get fixed. It is going to be rebuilt. It is going to be better than it ever was. You are going to show the rest of the country how it is done. <cheers> Because you represent the best of what this country has to offer. You understand the principal of hard work and self-reliance. You understand the difference between self-interest and selfishness. You are not selfish. You are all going to be working your own self-interest to you rebuild your lives. And in the process everybody else's lives will be rebuilt right along with yours. American exceptionalism is simply the result of our founding father's understanding. That our government is not to determine the equality of outcomes of life because we are not all the same. Our country was determined to permit equality of opportunity and what you do with it is your business. <applause> We are 235 years old. We are here on Independence Day. We are celebrating the greatest miracle in the history of human civilization.

And as I grow older, I just turned 60 — I know don't look it — I just turned 60. I become more in awe. More appreciation for this country each and every day. I am from Missouri. I am from Southeast Missouri. I am from Cape Girardeau. I know that people have asked me, "Do you think you would have succeeded as you have?" And who can deny my success? "Do you think you would have succeeded if you were born in the northeast?" Yeah, but not the way I have. I don't think there is any doubt the fact that I am from the heartland of this country. It allows me to be able to understand and relate to and be one of you. I have never changed. We are all part of a great part of this country that understands the concepts of hard work and self-reliance, respect for our neighbors, love, doing the best we can, playing by the rules, understanding none of us are perfect. We are there for each other when time requires it. Joplin, Mo., you are defining that. You are showing the world how it is done. I am honored. I am really honored to be here. We have this new little company that we have started. We wanted to bring a truckload in. We made sure. We didn't want to intrude. We wanted to add to ... we wanted to be a part of your event tonight. Show a little gratitude. Come and keep the spotlight on your city. The one thing that needs to happen. We must not forget what happened here. I know you are trying to tonight.

I understand that. People say, "What are you going to do?" What I am going to do is keep the spotlight on Joplin, Mo. And what you are doing, and how you are overcoming something that was just thrown your way. So, thank you all very much, I know you have a lot to do. You have a great band coming up. You have fireworks coming up tonight. You have a great future! You are Americans. We are all Americans. We are celebrating our 235th birthday. And remember, there is no stopping you what ever you want to be. You define it! You can do it! The best you can! Go for it! And I'll see you later. Thank you all very much! Have a great Fourth of July!

    <Applause>

Misty Gamble, her sons, River, 2, and Dylan, 9, and mother, Terry Gamble, stand in front of what will be Misty's new home on South Willard Street in Joplin with the first Samaritan's Purse crew to work on it. Crew members are (from left) Kyle Wing, Isanti, Minn.; Cathy Herman, Lakewood, Colo.; Howard Boersma, Porter, Wisc.; Nancy Centz, Milwaukee, Wisc.; Greg Jones, St. Louis; Sidney Anderson, Whidbey Island, Wash.; Stan Brensing, Olathe, Kan.; Stephen Bergen, Carthage; and Keith Herman, Lakewood, Colo.

PHOTO BY JOHN HACKER

32. A BLESSING IN DISGUISE

BY JOHN HACKER

A national relief organization is building 20 homes for survivors of the Joplin tornado in the next two years.

Misty Gamble, Joplin, was the first person in Joplin to get a home built by Samaritan's Purse, a North Carolina-based relief organization that first came to Joplin in the days after the tornado hit to help with the cleanup.

Samaritan's Purse, led by local case manager and volunteer coordinator Stephen Bergen, Carthage, is coordinating teams of volunteers to build a new home on the spot on south Willard Street where Gamble and her two children, River, 2, and Dylan, 9, lived prior to the tornado.

TEMPEST STRIKES

Before the storm, Gamble cared for her father in that same home until he died of esophageal cancer a year before the tornado.

"I took care of him in this house and he had passed away in the room with the fireplace," Gamble said. "That was a good memory of him because he spent a lot of time in front of the fireplace and everything. They were good enough to keep my dad's fireplace, this was my dad's home and they kept some bricks from it for a memorial to him. It really meant a lot to me."

Gamble said she and her children were visiting her sister, Amanda Seward, in Carl Junction for a barbecue when the tornado hit.

She said a few weeks before, she and her children had been visiting her sister and had been caught in their car driving home when a tornado warning sounded.

"I got in my car and left with the kids and got on 171," Gamble recalled, "I turned on the radio because it looked scary and they said get off 171 there's a tornado by the airport so that scared me enough where the next time I was up there, I was smart enough not to get in the car with the kids or else we would have either been here or else in the middle of the storm in the car."

She ended up staying in Carl Junction longer than anticipated.

She said friends and family went into Joplin after the storm passed and went to her home. They told her it wasn't safe to go home that night.

"The house wasn't completely gone but it was really badly damaged where they just tore the rest of it down," Gamble said. "I had no idea it was coming through my neighborhood. You know you don't really think stuff like that is going to happen to you until it does. There were people at my sister's and they said we'll go by and check your house out. They drove here and drove through the neighborhood and they didn't tell me really what happened, they just said don't go home, it's not good.

"I tried to come here to see my house but a lot of it was blocked off. We eventually made our way to this area and had to park over by the school and we looked and it was like, oh my gosh, just total disbelief of what happened. It was scary, I'm glad we weren't home."

*Misty Gamble (far right) took time off from her job on Jan. 20 to come out with
her mother, Terry Gamble, and sons, River, 2, and Dylan, 9, to thank the
Samaritan's Purse volunteers for the work they are doing.*

PHOTO BY JOHN HACKER

HISTORY OF SAMARITAN'S PURSE

Samaritan's Purse is a national relief agency founded in 1970 by Bob
Pierce.

Pierce had traveled through Asia after World War II and met a group
of courageous women living among lepers and orphans in China and min-
istering to them.

"Through their selfless love, God gave Pierce a vision for ministry,"
said the group's website, www.samaritanspurse.org "He dedicated himself
to finding and supporting other such Christians who were caring for the
poor and suffering in the distant corners of the world."

Pierce and Franklin Graham, son of the evangelist Billy Graham, built
the ministry until Pierce's death in 1978.

Stephen Bergen, the local case manager, said the group plans to build

River Gamble, 2, decided he was going to help build his family's home with the help of big brother Dylan Gamble, 9, as mom Misty Gamble looks on.

PHOTO BY JOHN HACKER

up to 20 homes and will stay in Joplin for up to two years to complete the mission.

Teams of volunteers are coming to Joplin from all over the world for the next two years.

Bergen said the group only builds for people who had homes in the tornado path and might have had homeowners insurance, but it wasn't quite enough to pay to rebuild their homes.

He said the homeowners must own their property. He said the group needs local volunteers to help as well.

"If someone here lives locally, they can call me, 291-1515 and we bring them in any Tuesday morning at 7:30 a.m. at Forest Park, Room 219 and I'll take them through their safety training and orientation, give them their shirt," Bergen said. "Then that way, they might not work that day but they will be on a list of people that we can call and use them to fill in. We don't require anyone to have any construction skills."

THE HOMES

The home the group is building for Gamble and her family will be a three-bedroom design and, unlike the original, it will feature a safe room, which can also be used as a utility room, in the house itself.

"That's going to make us feel a lot better and safer," Gamble said when she visited the construction site in January 2012.

Volunteers were putting the roof trusses on the home that day.

"Dillon, he's old enough to see what happened and know so whenever we hear about a tornado warning, he's scared to death," Gamble said. "I am too. I'm the mom, I'm supposed to be the brave one, but that (safe room) will help us feel secure."

ANOTHER FAMILY

Renoda Brewer came that same day to visit the home being built for Gamble and her family because Samaritan's Purse will be building a similar home for them on the lot where they lived at 2228 S. Pearl Ave., near the old South Middle School building.

Travis Porter accompanied his mother to the Gamble home.

Travis remembers May 22, 2011, like it was yesterday. He said he was having a father-daughter day with his 9-year-old daughter, Angelis Porter

"I took my daughter out," Porter said. "Her birthday was May 23 and it happened to be on a Monday, so we went out and did some things on Sunday. We went and saw a movie and came back, it was actually not a bad day, I had the top open on the car and everything.

"We got back and ordered pizza and I heard the sirens the first time and like everyone else in Joplin, I just ignored it. Then I heard it go off again and I kind of felt that rumbling and I was like ummm.

"I went outside and our neighbor had come out at the same time and we looked back and there was a big black wall. We looked at each other and said, I'm going back inside, and we both went back inside and I grabbed my daughter and we went to the bathroom. They wound up in the bathroom eventually after they all went outside."

Travis yelled to his mother and daughter to take cover, but like thousands of others that day, Renoda Brewer needed more proof.

"I had to see it with my own eyes, I had to go look, so I went to the kitchen and I looked out the back door," Brewer said. "I saw this black thing with things flying and telephone polls snapping and electrical wired snapping and it's literally in our alley. I turned and went to run and yelled for my dad and he was already coming and he was yelling get in the bathroom."

Renoda, Angelis, Travis and Renoda's 69-year-old father took cover just in time.

"As he came through the dining room, all the living room windows and the family room windows were already coming in from the front of the house, and the tornado was in the back of the house," Brewer said. "That tells you how many tornadoes were actually in it. There was more than one."

Renoda said Angelis was screaming for her daddy as the tornado passed overhead.

"She probably thought I was hurt because I was grunting, ahhh, ahhh, ahhh," Travis said. "Our bathroom wasn't really insulated or anything but we were in that plastic bathroom insert and the bricks from South Middle School were hitting the house and I was feeling that."

"They were hitting him in the side because he was laying over the top of her," Renoda added. "My dad was over on the floor in the bathroom and I was over him covering him up and they had to literally beat our bathroom door in so they could get us out."

"We weren't trapped for too long because fortunately it was an old house and it wasn't too hard to get through the door," Travis said.

Travis said Angelis' mother came and took Angelis out of the tornado zone.

Travis said the destruction in his neighborhood was indescribable.

"I still don't know how to describe what it was like when we got out," he said. "I ran from neighbor's house to neighbor's house and then to my aunt's house which was only a block down. Her house was totally smashed and we thought she was dead, but she survived."

Travis then ran to the Greenbrier Nursing Home, about four blocks from his home. The Greenbrier directly in the path of the storm and was leveled, killing or trapping the staff and the elderly and bedridden patients inside.

"I saw things that day I really wish I hadn't seen," Travis said. "That was bad, that was real bad."

The family stayed that first night in their damaged home.

"We heard the rafters breaking and everything else and we got out of there the next day," Travis said. "That night was really unreal. It didn't seem real. It's weird, it's something like you would see in a post-apocalyptic movie or something. You think it's fiction."

"What really got us was watching people go into people's homes and stealing," Renoda said. "They would have been in our house if we hadn't been there. It wasn't even 20 minutes after the tornado and someone broke into the people's house across the street."

"We heard our own house falling apart," Travis said. "We didn't really realize how bad it was until we got up the next morning. A wall had actually moved four or five feet more so it was coming down on one side. I finally got a hold of some friends and my uncle and my mom and her dad went to Grove with him, and I went to Seneca."

THE VOLUNTEERS

Bergen said Samaritan's Purse planned to help them build a home on their lot, but it would take a few months because they can stay at the FEMA trailers near the Joplin Airport until November 2012.

The group working on the Gamble Home in January 2012 was actual-

Betty Saltenberger brought cookies and other treats to the Samaritan's Purse volunteers. Here she gets a hug from Nancy Centz and Sydney Anderson.

PHOTO BY JOHN HACKER

ly one of the first groups of volunteers to come in for the Samaritan's Purse reconstruction project.

Bergen said volunteers are divided into teams of 10 with an experienced supervisor to help them learn the ropes. Volunteers are not expected to have any construction experience, just a willingness to learn.

Cathy Herman and her husband, Keith Herman, were traveling from their home in Lakewood, Colo., to visit their son in Nashville, Tenn., when they decided to stop in Joplin to volunteer. They were in Joplin between Jan. 16 and Jan. 21.

"I've worked with Samaritan's Purse seven times and when we heard about the rebuild, it was just Samaritan's Purse," Cathy Herman said "We really enjoy working with them. We feel they really do justice to the community and it's a joy. We get so much more out of it than what we give. This is hard work and it's work that we end up learning from. For a female to join a construction crew, I end up learning about the building and all kinds of things I didn't know before.

"My husband, Keith, worked for the Air Force; he was civil service. We've traveled quite a bit. Now we're retired and we do a lot of traveling. My son lives in Tennessee, so if we go to Tennessee, why not take a week off and help out. We went to Nashville and worked there last January and we're working here this January and we have a very good life and we've been blessed, we really have."

Cathy Herman said she was struck by the damage she saw in Joplin. She and her husband have helped at other disasters in the past, including Minot, N.D., where flooding and a tornado hit in 2011.

"It is heartbreaking, but people in Joplin, from what I've gathered, they have really come together and are working hard together," Cathy Herman said "They're going to end up with a better life and a better place. It's a terrible thing, but in the long run, hopefully they've gotten some kind of blessing from it."

Greg Jones, from St. Louis, said his mother had volunteered with Samaritan's Purse in New Orleans, so she encouraged him to work with the group when he said he was interested in volunteering somewhere.

"I checked it out and ended up here in October and helped repair a house," Greg said. "Samaritan's Purse is amazing in so many ways so I signed up to come back. I'm trying to go full time into contracting. Right now I'm contracting out of St. Louis but I'm trying to cut back and I've scheduled this year for once a month going some place to volunteer. I'm here for one week this time and I'm coming back in March with another church from St. Louis.

"Everyone loves seeing the families come and see us. The amazing thing to me is they get joy in seeing us do this but we get joy in doing this so it's like nobody loses, it's a win-win. It's a shame we have to have tornadoes to make us act like this."

FROM CLEANUP TO RECONSTRUCTION

Stephen Bergen said Samaritan's Purse was in Joplin immediately after the tornado hit and helped with the cleanup for about 40 days. The group helped 755 property owners clean up their land.

Samaritan's Purse officials then went back to North Carolina to plan and raise money for the reconstruction phase of the group's involvement in Joplin.

"We never come in and do the initial cleanup unless we have a plan to come in and do the rebuild," Bergen said. "We don't buy property and we won't allow people to go out and say hey, I brought property, now will you build me a home. We like to replace a home on the place where the home once stood and keep the family where they were.

"So we go in and if they have any FEMA funds or insurance money, we may be absorbing some of that to go towards construction, but Samaritan's Purse puts up the vast majority of money. Then the families move in mortgage free. That differentiates us a little from the other groups. "

Bergen said the group started in October 2011 helping people make repairs to homes that were repairable until it could arrange the proper construction permits.

"We made major repairs to six houses and then several others that we found that just needed a little bit of finishing up," Bergen said. "That was just so we could get our systems in place, keep the volunteers going and kind of keep the pipeline going for volunteers, so that last week when we poured our first foundation, we already had three or four months of volunteers lined up. We will take locals though, that's as far as out of town volunteers.

"This group was the first group to work on a new house. The foundation is sub-contracted out, so was the initial rough in of plumbing and electrical. We do that with local contractors. As far as out of town volunteers building a home, last week, Misty Gamble's home was the first one."

REBUILDING A NEIGHBORHOOD

Betty Saltenberger, 2404 S. Willard St., lives next door t Misty Gamble and is glad to see the Gamble family getting back into the neighborhood.

Saltenberger made a habit, each day, of bringing some kind of food out to the volunteers working on Gamble's home. One day it was milk and cookies, another day it was a pot of chili.

"I do it because I appreciate them coming to help Joplin," Betty said. "They're from far away and I want them to think of Joplin as a friendly place. One day I brought stew, but usually I'll bring cookies and milk over. I think they like it."

Betty's home was repaired fairly quickly; insurance paid the bill and they were one of the first to move back to the Willard Street neighborhood.

Betty said she and her husband, Roy, had plenty of warning from tornado sirens and television.

"I was in the hall linen closet when the tornado hit," Betty said. "I heard the sirens and then I saw on television they said it was down here on Gates, which I knew was about two miles from here. I knew it was time to do something. Yes we had plenty of warning with the tornado sirens so we said OK, get in the bathtub. I knew our bathtub was on an outside wall, no way, so we got in the linen closet and held the door. The door kept trying to come open and I bent the hinges holding on so tight. We could hear glass breaking and stuff coming through and the roof gone. But you know I wasn't scared. Isn't that funny? I thought I've done everything I can so whatever will be will be."

The Saltenbergers survived and emerged to a different world.

"There were two-by-fours sticking through the walls and of course the windows were broken and everything was soaked," Betty said. "The roof was gone and insulation was falling down on us and so we said OK, we're from the survival generation so you say OK, this happened, we better roll up our sleeves and get to work. That's what we did.

"We spent that night at the house, there wasn't anyplace to go. You couldn't have gotten there anyway. It wasn't really scary, we were home. We had one room that had a roof on it. That's where we stayed that night and luckily it was a bedroom that had a bed in it.

"It was a strange night. It was strange because there were people knocking on the door all night long and asking are you OK, are you OK? We made it though and we didn't get a scratch so if you have your health, you have it all.

"The next morning, the first thing I did was go down and rent a storage unit and went out and found a motel room. Then really, through all of this, we had nothing but good luck. See that house down on the corner? Those people that live near here just built it. It was almost finished on May 22 and it wasn't damaged very much so they came up one evening and said how would you like to move into our house while your house is being built, so that's what we did, we moved down there and then there was a group from Carthage that came and wanted to rebuild our house and they did."

Betty said she knew Misty and her boys before the tornado and she's glad they're moving back to the neighborhood.

"I figured the people that wanted to come back would move back," Betty said. "It's getting built back and now they're building on that little house across the street and that's a new house over there and another neighbor upgraded their house. It's really going to be a nice town when we get through.

"Everything was just messed up, but you know, Joplin's going to be a better place because of it because people are not building back what they had. Everybody's upgrading so it's kind of a blessing in disguise."

33. WE WILL NOT BE KEPT DOWN

By Mary Jean Miller

There have been a lot of horror stories that have come out of Joplin, Mo., as a result of the May 22, 2011, EF5 tornado. Stories of entire houses being decimated, family and friends missing, and far too many losing their lives. Now, a year after our lives were forever changed, we're rebuilding our town and our lives. It hasn't been easy, and we still have a lot of progress to come, but Joplin is coming back, and we're coming back stronger than ever.

My family was lucky in that the tornado missed us by about four blocks. I can still remember standing in my bathroom, power out, and hearing that monstrosity as my father ran in and told my brother and I to get in the bathtub. I will never forget that moment when I started to wonder if, after all these years of tornado scares, this was it.

After the tornado passed, my mother left to drive to the Kum and Go that she manages in Neosho because she knew that there would be a large flux of people coming in for necessities such as bottled water. My brother and father jumped in our truck and went to get a precursory look at the damage. I waited at home, phone in one hand and solar powered radio in the other.

As I desperately sent out text messages to my friends to make sure everyone was OK, I listened to the radio and began to realize the extent and the magnitude of what had just taken place. Slowly but surely, I got messages back from my friends, and from them I heard what had transpired. A tornado had wiped out the middle of town. The high school was gone. 20th Street looked like a war zone. One of my friends, Michelle Barchak, had only an instant to shoot off a quick message to me. Her house was gone, but she and her family were all right. Luckily, they had taken refuge in the basement, by the only wall that hadn't been toppled. Due to the gas leaks, they were in the process of running to her grandparents' house. Another of my friends, Sarah Kessler, I didn't hear from at all. I was terrified. She had lived only a block from the high school, and when I called in to the radio station to confirm the destruction of JHS, they said it was a complete mess. My home didn't have to be hit for me to be in a state of complete shock. In between frantically trying to call people on phone lines that were down and relaying information to a college friend who was out of town, it had slipped my mind that Sarah was not at home, but at Missouri Southern State University, attending her brother's senior graduation. It wasn't until later that night that she got cell phone service and could text me, but I remember almost crying with relief when I read the message saying that she was OK.

That night passed in a blur, but at the same time it lasted a lifetime. The next two weeks would prove to be some of the most trying times in my life so far. My father, brother, and I ventured out early on May 23rd, driving over downed power lines and trees into the heart of the destruction to help people salvage what they could. I can remember driving past places I used to know, streets I used to recognize, and being completely numb. It was all so overwhelming that my mind shut down. I became mechanical, simply working and ignoring the devastation around me as best I could. My family and I worked for almost two straight weeks, going out early in the morning and working until dark. We became accustomed to the itch of fiberglass insulation digging into our skin, constantly watching where we were walking so we wouldn't impale our feet on nails, and breathing the ever-present mixture of wet drywall and destruction that a tornado leaves in it's wake.

At night I stayed up contacting members of Joplin High School's Key Club, the club I had been elected to lead before the tornado hit. I was relieved to find that, while about half had lost homes, everyone was all right or just had minor injuries.

Eventually, the residents of Joplin, Mo., stopped salvaging and began cleaning. Summer progressed, and with it, so did the building of the new schools and the promise that school would resume as planned on August 17th. With the juniors and seniors being at the 11/12 center in Northpark Mall, and the freshman and sophomores being at the 9/10 center in Memorial School, I was presented with a challenge. As president of Key Club, I was faced with the daunting task of figuring out how our club was going to function being at two separate campuses. In the past we'd always held club meetings as a group, and our District Board had a requirement that at least some percentages of club meetings be held as a single entity. How were we supposed to unite the two groups of students? The answer was uncovered during a summer meeting between the Key Club officer board and our new sponsor, Tim Oster. We would be getting laptops, generously donated by the United Arab Emirates. We were going to take 21st Century Learning a step further. Our Key Club meetings would be held over Skype.

When the first meeting rolled around, I was very nervous. I was very limited in my knowledge of Skype, and I'd never heard of a large group at our school using it to hold a meeting. However, when we connected the campuses and the separate groups could see each other on the Smart boards, I couldn't help but grin. This was actually going to work.

Throughout the year, Key Club utilized our available resources and, while our numbers dropped due to the tornado, we maintained the club. As a result, we had the opportunity to see first hand the effects of our community service. We regularly went out and helped in any way possible. There was so much to be done, and we jumped right in and got to work. I'm happy to say the Key Club has lived up to our pledge by "building our home, school, and community." While that may have been a little more literal than originally intended, we have truly given back to the community as much as we can, and we plan on continuing to do so.

Looking back I can say, without a doubt, a lot has changed in the span of a year. There are the normal things, such as planning for graduation and college, and then there are things like rejoicing with friends because their new home is almost built. There are times where I am bleak and there are questions that can't be answered. Most prevalent is the question of why. Why Joplin? Why us? I don't have answers to these questions, and I likely never will. However, it's not hard to look around and see that Joplin is truly strong. We have accomplished so much in the span of a year. Alice Morse Earle said, "The clock is running. Make the most of today. Time waits for no man. Yesterday is history. Tomorrow is a mystery. Today is a gift. That's why it is called the present." Our past is that we have suffered great losses. While we may not know exactly what is to come, we do know that our future is a bright and hopeful one. We may be recovering, but each day is a chance for something great. As awful as it was, we can't dwell on May 22, 2011, forever. It will always be a part of Joplin, and I will never forget that day, but the future is calling. Let's embrace our past, because we can't change it, and walk into our future with open minds and soaring ideals. We are Joplin, and we will not be kept down.

Mary Jean Miller is a 2012 graduate of Joplin High School.

34. THESE ARE MY STUDENTS; THIS IS MY SCHOOL

By Randy Turner

The bare walls of a classroom without children can be the scariest thing for a teacher.

When August arrives, teachers have to find a way to make what is essentially just another room into an educational Shangri-La where children will come for nine months to learn the lessons of life.

I have never been good at this. Trained for 22 years as a newspaper reporter and editor, when I entered the classroom I had no concept of colorful bulletin boards and posters with inspirational sayings.

And this year, though I am loath to admit it, the last thing I wanted to do was to decorate a classroom.

This is not my building. This is not my room.

My school, Joplin East Middle School, met its demise Sunday, May 22, when a tornado ripped its way through my city, destroying everything in sight. As I looked at the bare walls of my new classroom, located in a spec building in an industrial park, I have to admit I was thoroughly depressed, a feeling quite familiar to those who have dealt with the aftermath of the tornado. And it was something I had to put behind me, since in a few short hours the East Middle School Family Picnic was scheduled to introduce students and parents to the new facility.

Since depression doesn't get the job done, I reached into a cardboard box and pulled out a stack of old papers — some of the best written by my students over the years — the papers that have hung proudly on my Writers' Wall of Fame.

I had room to put 20 papers on my new bulletin board. These would be the papers that would set the bar high for my new students when they entered the classroom Aug. 17. Somehow these papers had survived the tornado, offering teenagers' thoughts from years past.

I reread them before I put them on the wall — Amy's modern-day short story "Laptop Love," Dylan's research paper on Emmett Till, Sarah's poem that appeared in a national publication, Steve's essay on child abuse, Katey exploring the horrors of cyber-bullying.

I grabbed the tacks and placed Mary Jean's short story about a "Jade Tiger," Jessica's award-winning patriotic essay about the American flag, and Sarah's essay on students treating each other hurtfully, on the bulletin board.

Two papers were filled with unintentional irony. Laela criticized the antics of the Westboro Baptist Church. A little more than a year later, church members protested at the Joplin Tornado Memorial Service, a service designed to bring the community together... a service that meant a lot to Laela, who lost her home in the tornado.

Sabrina R. wrote about the need for each student to have a laptop. Because of the tornado, Joplin High School students will have laptops when they return to school.

The last two papers I put on the Wall of Fame did not look like the others. While the first 18 papers had been stored safely away in folders, the last two were on the Wall of Fame when the tornado hit.

At first, I thought they were too battered and dirt-covered to be on the wall, and then I realized that is exactly why they had to be there.

Miranda's paper talked about censorship at school, with several words cleverly blacked out. Sabrina S.'s paper was a touching tribute to her friend, Clayton, who had been killed in a tornado three years earlier.

As I placed the final paper on the Wall of Fame, I heard voices in the hallway. Students and parents were arriving early to receive their first look at our new facility. One girl raced into my classroom and shouted, "Mr. Turner, I'm in your class this year!" and proceeded to tell me what she had been doing all summer.

Before long, the classroom was filled with students, former students, and parents. The conversations, surprisingly, were not centered on the tornado, but were about the new educational adventure we would be beginning in six short days.

As the East Middle School Family Picnic continued, I watched the interaction between students, parents, and my fellow faculty members. The value of education to a community had never been spelled out more clearly. The depression of a few short hours earlier had vanished.

It was a building that was destroyed by the tornado. My school is alive and well.

35. SCHOOL BEGINS TODAY IN JOPLIN

BY RANDY TURNER

A pre-claustrophobia nervousness settled over me as I wheeled my car into a space in the parking lot at Missouri Southern State University Monday morning.

It was the first day for teachers to report back to work in the Joplin School District and that meant the annual pep rally. In past years, the event was traditionally held in the high school auditorium, but that high school no longer exists, thanks to the tornado that hit our city May 22.

The second I opened my car door, I could hear shouting, intermittent applause, and music, punctuated by the pounding of a bass drum.

At first, I thought it was an early MSSU band practice, but as I took the crosswalk to the building where our district meeting was scheduled, the purpose of the noise became clear.

The sustained applause was for teachers returning to work. As someone who has written numerous times over the past few years about the constant barrage of attacks on public schoolteachers, this was a pleasant surprise.

Our community was showing its appreciation.

When we entered the auditorium for the program, we saw Gov. Jay Nixon standing in the wings. The rest of the morning is something teachers in the Joplin School District will never forget.

During that time, we heard a powerful rendition of the National Anthem by one of my former students, high school junior Hannah Cady, an uplifting speech by the governor, and the remarkable chronicling by our Superintendent, C. J. Huff, of how the school, the community, the nation, and the world, had combined to produce the miracle of a school district that had 10 buildings either destroyed or heavily damaged, starting on time.

We left the auditorium ready for whatever challenges may come our way as we begin the 2011-2012 school year. In about an hour as I write this, classes are scheduled to begin.

Some will be held in a refurbished building at the mall, some will be in buildings that have not been used as schools in a couple of years. Modular buildings dot the landscape at a large number of the schools as we open our doors.

The school where I teach, East Middle School, another victim of the tornado, has been moved to a spec building in an industrial park.

But it's school. The teachers are ready, and maybe for the first time after a summer in which everything has revolved around the destruction of the Joplin Tornado, the students are ready, too.

Three short months ago, we were looking at once proud structures that had been reduced to rubble by the fury of nature.

Today, thanks to school administrators and board members who had a dream, and to the people of the world who made that dream come true, school bells will ring again in Joplin.

36. THE TOUGHEST TOWN ON GOD'S GREEN EARTH

THE FOLLOWING SPEECH WAS PRESENTED BY MISSOURI GOV. JAY NIXON AT OPENING DAY CEREMONIES FOR THE JOPLIN SCHOOL DISTRICT AUGUST 15, 2011.

Good morning! It's great to be here for the start of a new school year in Joplin, Mo., — the toughest town on God's green earth.

Less than three months ago, I stood on this very same stage, in this very same spot, for a memorial service. That was one week after the tornado had struck.

What you have accomplished in the 85 days since then, is astonishing — far beyond what anyone would have thought possible. Except maybe one person.

When C.J. Huff told me back in May that you were going to start school on time, I sincerely wanted to believe him. Well, he's a man on a mission, and a man of his word.

He says you're expecting 92 percent of the students to return this year. That's a great number — for any school district in America.

PHOTO COURTESY
THE STATE OF MISSOURI

And we all know that this wouldn't have been possible without each and every one of you here this morning. Whether you are a principal or a parent, a secretary or a science teacher, a coach or a civic leader, a cheerleader or a trumpet player, your determination, sweat and optimism were crucial to this mission.

It's a testament to Joplin's commitment to its schools and its children. It reflects the strength of our partnership, which has brought every possible resource to bear to help Joplin recover and rebuild. And we're not done yet.

You are helping the healing process for this community, because going back to school means getting back to normal.

So today is a milestone, and a cause for celebration.

We're celebrating the fact that life in Joplin is not a tornado emergency anymore.

We're celebrating the mountains Joplin has moved — literally — in just 85 days.

Mountains of what Joplin used-to-be have been moved to make way for the Joplin soon-to-be.

It's exciting to see the "Now Hiring" signs popping up along Range Line Road.

And it's great seeing all the cleared lots, just waiting for new houses and families to come back and rebuild their neighborhoods.

A lot of progress has been made, and we're not stopping now. Not 'til every ounce of rubble is out of here.

This hasn't been an easy time. Some of you lost your homes and possessions. Some of you lost friends and family members.

Getting ready for school has meant putting your needs and emotions second, and the needs of your students first. Because you have to be strong for them.

They'll be looking to you every day for reassurance, for guidance and for discipline.

Some days they'll need a shoulder to cry on; other days, they'll need a firm hand to keep them on track. And as we all know, students rise to meet our expectations.

Today is also a celebration of the mountains you will move in the next month, and the next year, and the next decade. Because much remains to be done in our schools.

We want Joplin schools to be the pacesetter, to lead the statewide push to move all Missouri public schools into the nation's Top Ten by 2020.

We need to educate our children for the challenges of global citizenship in the 21st Century; to rebuild a strong and competitive economy; and to reclaim America's place as one of the most innovative, well-educated and prosperous nations on earth.

Our goal is nothing short of excellence, and together, we will make it happen in Missouri, starting right here in Joplin.

Right now, you are the glue holding things together in the wake of so much loss. In about 19 minutes, 14,000 people were made homeless. Thousands lost their jobs; hundreds lost businesses. A hundred and sixty people lost their lives.

But Joplin didn't lose its faith, or its heart, or its soul.

The schools are the heart and soul of Joplin. In a very real way, you are the key to the future of this community: to its stability, its growth, its prosperity.

When the schools come back, stronger and better than ever, more families will want to stay and raise their kids here. Families like Leanne and Randy Ford and their two sons: Duncan, who's 15, and Grayson, who's 17.

The tornado destroyed their home, all their belongings, and Randy's dental office. In those first chaotic weeks, they did some soul-searching. They thought about moving to Carthage, or Webb City, or even to the West Coast.

In the end, they knew there's no place like home, no place like Joplin.

When families like the Fords stay and rebuild, businesses stay and rebuild. Family-owned businesses like Jim Bob's Steak and Ribs have already started.

I visited the Gambles at the end of June, to let them know the state stood ready to help local business owners rebuild, so they can start rehiring folks so eager to get back to work.

And while we were standing there, looking at the spot where the restaurant once stood, the mailman walked up. He handed them their mail. And then he asked them if they knew where his bass was.

The mailman had caught a big old bass and had it mounted. His wife didn't consider it home decor, so he hung it on the trophy wall at Jim Bob's.

The Gambles actually found that bass in the rubble, and promised it would have a place of honor as soon as they reopen.

I tell that story because it says so much about the kind of friendly, close-knit community Joplin is. The eyes of the world are on Joplin once again this week, and there's a lot of wonderful things for folks to see.

They'll see the transformation of a big, empty box into a sleek, high-tech high school. Thanks to the generosity of people all over the world, Joplin will be getting 2,200 new laptops — one for every high school student.

They'll see hundreds of little kids marching down the halls at Cecil Floyd, Duquesne and Emerson elementary, with brand new backpacks stuffed with donated school supplies.

They'll also see the best of the human spirit in action. They'll see what people with common sense can accomplish when they put the common good before self-interest. And they'll see the unstoppable forces of tenacity and teamwork.

And what an outstanding team we've got here in the Joplin schools.

Educating our children is a high calling, and those who answer the call are heroes in my book. Public schools have always been, and will always be, a beacon of hope and opportunity for all.

No one is turned away. Some children come to school hungry or homeless. Some bear the burdens of poverty and neglect.

But when a child of want, and a child of wealth, walk through Joplin's schoolhouse doors, they enter as equals, both precious in the sight of their Creator.

We must work together to help each child fulfill the promise God has placed in them, and to carry out the sacred trust He has placed in us.

Here in Joplin, we are a team. The team includes everyone in this auditorium, and thousands more. It includes the legions of carpenters and masons, electricians and plumbers who worked around-the-clock to get the walls up, the lights on, and the water running in every school.

It includes scores of business that dug deep for cash, football gear, books, whatever it took to get Joplin schools open for business, even if their own businesses were still struggling to get back on their feet.

The team includes the doctors and nurses, technicians and cooks who have pledged to stay and care for this community until a new hospital is built.

The team includes every family and every student, whether they're living in a FEMA trailer or a house upon a hill. And it includes the hundreds of churches and thousands of pilgrims still making their way to Joplin.

More than a thousand Boy Scouts from across the Midwest put in 10,000 hours in Joplin's schools a couple weeks ago: painting playground equipment, spreading mulch and picking up debris. The temperature hit one hundred and six that day.

A fifth-grade teacher drove down from Central Michigan — 850 miles each way — to help unpack and assemble furniture at the new high school, before her own school was back in session. There are hundreds more stories like these.

Disasters happen every day around the globe. So what is it about Joplin that draws people so powerfully?

I'll tell you what it is. The people of Joplin never acted like victims. Not one; not ever.

Yes, a terrible tragedy occurred, and the losses were staggering.

And you stepped up with courage, determination and true grit. You started looking for opportunities to make Joplin even better.

As great as the needs were, and will be, you never took it for granted that the world owed you something. You know that the only way to get anything in life is to work hard for it. And you worked hard for it.

You put your shoulders to the wheel and haven't stopped. If you did, you might collapse. So don't. School starts the day after tomorrow!

When the world sees so many positive, tangible signs of what your hard work has accomplished, it inspires confidence.

Folks can see that an hour spent in Joplin makes a difference in Joplin; that a dollar planted in Joplin, blooms in Joplin. That makes them want to be part of Joplin's comeback story.

And finally, I think what draws folks to Joplin is that you have made it so easy to help you.

You're organized. You're energized. And you never forget to count your blessings. This is how all good parents raise their children, and all good shepherds raise their flocks.

I know you want the lessons the children learn in class this year to stay in their heads as long as possible. You want your students to use their Joplin education as a springboard to their dreams, whether they want to be doctors or dancers, engineers or entrepreneurs.

This year, you are teaching them life lessons, by the example you have set.

You are showing them that from great adversity, great blessings flow.

You're showing them that when you get knocked down, you pick yourself up, dust yourself off, and keep on going.

You're showing them that hard work really can turn dreams into reality.

And I guarantee you: those lessons will stay with them for the rest of their lives.

Not in their heads, in their hearts.

There's a lot of uncertainty in this life. We can't control the weather. We don't know when the first kid will be able to dive into the swimming pool at Cunningham Park, or when the first new house will be finished.

We don't even know how many children will show up at the right schools — or the wrong schools — on Wednesday.

We can't see the future, but one thing is clear. Brick-by-brick and board-by-board, Joplin is rising:

- one life;
- one house;
- one business;
- and one school at a time.

The spirit of Joplin, Mo., can move mountains. Just watch us. Thank you.

C.J. Huff is flanked by Gov. Jay Nixon during a speech at opening day ceremonies for Joplin Schools on Aug. 15, 2011.

PHOTO BY JOHN HACKER

37. AN OPPORTUNITY TO MOVE FORWARD TOGETHER

JOPLIN SCHOOLS SUPERINTENDENT C. J. HUFF PRESENTED THE FOLLOWING SPEECH AT OPENING DAY CEREMONIES MONDAY, AUG. 15, 2011.

So to explain my thoughts to you, I am going to have to go back to the Joplin High School Auditorium in August of 2008 at the same event. That was the day I had my first opportunity to meet all of you. Those of you who were there that day will remember it was more of a roast of a new guy in town as opposed to a kick off event.

I remember now a skit where one of our young students was asked to play yours truly dressed up in a makeshift diaper. And whoever wrote the script — Cosetta — thought that it might be cute to make fun of the unfounded rumors that I might be slightly directionally challenged. It was all in good fun.

When it was my turn to speak to you — 1,100 of you. My message was a simple one. I wanted to define our current reality. I shared what I had already learned about you and our district by talking to our patrons, our parents, and our students of the Joplin Schools. Then I left you with my one wish it went like this:

"But if I could have one wish to today to make our district even stronger for our kids it would be this: I would wish that everyone left this auditorium today feeling as though they were on the same team. Not NEA, MSTA, Independent, Republican, Democrat, classified, certified. Not elementary, not secondary, not Royal Heights, not McKinley, not North, South, or Memorial. Not teacher, not administrator, not workman. If I could have one wish come true it would be that we could all leave here together working as one unit. One cohesive team working together toward a common goal. Each of you is a part of the whole. I want to make this point very clear. You are all educators in Joplin School District because we all come to school every day to do good things for kids. This is my one wish in 2008."

In the early morning hours on May 24, I laid awake on a nurse's cot in the middle school counselor's office doing what I am sure many of you were doing at that hour. Wanting to be with my family, worrying about the thousands of members of our schools that had yet to be accounted for.

<pause, moment of tears>

Just trying to make sense of it all. Trying to figure out the answer to the question of what do we do now? What do we do? So I did what any good superintendent who believes of the possibilities of 21st Century teaching-learning tools would do. I got up from my cot and walked over to the computer and Googled "disaster response for dummies."

<Applause>

No luck. So I had to go to plan B. Plan B. I took a look at my team — all 1,106 of you. You may be surprised to learn that I have been paying attention these last three years. What I came to realize at 2 a.m. on May 24, is that we have a phenomenally, talented team. I have watched departments work together to overcome other natural disasters: blizzards, ice, and freak windstorms.

We have even moved a few buildings: North to old South, old South to new East, Memorial to new South, old South to new North, Washington to Memorial just to name a few. It was good practice. We worked together, side by side. And accomplished those moves ahead of schedule and injury free.

I have seen teachers, grade levels, departments, and buildings pull together to accomplish amazing things around assessments, PBIS, RTI, graduation rate, PLC, ALL training, and Bright Futures. Great things were happening to Joplin Schools right up to the afternoon of May 22, 2011. Which culminated in the graduation of the second largest class in last fifteen years over 450 students who had received in excess of $3.2 million in scholarships.

All of that changed at 5:41 that day. But by early in the morning of May 23, following the aftermath of that storm, our good works continued. The transportation department went to work. Our bus drivers came in and turned our buses into ambulances and rescue vehicles. They saved lives.

The technology, maintenance, and payroll departments did the unthinkable. With hard hats and flashlights they waded through water, and sifted through debris in the basement of the administration building to restore power, bring our servers on line. And they made payroll on time.

So at 2 a.m. on May 24, as I reflected on our school family and our achievements, it became clear that my one wish had been granted. We had become one cohesive team — one cohesive team working together towards a common goal. For in the Joplin Schools we do the work that needs to be done. When it needs to be done — for every child — every day — no matter what. Nothing stops us. <applause>

Because of who we are, we have made people from all around the world believers. Together we have made possible what so many people believed was impossible. Our children are coming back to us in one day, 22 hours, 35 minutes, and eight seconds. <applause> Aug. 17 is going to happen. I now am looking past that day and I challenge each of you to look past Aug. 17 as well. On this day as we begin looking forward, if I could ask one thing, one wish, I would wish for you to have faith; faith in your abilities to make a difference in the life of every child. Everyday no matter what. Faith in your colleagues, faith in your community, and faith in my leadership and the leadership of your board of education to guide us towards that collective vision for the future of the power of the kids. To illustrate this idea of faith, I would like to read to you what I shared with the class of 2011 on their graduation day:

"When you walk to the edge of all the light you have and take that first step into the darkness of the unknown. You must believe one of two things will happen. There will be something solid for you to stand upon or you will be taught how to fly." If there is one thing you have learned about me these past three years I hope it is this: I will never ask anyone in this room to do anything that I wouldn't do myself. Today I ask that you take that step with me into the darkness of the unknown. I ask that you grant me one more wish. I ask that you have faith in the school family that we have become. Aug. 17 marks not only the start of what promises to be an outstanding school year but also an opportunity to move forward, fearlessly, courageously, boldly, and, intensely focused — together. I thank you in advance for the good things you are going to do for every child every day — no matter what. Now let's get to work. God bless.

PHOTO COURTESY THE STATE OF MISSOURI

38. A DAY OF MIRACLES: JOPLIN SCHOOLS START ON TIME

By Randy Turner

It was the first day of school at East Middle School and a sixth grader did not know where the office was in our new building.

He asked eighth grade science teacher Mike Wallace for directions. Wallace, glancing down at the end of the hall, told the youngster, "Go down the hall and turn right at the governor."

Whether the child knew who Missouri Gov. Jay Nixon was, I have no idea, but the presence of the governor in our hallways and the national media at every new or refurbished building in the Joplin School District made our first day of school Wednesday a memorable one.

Normally, so much media might be considered intrusive, but not on this day, just three months after an EF5 tornado destroyed or heavily damaged 10 of our 19 schools.

On this day, the national and world media were welcome because it was so important to thank the world for making it possible.

In the days after the May 22 Joplin Tornado, the idea that school would start on time seemed an impossibility. Joplin High School, a center of the community, had been blown apart by nature's fierce fury, leaving the words "Op High School" for all to see.

That did not last long. Within a couple of days, someone had added two letters to that sign, an H and an E, turning it into Hope High School, and setting the stage for the complete resurrection of the Joplin School District.

The effort began with school administrators and board members who had to create solutions because there was no blueprint for how to deal with this kind of devastation.

Teachers and staff were brought into the equation and the Joplin community, parents, students, business owners, and people who had no connection to elementary and secondary education except for paying the taxes that support it. The restoration of Joplin schools and the idea that they could open on time, only 87 days after the tornado, became the goal of an entire community.

And that community extended far beyond the city limits of Joplin. There was much need in this community and in this school system and people from across Missouri, the nation, and the world, stepped in to take care of that need.

Millions in donations came, brought about in part because of the national media that brought attention to the difficulties we were facing.

The United Arab Emirates chipped in with a half-million dollars and the promise of another half-million in matching funds to provide laptops for every Joplin High School student as a part of the school district's One-to-One initiative.

Most of the effort was steered successfully through the district's Bright Futures program, an initiative started two years ago to help provide equipment for schools and to cover the needs of the poorest children in our community.

Bright Futures' success had already been imitated in neighboring school districts well before the tornado. Its expansion to meet the challenges of tornado recovery should guarantee it will be imitated across the nation.

So when we saw reporters with their cameras and notebooks approaching us and our students Wednesday morning, we met them with

PHOTO COURTESY THE STATE OF MISSOURI

deep gratitude.

They were the ones who allowed us to express our thank you to a world that adopted the Joplin community and made it their own.

A simple thank you can never repay the many acts of generosity that made opening day in the Joplin Schools a success, so we are going to try to show our appreciation in the best way we can, by giving 100 percent of our effort to make the best use of the schools that the world made possible.

39. BACK TO THE COUNTRY

BY GARY HARRALL

May 22, 2011, turned my world upside down. But here I am a year later still picking up the pieces of my life.

I look at the tornado as a blessing to me in hindsight. Out of this tornado, I was able to fulfill my dream of owning a house out in the country with property just like I had as a kid. I was able to get me a better reliable vehicle. Now I have a better paying job. Shortly after the tornado, I met a girl who once again turned my life upside down. Her name is Kelley. We went out a few times after the tornado but I didn't hear from her again until around July 4. I was in Granby watching the 4th of July parade (I was actually supposed to be in it, but the tractor I was driving broke down) when I got a text message from her. We started dating. I fell for her and vice versa. I asked her to marry me on Dec. 9. The date of the wedding was April 21, 2012.

That has been my life since the May 22 tornado.

40. NOTHING STOPS US

By Denton Williams

May 22 will be forever remembered in my mind as the single greatest natural disaster to ever happen in my life. The true magnitude of the damage was unlike any other. You couldn't even drive to the other side of town without driving through the destruction.

As for me, I was one of the lucky ones. My house was not destroyed in the tornado, and I only lost my fence and my pool. We rode the storm out in the closet, and all I could do is worry about my friends. Especially Rylee Hartwell, who was shopping at Walmart at the time. The phone lines would be dead for ten minutes, and then all of the sudden, they'd work for about three minutes and then they wouldn't work again.

While we first began riding out the storm, we watched the lights flicker once.

"Oh, here we go!" my mom told me.

Just after that, the lights went dark, and I couldn't see a thing, just the small amount of light shining through the window in the other room.

After we saw on the world news how bad the damage was, we were horrified. We didn't know how long it would be until Joplin got power back, let alone rebuild.

We were absolutely amazed at the amount of help from all over the country. There were so many donations being made, that eventually they had to start limiting them because the places were overflowing with supplies!

Branson was a huge help to Joplin, by holding a televised event: "Branson Cares for Joplin Telethon." This brought so many funds for the Joplin High School Band, and St. John's Regional Medical Center. So many great acts were featured, and as a soon-to-be band member, and a St. John's volunteer, I was lucky enough to go with my mom to see it live! So many donations and funds were raised, it was really incredible.

Despite Mother Nature's best efforts, the Joplin High School Band was able to have Band Camp, without delays. The band began learning the first marching show since the May 22 Tornado, Elvis Live!

Within a week after the tornado, C. J. Huff, superintendent of Joplin Schools, announced that Joplin would hold its first day of school on Aug. 17, as planned. Against all odds, Joplin was able to renovate an old Shopko building at the mall into an incredible high school for the juniors and seniors, which was later known as "Northpark High School 11th-12th Grade Center." The "9th and 10th Grade Center" moved into the old Memorial Middle School, in downtown Joplin. East Middle School, which was also destroyed by the tornado, relocated to a warehouse east of town.

Thanks to the donation from the United Arab Emirates, the Joplin High School was able to purchase each student a MacBook laptop computer. Providing each student the chance of learning in a "21st Century Learning Environment." Presentations, essays, and projects that students could only work on at school, can now be finished at home. Students working on group projects are now able to communicate with their group partner by using Skype, allowing students to see their peers, as well as hear them.

Progress in rebuilding Joplin has been advancing at a rapid pace. Walgreen's and Walmart were the first major businesses to reopen, followed by Home Depot and Academy Sports and Outdoors. The cleanup of Joplin progresses quickly and we are beginning to see houses, businesses, schools, all kinds of buildings to fill up the empty landscape that Joplin was left with after the tornado.

I am proud to say that I live in Joplin, Mo., and I believe that Joplin will live in all of our hearts forever; I know it will in mine. Joplin has so many great qualities that have gotten us through the tornado: hope, perseverance, love, pride, the ability to look toward the light at the end of the tunnel, and the idea that "Nothing Stops Us." It hasn't before, and it won't now, or ever.

I'd like to personally thank everyone who has helped the people of Joplin over the past months, and I can't wait to see Joplin when it's rebuilt: bigger and better than ever. Joplin is now getting out of the recovery stage, and we are rebuilding rapidly. It makes me proud to be here.

Denton Williams will be a sophomore at Joplin High School during the 2012-2013 school year.

Hundreds of people gathered in Cunningham Park on Sept. 11, 2011, to witness the unfurling of a battered flag recovered from the site of the World Trade Center after the Sept. 11, 2001, terrorist attacks. The flag sat in storage until 2007, then was brought to Greensburg, Kan., where residents there started stitching it back together after a tornado ravaged that town in southwest Kansas. That job was finished in Joplin as hundreds of people added stitches of their own on the 10th anniversary of the Sept. 11 attacks.

PHOTO BY JOHN HACKER

41. TORNADO-BATTERED JOPLIN HONORS VICTIMS OF TERRORIST ATTACKS

BY JOHN HACKER

While nearly everyone else in the nation remembers Sept. 11, 2001, for the terrible terrorist attacks on New York, Washington and Pennsylvania, Jeff Parness, a New York native who lost his best friend in the attacks on the World Trade Center, prefers to remember Sept. 12.

On the 10th anniversary of those attacks, Parness urged Joplin residents not to dwell on May 22, 2011, but to remember May 23.

The hands of firefighters hold high the National 9/11 Flag for all to see at the moment the North Tower of the World Trade Center collapsed 10 years ago.

PHOTO BY JOHN HACKER

Carter Mackey, 5, Neosho, was one of dozens of people who got the chance to hold the National 9/11 Flag during ceremonies to mark the 10th anniversary of the terrorist attacks at Cunningham Park in Joplin. Mackey's older brother, Derek Lawrence, is a Joplin firefighter who came in to work on May 22, 2011, after the tornado struck to help victims of that storm.

PHOTO BY JOHN HACKER

"This community will always remember May 22, but never forget May 23, and the compassion and the love and kindness and the neighborliness and the volunteer spirit because that's what America is all about," Parness said at a memorial service to mark the milestone anniversary of terrorist attacks on New York City and Washington, D.C., and the attempted terror attack that ended with passengers fighting their hijackers and crashing their plane in Pennsylvania.

"On Sept. 11, think about that. Drive around your community and look at these beautiful Stars of Hope," Parness said. "Knock on your neighbor's door and say, 'Is there something I can do for you?' That's what will show the world who we really are."

Parness is founder of the New York Says Thank You Foundation. He was in Joplin on Sept. 11, 2011, with the National 9/11 Flag, a 30-foot American Flag that was hanging from a building near Ground Zero in New York City on that fateful day and nearly destroyed the terrorist attacks at the World Trade Center.

In 2007, he brought that flag to Greensburg, Kan., right after an EF5 tornado leveled that community and residents there stitched the flag back together. Since then, the flag has been on a tour of the country, and people in places where tragedy has struck, such as Mena, Ark., Fort Hood, Texas, Washington, D.C. and other places have sewn patches into the flag.

That process was completed on Sept. 11, 2011, in Joplin.

Quinton Anderson, a Joplin High School senior who was seriously injured in the May 22, Joplin tornado which killed his parents, got the chance to sew one stitch into the huge flag at a memorial service for 9/11 victims at Missouri Southern State University. Anderson was hospitalized for five and a half weeks, but walked into the new Joplin High School at the Northpark Mall on the first day of his senior year.

"It represents the American spirit," Anderson said. "No matter what happens to us, we'll rebuild and come back stronger. I don't really feel like I deserve to do this, I'm just a person. I might have a story, but it's just a story. I'm still who I am and I don't feel like I deserve to be able to do that."

Grace Anderson, Quinton's sister, and her boyfriend, U.S. Army soldier Shawn Stilliens, also got to sew in one stitch each.

"I felt honored when they asked me to do it," Grace Anderson said.

"It's a special thing," Stilliens added. "It goes back 10 years, this flag does, and it's an honor to be able to help repair it here in Joplin."

Prior to the memorial service at Missouri Southern, the flag was displayed at Cunningham Park during the time when 10 years ago, airliners were flying into the World Trade Center towers.

Hundreds watched in the park as firefighters and dozens of others held the flag with the shattered remains of St. John's Regional Medical Center as a backdrop. The crowd observed moments of silence at the times when the South Tower fell, then when the North Tower collapsed.

Carter Mackey, 5, Neosho, was one of dozens of children who got the chance to hold the flag during this time.

Mackey's older brother, Derek Lawrence, is a Joplin firefighter and responded, even though he was off duty, when the tornado hit Joplin on May 22.

Heather Mackey, the boys' mother, said she was proud of her youngest son, who stood up there dressed in a firefighter's jacket and red plastic firefighter's helmet.

"It was an honor," she said. "It's important because we support our country and our city and our neighboring city."

Vincent Alejandro, a New York native who now lives in Carterville, said it was important for him to be here as well.

Alejandro was in Germany working as a contractor on a U.S. Army base when the terrorists hit his home state in 2001. He responded to help relatives who lost their homes in Joplin when the tornado hit in 2011.

To help deal with the loss in Joplin, Alejandro painted the Hope Wall at 20th and Main streets in Joplin.

"This means everything," Alejandro said as the firefighters unfurled the battered flag. "I knew I had to be there as a vet, a New Yorker and now a Joplin resident. With everything that's happened, I just had to be here."

HISTORY OF THE FLAG
COURTESY NEW YORK SAYS THANK YOU FOUNDATION
HTTP://NATIONAL911FLAG.ORG

"And the rocket's red glare, the bombs bursting in air, gave proof through the night that our flag was still there."

Those familiar words rang true in New York in the days following September 11, 2001 when the remnants of a 30-foot American flag hung torn, tattered, and blowing in the wind at 90 West Street across from

Ground Zero for the entire world to see.

In late October 2001, Charlie Vitchers, a construction superintendent for the clean up effort at Ground Zero, sent a work crew to take down the tattered remains of the American flag. The remains were placed in a storage shed where they sat untouched for seven years.

On the 9/11 Anniversary in 2008, Charlie, who volunteers as a construction coordinator for The New York Says Thank You Foundation, brought the torn remains of the Flag with him to Greensburg, Kan., a town 95 percent destroyed by an EF5 tornado. As hundreds of New York Says Thank You volunteers spent the 9/11 Anniversary weekend helping to rebuild Greensburg, the residents of this small Kansas prairie town joined disaster survivors from across the United States to stitch this very special American Flag back together using flags salvaged from the Greensburg tornado.

In doing so, they literally stitched together the two communities shared stories of tragedy and triumph and created a new and living piece of American History.

The goals of The National 9/11 Flag Tour are:

RESTORE

We will restore The National 9/11 Flag back to its original 13-stripe format using pieces of fabric from American flags scheduled for retirement in all 50 states. This historic grassroots restoration effort will comprise a two-year, 50 state, National 9/11 Flag Tour lasting through the end of the 10th Year Anniversary of 9/11.

EMPOWER

We will empower local service heroes in all 50 states with the once-in-a-lifetime opportunity of placing stitches in The National 9/11 Flag.

We will honor wounded warriors, military veterans, first responders, educators, students, volunteer service leaders, and those who lost loved ones on 9/11 with the privilege of participating in the historic restoration of The National 9/11 Flag.

INSPIRE

We will inspire 300 million Americans with The National 9/11 Flag's rich visual history through public and private displays at leading venues

Lori Sullivan, Mena, Ark.; Wendy Hauser, Chicago; Carolyn Deters, Glenwood, Iowa; and Patty Lanni, Omaha, Neb.; all volunteers with the New York Says Thank You Foundation, prepare patches for stitching by area residents at a ceremony held Sept. 11, 2011, at Missouri Southern State University in Joplin.
PHOTO BY JOHN HACKER

nationwide.

We will educate generations of young people with the flag's powerful message of service and sacrifice and overcoming historic challenges by working together.

We will deepen our sense of citizenship and national pride.

We will bolster the spirit of volunteerism on the 9/11 Anniversary and year-round.

ABOUT THE FOUNDATION

The New York Says Thank You Foundation is proud to be the national custodian of The National 9/11 Flag.

Started in 2003 at the suggestion of a 5-year-old boy, The New York

Says Thank You Foundation has grown into one of the nation's leading organizations to transform the 9/11 Anniversary into a positive, hands-on platform for national volunteer service.

Each year on the 9/11 Anniversary, The New York Says Thank You Foundation sends large groups of volunteers from New York City to help rebuild communities around the United States recovering from disaster. It's the group's way of saying "Thank You" for all the love and support Americans from across the country extended to New Yorkers in the days, weeks, and months following Sept. 11.

The Foundation's core volunteer group consists of FDNY firefighters, many of them survivors of the World Trade Center, as well as Ground Zero construction workers, 9/11 family members, NYC schoolchildren and scores of New Yorkers impacted by the tragedy of 9/11 and the humanity we experienced as a nation on 9/12.

At each 9/11 Anniversary rebuilding effort, the group is joined by hundreds of local volunteers as well as by a growing group of disaster survivor volunteers from all the communities assisted by New York Says Thank You on previous anniversaries of 9/11 who continue to volunteer each year as their way to "Pay It Forward."

Recognized in 2009 by President Obama, New York Says Thank You Foundation's volunteer rebuilding efforts have been featured on over 500 television news programs nationwide including ABC World News Tonight "Persons of the Week," CBS Evening News, NBC Nightly News, CNN, and Fox. The organization's projects have also been featured in The New York Times and local newspapers across the United States. To date, 7,000 people nationwide have participated in The New York Says Thank You Foundation's 9/11 Anniversary community rebuilding projects.

The secret to New York Says Thank You's growing national "pay it forward" movement is very simple: What we do is not about 9/11. What we do is about 9/12.

For more information, visit www.NewYorkSaysThankYou.org.

42. ANTI-MUSLIM SENTIMENT CLOUDS GIFT TO JOPLIN SCHOOLS

BY RANDY TURNER

It was one of those feel-good stories that have popped up day after day since the May 22 Joplin Tornado.

The United Arab Emirates embassy pledged half a million dollars to the Joplin Schools for the One-to-One program, which is designed to give every high school student a laptop for the 2011-2012 school year.

That pledge is backed by an additional pledge of another half million if other donors can match the original amount.

The following passage was included in the school district news release:

"The entire world was touched by the devastation caused in Joplin by the May 22 tornado. Given the scale of the disaster, including the destruction of the community's only high school, we felt it was important to provide assistance," said Yousef Al Otaiba, UAE Ambassador to the U.S. "The One-to-One initiative is a truly innovative idea that will not only give current students the tools they need to start the school year, but position future Joplin Schools students on the cutting-edge of learning."

Joplin Schools and the UAE Embassy anticipate this grant as the start of a longer-term partnership between the two organizations. JS and the Embassy hope to work together to develop programming that will deepen cultural understating and awareness between the U.S. and the UAE.

At least $500,000 and probably $1.5 million being used for the benefit of students whose lives have been forever changed by the cataclysmic forces of nature.

Who could argue with such an outpouring of humanity? Who could argue with the evidence of the effect Joplin has had on the world?

Sadly, some of those who are arguing come from within Joplin. They lurk on the comment sections of blogs, including mine, and the local newspaper.

Deep torrents of bigotry are unleashed in these comments, almost always by people who hide behind the cloak of anonymity.

The first reaction on my blog, The Turner Report, was what I expected when I printed the school district's news release on the gift:

The same country that brought us the 9/11 hijackers!

Another one wrote:

Did Joplin Schools sell their souls?

Those are the ones that I allowed to remain on my blog. I do not intend to become a surrogate for the type of hatred that runs rampant among certain elements in our society. Other comments, which contained profanity and anti-Muslim slurs were removed immediately.

The Joplin Globe apparently took a different approach. Its story on the gift, on the homepage of its website, has been scrubbed of all comments.

I don't pretend to speak for the Joplin School District, Joplin High School or this city. As an educator, my job is to make sure that students get past blind hatred and prejudice and learn to reason. There are times when I wonder if I am swimming against an overwhelming tide.

It is difficult to promote reason when our culture is dominated by conversations in which those who can shout the loudest and have the catchiest soundbites are prized more than those with the ability to discuss an issue using the force of reason.

Our culture is a recipe designed to pull us apart, not bring us together.

But I have watched over these past two-and-a-half months as the most horrific event in Joplin's history has brought together not only the people of Joplin, but the people of the world.

The basic tenets of love, decency, and generosity are not limited to one country, one religion or one color.

When someone reaches out with a helping hand, we should never respond with slurs and undisguised hatred.

The correct response to the gift of the United Arab Emirates, the one which has been overwhelmingly provided by those in Joplin who do not hide their venom behind fake names or "Anonymous" is "thank you."

43. I'M PROUD TO BE A RISING JOPLIN EAGLE

By Micaela Tennis

On that forsaken day that I wish had never happened, I frantically called every single number in my contacts list on my phone. Some friends didn't answer, but later I was relieved when they called back. Phone service was sporadic that day, due to so many people trying to locate or contact their loved ones. "I'm sorry all circuits are currently busy. Please try your call again later." Reliability and service, you failed me that day.

It was such a radical summer, full of emotional roller coasters, tears, and confusion. There was a sense of unification in the air. Joplin was a family, a community. Before it hadn't been that obvious, until we lost so many things we held dear. I had wondered, the week before the school year began, what it had in store. Certainly it wasn't going to be the same, at all. I was excited, to get back into a schedule, even though it wasn't going to be the Joplin High experience.

Six a.m. finds me with the alarm going off, yelling at me to get up. The sound was so haunting it seemed, or maybe I was overreacting. Snooze, I'm sure I used you more than five times that day. It was Aug. 17, 2011. Summer ended when I got out of the bed, 87 days went by in a blink of an eye. I looked back, the bed seemed so comfortable, I wanted to go back, and sleep. Gabriel was already up, and was sitting on the couch watching his favorite shows. I'm sure he didn't know about school starting but he would soon find out.

I will never understand why how you look on the first day is, and was, so important to me. I mean I had respect for myself, and I wanted to look nice, but now that I look back, it probably wasn't the best fashion choice. But then again I thought of those who lost their homes that summer. What would they look like? I wasn't trying to be judgmental, and I know that sounds bad, but you never know. It's 6:45 now, 15 minutes until I have to leave. Add the finishing touches to my look.

I felt so unprepared for this day. I didn't have a backpack I could use, and I had no school supplies. I was always used to going to my grandparents house every morning to get ready for school. But now since it's been long gone, I had to adapt. I didn't think about what I was going to say to my friends when I got there. I wasn't scared, I just didn't know what August 17th had in store for me.

I knew that leadership was going to play a huge role in my life this year.

I had always felt that God had given me this gift of leadership. But that's just my religious-based perspective. There was and is a reason for everything that happens in life, even if you walk away from it without learning anything. I was involved in JHS Student Council, and that's where I had the opportunity to display and practice my leadership skills. I had hopes that this year would be the year that I would establish myself as a leader to my school and my community, regardless of if I were not a class president.

I arrived at the 9/10 campus 30 minutes early. Just so I could be reunited with the friends I hadn't seen since May 20th. I felt like I was in summer school all over again, being at Memorial. The usual "catch up on the summer's gossip" didn't suffice for me. I asked my friends how they were doing, what I could do to help them out. The atmosphere was entirely different. It was difficult to grasp the concept that this was an actual high school at one time. No "Eagle Alley" filled with different types of people talking, having a good time. No alphabetically ordered hallways telling me where my classrooms were. Compared to Joplin High, the 9/10 Campus seemed so much larger. Walking with my friends I started to miss the normal schedule. But then again, I suppose adaptation was going to play a major role in my life this year.

At 8:15 a.m., the bell rings. I believe the monotone ring was more haunting than that of my alarm clock ... first hour was Spanish. I didn't even take into consideration until I was sitting in class that my teachers, too, had been affected. I felt so self-centered. I was much better off than others; I didn't lose much of anything aside from my grandparent's house. But then again, I grew up there. They lost everything in their classrooms. Some things were family photos, or decorations for the classrooms, textbooks, lesson plans, and the memories. I'm sure that they felt separated from the other teachers at the 11/12 Campus. Teachers oftentimes reference to the items at the High School that still lingered there. You could tell that it was still difficult for them to talk about the things in their other classrooms. It's never going to be easy for anyone that experienced what happened on May 22. No one can ever know what it is really like to experience something of this magnitude.

As the day continued, I started to miss the upperclassmen that I saw every day. It wasn't the same. Sophomores were the big dogs this time, and I couldn't determine if that was necessarily a good thing. I missed being bossed around by the upperclassmen, but of course then I was just an innocent little freshman. I knew that I would see them again, just not as often as I would have liked.

Lunchtime was entirely different. No exceedingly long line stretching to the back of the cafeteria. I never thought smaller could be better. Yet, it still wasn't the same. Sometimes you wish that you had the ability to go back in time and change everything. Oftentimes, I wished I could go back and change something, maybe that would have altered the possibility of a tornado ... or if maybe you could go back and experience freshman year all over again.

It's 1:30 p.m. now, class has started, communication arts, to be exact. I couldn't have asked for a better first day of school. I still had seventh hour to go to, Drama class! I have always loved meeting new people. The teachers were so kind, they asked us, did you do OK with the tornado? Did you lose your house? How was your summer? The conversations always seemed so formatted. I, of course, asked the same questions to my teachers. I knew it wasn't my business, but I didn't want my teachers thinking I didn't care about others.

At 2:20, passing time to seventh hour, I found it very difficult to get from one side of the school to the other in five minutes time. I took the outdoor route, it was a very, very hot day in August, but it felt wonderful! I walked quickly to class; I have never been late to a class in my life. There was a new drama teacher this year, Mrs. Brim. I felt empathetic for her. She was new to the Joplin School district, so I can understand the challenges that she would face for the upcoming year. Costumes, props, and make-up were destroyed during the tornado, and possibly that drama wasn't going to be the focus. I felt that the drama department wasn't going to be as successful as before. I didn't want to come across as a rude student, but that's just how I felt about the drama department.

At 3:15 p.m., the final bell rings. This time the monotone sound wasn't as haunting as it was that morning. I wish the day could have been longer. I loved school and all, but I wanted to be with my friends. I had to start riding the bus home after school every day, because my whole family's schedule got flipped around. I rode the wrong bus home, that was a big mistake, but of course that would happen to me. As I was sitting on the bus, unaware of my surroundings, I thought about how the whole atmosphere of the school was different. The word separated came to my mind. I wondered when the entire Joplin High School student body was going to be reunited again. I knew it was going to be a great year, full of adventures, new beginnings, trials, and hardships. And if this year were going to be filled with trials, I would have my friends right there with me.

I never planned for a tornado to happen, it just wasn't in my schedule. Hmm, let's see ... go to May, hmm ... the 22nd is a Sunday, that sounds like a wonderful day to have a tornado. Now, what time will that be, 5:41? Sure! No. I am incredibly blessed to have my friends and family still with me today. Never again would I take anything or anyone for granted. Joplin is a family, a stronger community that is quite prominent. Thank you to those who donated or spent their summer here in my hometown to help us get back on our feet. You will never understand my appreciation towards all of you. I'm proud to be a rising Joplin Eagle.

Micaela Tennis, 15, will be a junior at Joplin High School during the 2012-2013 school year.

Maria Kumbier and her children, Asa Kumbier, 9, and Coe Munch, 12, stand together with their lights held high during the ceremony held Tuesday, Nov. 22, 2011, at Cunningham Park marking the six-month anniversary of the EF5 tornado that devastated Joplin.
PHOTO BY JOHN HACKER

44. THE SIX-MONTH ANNIVERSARY: NOV. 22, 2011, IN CUNNINGHAM PARK

By JOHN HACKER

Six months after the tornado tore its deadly path through Joplin, hundreds of people gathered at a park that has come to symbolize Joplin's recovery to remember, mourn and try to move forward.

On Nov. 22, 2011, city, state and federal officials gathered with residents in Cunningham Park to mark six months since 161 Joplin residents and others were killed in the May 22 storm.

Chris Piquard, who lost his mother, Marie Piquard, in the storm, attended with his father, Lloyd Piquard, to remember and move on. The two saw the name of their mother and wife on a temporary version of a bronze plaque that will soon grace Cunningham Park as part of a series of memorials around the park at 26th Street and McClelland Boulevard.

"The milestone is hard," said Lloyd Piquard. "It makes it hard on me, but I know where my wife is, she's in heaven with Jesus."

Chris Piquard said it was important to remember those who died on the six-month anniversary of the storm.

"I think it's something that memorializes not just the fact that Joplin, most of it was destroyed, but the fact that we did lose those loved ones and they will be remembered," Chris Piquard said. "It's a milestone that we've come to, and I think closure is something that we're never going to get as far as we're never going to forget who was lost or what has happened, but it is a milestone that we came to and it is a part of the recovery that Joplin needs to go through."

City officials joined Missouri Gov. Jay Nixon, U.S. Rep. Billy Long and local clergy to lead the ceremony that saw hundreds bring lawn chairs to brave chilly temperatures and remember.

Joplin Parks Director Chris Cotten spoke about the trees that were uprooted in the park.

"On the morning of May 22, 2011, 61 oak trees stood tall and proud in Cunningham Park," Cotten said. "More than likely, some of them had stood prior to Cunningham Park's establishment in 1890. They had witnessed countless family events, observed babies napping under their branches, watched young children grow old and shared lovely spring days and crisp fall evenings with our seniors as they entered the twilight of their lives. By 6 p.m. that evening, like the city of Joplin, they stood broken and shattered.

"The largest of those oak trees had a width of 43 feet, stood 50 feet tall and had a canopy of 60 feet. If it was not the oldest tree in the park, it was certainly one of the oldest. Like the mighty oak tree, strength and courage among Joplin residents were not lacking immediately following the tornado's aftermath."

Cotten said the city plans to plant 161 trees in a rebuilt Cunningham Park, one for each of the people killed in the storm.

He also talked about a bronze plaque, containing the names of all 161 victims, which will be placed in the park.

He also described a new fountain that has been set up in the park.

"In November of 1908, the work of installing a fountain, purchased by the Women's Park Association for Cunningham Park, began," Cotten said "That fountain was nine feet in diameter and the water was to fall from

The band Live Wire performs its Joplin tribute song "Miracle of the Human Spirit" on stage at the ceremony on Nov. 22, 2011, at Cunningham Park marking six months after the May 22, 2011, tornado.

PHOTO BY JOHN HACKER

three levels. In May of 1909, that fountain came to life in Cunningham and was described as located at the foot of a slope in the southeast corner of the park. For reasons lost to us through time, that fountain was removed in the 1920s, but the base was left behind. For years and years it was used as a planter and its history as a fountain was forgotten.

"After the storm, its true history was again discovered, and today, some 80 years after its predecessor was shut down, water will again flow in this fountain basin."

Now a new fountain has been installed with three levels, the top level with five streams of water, the middle level with 22 streams and the bottom with 11, to mark the date 5-22-11.

Governor Jay Nixon compared Joplin to the "the house of the wise man described in the gospel of Matthew."

"The rain descended and the winds blew and beat upon that house

Ron Sifferman takes a picture of the prototype plaque honoring the 161 people killed in the May 22, 2011, Joplin tornado as his wife, Coleen Sifferman, looks on. Coleen Sifferman lost her mother, Lorna "Kay" Miller, in the tornado and her name was among those on the plaque dedicated Nov. 22, 2011, in Cunningham Park.

PHOTO BY JOHN HACKER

and it fell not for it was founded upon a rock," Nixon told the crowd. "The storm shook Joplin to the core, but its rock, its foundation of faith could not be moved. In six short months, the tornado's wounds, some still visible, some hidden deep within us are healing. Brick by brick and board by board, Joplin is rising from its granite foundation of faith. And everywhere we look, we see change.

"Cunningham Park has been transformed into a vibrant oasis of beauty and peace, a living memorial to those who lost their lives and the tens of thousands of volunteers who opened their hearts in Joplin's hour of need."

Nixon talked his admiration of the "unwavering courage, compassion and true grit," shown by Joplin residents.

"Your fight and your faith have proved to the people of our state, our nation and the world that the spirit of Joplin is unbreakable," Nixon said. "From day one, help was here when and where it was needed most. In all, more than 400 first-responders and law enforcement agencies from every corner of our state and many other states dropped everything they were doing to help Joplin. We owe these brave men and women an enormous debt of gratitude.

"The success of our partnership is a shining example of what we can accomplish when people of good faith rally around a common goal. I know that Joplin's journey has really barely begun, and I'm here to tell you that we'll be here with you until that job is done."

Joplin Mayor Mark Woolston talked about the strength he had seen in Joplin's residents in the reconstruction work that happened in the summer and fall of 2011.

"In the immediate aftermath of the tornado, city staff, school district personnel and the Chamber of Commerce set the tone that this is not the type of community that is going to let a little EF5 tornado kick our ...," Woolston said, pausing instead of using the word he used on CNN immediately following the storm. "We're not going to let this storm defeat us. That is just as true today as it was the first day following the storm.

"The sense of community that has been realized here is, to my knowledge, unmatched anywhere in the country, and that sense of community is what brings us here tonight. Not only have we lost 161 members of our community, we've lost a part of ourselves. That loss is something from which we are not ever likely to recover. Though we may never recover form the loss of 161 lives, we will, slowly, but surely, move forward. As we move forward to Thanksgiving, let us be thankful for the lives that were spared. For those that avoided destruction, for those that volunteered to help us and for those who continue to help us recover. In this community, we care for one another."

REMARKS BY CHRIS COTTEN, JOPLIN PARKS DIRECTOR

Throughout literature and history, oak trees have been regarded as wise and humble. This is primarily due to their extended age and wrinkled appearance, which evokes itself to our parents, our grandparents and great grandparents, who have known and witnessed many things.

In many cultures, the oak tree is seen as the mightiest of trees and symbolizes strength and courage. In Christianity, the oak tree is used to represent Christ's steadfastness, and in Judaism, it stands for divine presence.

On the morning of May 22, 2011, 61 oak trees stood tall and proud in Cunningham Park. More than likely, some of them had stood prior to Cunningham Park's establishment in 1890. They had witnessed countless family events, observed babies napping under their branches, watched young children grow old and shared lovely spring days and crisp fall evenings with our seniors as they entered the twilight of their lives. By 6 p.m. that evening, like the city of Joplin, they stood broken and shattered.

The largest of those oak trees had a width of 43 feet, stood 50 feet tall and had a canopy of 60 feet. If it was not the oldest tree in the park, it was certainly one of the oldest. Like the mighty oak tree, strength and courage among Joplin residents were not lacking immediately following the tornado's aftermath. As we work to rebuild Cunningham Park, we will plant 161 trees to keep alive the memory of our friends, that due to circumstances beyond our control are not here with us today. A bronze plaque with the names of those we lost will stand here and solemnly remind us of that fateful day. Today we unveil a simile of that plaque so that the families of those we lost may have one last chance to make any adjustments to the names of their loved ones before their names are permanently attached to the new Cunningham Park.

Joplin is a diverse community with many different ethnic and religious beliefs. Likewise there will be a diverse tree population planted in Cunningham Park that will represent what we lost. That being said, this tree, a Shumard red oak, the symbol of strength, courage and wisdom will be planted for future generations to appreciate for years to come. The Shumard is considered to be an attractive, fast-growing shade tree. The trees typically will reach over 100 feet of height, with crown width of up to 60 feet. Some have been known to live for over 400 years. At some point in the future, long after we are gone, children will once again play under trees with full canopies in Cunningham Park. Families will picnic under their branches and couples, young and old, will sit and admire the beauty of Cunningham Park.

In November of 1908, the work of installing a fountain, purchased by the Women's Park Association for Cunningham Park, began. That fountain was nine feet in diameter and the water was to fall from three levels. In May of 1909, that fountain came to life in Cunningham and was described as located at the foot of a slope in the southeast corner of the park. For reasons lost to us through time, that fountain was removed in the 1920s, but the base was left behind. For years and years it was used as a planter and, over time, its history as a fountain was forgotten.

After the storm, its true history was again discovered, and today, some 80 years after its predecessor was shut down, water will again flow in this fountain basin. This time the water will flow from the top level in five streams, from 22 streams at the second level and finally from 11 streams at the third and last level. As City Manager Rohr discussed, flowing water symbolized a regenerative spirit and this fountain symbolizes not only how the city will regenerate, but also shows that we will not forget.

REMARKS BY JOPLIN MAYOR MIKE WOOLSTON

In a little less than two days, we'll gather with our loved ones to celebrate Thanksgiving. And this year, in spite of what we've been through, we have so much for which to be especially thankful for. But this evening we gather to acknowledge and memorialize the loss of 161 members of our community.

Those with whom I'm acquainted know that I'm not very good at expressing my feelings. I've always found it difficult to convey to people how I felt about them. I think this event tonight offers that opportunity.

Not only for me, but for all of us to talk about the pain we feel, to acknowledge the loss we've suffered and to continue the healing process. Make no mistake, the tornado of May 22 affected all of us, some lost their jobs, some lost their homes, some lost their loved ones, but none of us lost hope.

Since the storm there have been many anecdotes being told about family helping family, which you might expect; friends helping friends, which is a pleasant surprise; and of some people helping complete strangers, something which, for many of us, was completely unexpected. In the immediate aftermath of the tornado, city staff, school district personnel and the Chamber of Commerce set the tone that this is not the type of community that is going to let a little EF5 tornado kick our ... We're not going to let this storm defeat us.

And that is just as true today as it was on the first day following the storm. The sense of community that has been realized here is, to my knowledge, unmatched anywhere in the country, and that sense of community is what brings us here tonight. Not only have we lost 161 members of our community, we've lost a part of ourselves. That loss is something

Joplin Mayor Mike Woolston speaks at the ceremony on Nov. 22, 2011, at Cunningham Park marking six months after the May 22, 2011, tornado.
PHOTO BY JOHN HACKER

11.22.11
JOPLIN
SIX-MONTH REMEMBRANCE

"The Miracle of the Human Spirit"

from which we are not ever likely to recover. And though we may never recover from the loss of 161 lives, we will, slowly but surely, move forward. As we move forward to Thanksgiving, let us be thankful for the lives that were spared, for those that avoided destruction and those that volunteered to help us, and those that continue to help us recover. In this community, we care for one another.

REMARKS BY GOV. JAY NIXON

We gather together to mark a milestone in Joplin's journey of recovery and rebirth, six months to the day. We gather to remember those who the storm has taken from us and reflect on the kindness of our fellow man and to rekindle the spirit that has carried us so far, so fast. There's no doubt that the last six months have been some of the most difficult and most rewarding of our lives.

Joplin's a bit like the house of the wise man described in the gospel of Saint Matthew. The rain descended and the winds blew and beat upon that house and it fell not, for it was founded upon a rock. The storm shook Joplin to the core, but its rock, its foundation of faith could not be moved. In six short months, the tornado's wounds, some still visible, some hidden deep within us, are healing. Brick by brick and board by board, Joplin is rising from its granite foundation of faith. And everywhere we look, we see change.

Cunningham Park has been transformed into a vibrant oasis of beauty and peace, a living memorial to those who lost their lives and the tens of thousands of volunteers who opened their hearts in Joplin's hour of need.

Businesses from Range Line to Main Street have opened their doors and are hiring again. The new high school is bustling with activity. Families are starting to move out of the FEMA mobile homes and back into the community. More new houses are springing up each and every day. In Joplin, the sun rises every day on a different place and sets every night on a better place. So much change, so much progress, none of it has happened by accident. From those first terrible moments in the storm's wake, the rescue, recovery and rebuilding of Joplin have been a team effort. Some things are just too big to tackle alone. And the simple truth is that we are stronger together than apart. Teams who work together, win.

11.22.11
JOPLIN
SIX-MONTH REMEMBRANCE

Gov. Jay Nixon speaks at the ceremony on Nov. 22, 2011, at Cunningham Park marking six months after the May 22, 2011, tornado.

PHOTO BY JOHN HACKER

The astonishing progress we see all around us is a testament to the resilience and resourcefulness of this community. I've said it before and I'll say it again, Joplin is the toughest town on God's green Earth.

From day one, you have shown unwavering courage, compassion and true grit. Your fight and your faith have proved to the people of our state, our nation and the world that the spirit of Joplin is unbreakable. From day one, help was here when and where it was needed most. In all, more than 400 first-responders and law enforcement agencies from every corner of our state and many other states, dropped everything they were doing to help Joplin. We owe these brave men and women an enormous debt of gratitude.

The success of our partnership is a shining example of what we can accomplish when people of good faith rally around a common goal. I know that Joplin's journey has really barely begun, and I'm here to tell you that we'll be here with you until that job is done.

Everything has progressed faster in Joplin thanks to the tremendous outpouring of volunteers.

The numbers are staggering. At last count, 113,167 volunteers have logged 688,774 hours of service. They came from all faiths and all walks of life, from Alaska to Florida, from Sweden to Japan, each one so moved by Joplin's story that they wanted to be part of it in whatever way they could. Cajun chefs drove up from Louisiana to make gumbo for hungry volunteers. It was good too.

Missouri cattlemen grilled steaks for firefighters and police. Church groups and chainsaw crews came from Iowa, Nebraska, Colorado and Tennessee, heavy equipment operators brought backhoes and forklifts, buckets and cranes. Crewmembers of the USS Missouri took a week of shore leave to help haul debris. A thousand Boy Scouts painted playground equipment in sweltering, 106-degree heat. Inner-city teens came from Philly to help sort clothing.

Americorps volunteers sifted through the rubble and found two Purple Hearts and reunited them with the heroes that had earned them. A little girl in Indiana emptied her piggy bank and sent her life savings to a church in Joplin, $52 in nickels and dimes.

Joplin is living proof that the Lord helps those who help themselves. Just moments after the storm had passed, the people of this community mobilized to help one another. And when volunteers began to arrive, you made them feel welcome; you never took their generosity for granted. And because of that, donations and volunteers are still pouring in. Ask any one of them and they'll tell you the same thing. They got much more than they gave. Some day, it will be Joplin's turn to pay it forward and teach another community in crisis just how it's done.

The lesson of Joplin is clear, with teamwork and tenacity, the impossible is possible. By rebuilding Joplin stronger and better than ever, we will honor the memory and fulfill the legacy of those we lost. Soon it will be too cold to pour concrete and lay sod. The line of pickups at McDonalds will be shorter, the motels not quite so full and as winter settles in, we may not build as much with bricks and mortar, but we can build something different, one to one. They say that a lot of life goes on around the kitchen table. I think there's real truth in that, so take care of one another in the gray days of winter. Make a double batch of chili and share it with a neighbor. Take time to thank the teachers playing backstop for your kids. Remember those still grieving who may need a willing ear. Small acts of kindness make a big difference.

But before we know it, the days will grow longer, the nights warmer, flowers will bloom again, the trees we planted will send out new leaves and Joplin's forward progress will continue. So today, in the spirit of Thanksgiving, let us give thanks for one another, for the lessons and the mercy and for the lives filled with purpose and compassion and let each of us humbly seek God's blessing for the hard work that lies ahead. God Bless you Joplin forever.

REMARKS BY CONGRESSMAN BILLY LONG

It's an honor to be here to speak to the greatest people in the United States of America. Whenever I was elected, there are 435 congressional seats, and when I was elected, I said I've got the best one of them and you all have proved that to this whole country.

How many of you remember where you were on May 11? I remember where I was on May 11, I was in my office in Washington, D.C. There were a group of folks who wanted to come in and see me that day, they were called the Joplin Coalition, Rob O'Brian, Mike Woolston, the Mayor and Steve Stockam from the Regional Airport. And what were they there to see me about in Washington? They wanted to make their town, that they were so proud of, a better place to live in for all of their citizens, and work to improve Joplin. They were so proud of this area.

How many remember where you were on May 19? I remember where I was, I was in Joplin, Mo., May 19. What was I doing on May 19? I was meeting with that same group, the Joplin Coalition, that was so proud of what they were doing. They were looking forward. They were trying to make this a better community for their citizens, this area that they were so proud of, their hometown.

That was on May 19, then came May 22.

That morning I was in a church in Mount Vernon, their 145-year-old celebration, the First Baptist Church. It was a beautiful morning. Great event, they were adding on to their church.

That evening, May 22, where was I? My oldest daughter was having her birthday, we went over to some friends house and we sat down and we got the news. The next morning we were over here at daylight and found 450 first responders huddled in the fire house at the emergency operations center from all over the area, people from all over our great state, our great country, and yes, the world, came in to help Joplin. But the real first responders had been there the night before, the people who went and cleared that hospital out in 90 minutes, in their pickup trucks.

We had first responders created immediately because those are the types of people who live around here in Joplin and you need to be proud of your community, proud of yourselves. Fifty-four percent of the school capacity gone, thousands of homes gone, hundreds of businesses gone, 161 lives cut short, but their memory will never wane. Those 161 folks that we lost touched thousands and thousands of people throughout this community. I just want to thank you all for how strong you've been, how strong you've shown the rest of the county how it's done.

Here we are six months past May 22, there is not a day that goes by that someone doesn't come up to me in the halls of Congress, on the floor of Congress and say, 'Billy, how's Joplin?' How's Joplin? They're still concerned, they say, you know, we can't believe the people in Joplin, the attitude of the people in Joplin. How they reached out and pulled themselves up by their bootstraps and helped themselves. They're a remarkable bunch and I say, yes they are a remarkable bunch. I had breakfast week before last with Janet Napolitano, the Secretary of Homeland Security and Peter King, the chairman ... I walked in the room and Peter King, was there, the first thing he said was, 'Billy, how's Joplin?' A few seconds later, Secretary Napolitano came in and said, 'Billy, how's Joplin doing? Whatever you need, we'll get you.'

Like I said, those 161 people that were tragically killed, their lives cut short through this horrific, horrific event, they would be so proud of you and I'm so proud of you and God bless you.

45. COME HOME TO JOPLIN

THE FOLLOWING SPEECH WAS GIVEN BY JOPLIN CITY MANAGER MARK ROHR AT THE
SIX-MONTH MEMORIAL SERVICE NOV. 22, 2011, AT CUNNINGHAM PARK

I don't know if everyone remembers where that term came from, "the miracle of the human spirit," was the one-week moment of silence we held right over there. At that point of time, before we observed the moment of silence, I had the opportunity to say a few words and I tried to describe what I had seen in that week since the tornado. It was the outpouring of love and support that I had seen, and it occurred to me that the perfect term for that outpouring of support and what we had seen was the miracle of the human spirit, and it's grown exponentially since then.

We saw a lot of support that first week and it's grown over and over since that point in time. We're thankful to the guys for putting that song together, it's a wonderful song.

I want to personally thank everyone here for coming out today to be participants in this very important moment in the city's history. We gather here today to pay tribute to those that we have lost as a result of the May 22nd tornado.

Joplin City Manager Mark Rohr speaks at the ceremony on Nov. 22, 2011, at Cunningham Park marking six months after the May 22, 2011, tornado.
PHOTO BY JOHN HACKER

We gather here today to thank the many that have come to Joplin to help our town and we gather here today to look towards Joplin's future. I asked you on May 29, right over there, to honor those that we've lost by channeling our efforts and feelings and emotions for the departed into our overall recovery efforts. You, the citizens of Joplin, have done so in ways, and to extremes, that I never dreamed of at that moment of silence observation held that day.

Joplin stands as a shining example to our state, our country and to the world of what the time-honored American virtues of compassion, hard work and dogged determination can accomplish.

Today we dedicate the first of 161 trees in Cunningham Park that will serve as the living embodiment of the spirits of those that we have lost. These trees will be nurtured by our tender hands, and those of our children, and our children's children, in this hallowed ground that we now sit on.

They will transcend the temporal limitations of those of us in attendance here today as a living reminder of those no longer with us. I dare say that these trees will be among the most well-kept in the state of Missouri, Mr. Governor. (long pause)

To the 113,000 registered volunteers that have come to Joplin's aid, mere words and actions expressing thanks are inadequate in acknowledging your efforts. You have reaffirmed my faith in mankind, but more importantly, you have demonstrated to the world what can be accomplished by setting aside egos, agendas and the demands of your own lives to help your fellow man. It is a lesson in life that we all need to remember and we all need to live long after the fog and the emergency and its aftermath have lifted. You, the volunteers, are the living embodiment of the miracle of the human spirit.

In a humble attempt to express our gratitude, we have created a memorial to our northeast that reflects, in concentric circles, the four stages of our disaster recovery, along with a metal band representing the miracle of the human spirit.

At the center of the memorial we would like to have a bronze sculpture with figures representing the volunteers and actual debris from the storm cast in bronze. This debris will serve as a touchstone for you and succeeding generations to come to return to Joplin and commemorate your experience in this very special human movement. In the same manner that you helped Joplin, your offspring can demonstrate their participation in this unique effort by simulating their assistance in lifting the debris in the sculpture.

We are also blessed here today to dedicate two distinct water features in Cunningham Park. The use of water is intended to demonstrate the growth and regenerative properties of that element. What really do we all have but this moment in time amongst our friends and relatives, and our hopes for a bright and verdant tomorrow?

The tornado can take away that which we own, but it cannot strip away our values, beliefs and our hopes for a better future. On that fateful day in May, nature let loose a powerful force that cleaved our city in two and rendered unspeakable damage. But in doing so, it unleashed an even-more powerful force, much stronger than the winds that day. It is a force that has drawn this town together and has united us in a common effort that will make Joplin better than it was before.

We are forever linked by our common experiences on that very uncommon day. We are brothers and sisters of the storm, we are survivors that will not be defined by the tornado, but rather the manner in which we responded to our circumstances that were thrust upon us and in that spirit, I say to those Joplinites that have sought refuge elsewhere, you may have been welcome in your new circumstances, but those who surround you can never fully identify with what happened to you like all of us here today can. And I bid to you today, come home to Joplin, come home to Joplin, come home to Joplin.

Thank you.

An aerial photo of Cunningham Park from February 2012.
PHOTO BY JOHN HACKER

46. CUNNINGHAM PARK, JOPLIN'S FIRST PARK

BY JOHN HACKER

Cunningham Park was Joplin's first park, and it was the park most heavily damaged in the May 22, 2011, tornado.

Even as it lay devastated, Cunningham Park became a place people gravitated to in the weeks after the tornado.

The news media, using the ruined St. John's hospital building as a backdrop, used the park as a staging point. News conferences were held there daily for a week after the storm.

On May 29, 2011, one week after the storm, hundreds gathered for a moment of silence.

On Nov. 22, 2011, six months after the storm, hundreds gathered on its lawn once again to mark an anniversary and milestone.

Uncovering the history of Joplin's first park is a tricky endeavor and requires piecing together information from a number of sources.

Brad Belk, historian and director of the Joplin Museum Complex, said no one thought to put any sort of marker in Cunningham Park telling who Thomas Cunningham was back in 1898 when Cunningham decided to donate a seven-acre grove to the city.

Belk, citing Joel T. Livingston's two-volume 1912 book, *The History of Jasper County, Missouri and its People,* said Thomas W. Cunningham was mayor of Joplin in 1897 and gave the piece of land then known as Cunningham's Grove to Joplin on July 5, 1898.

"This beautiful grove was greatly used by the citizens for picnics and celebrations, and it was Mr. Cunningham's idea to preserve the grove so that the people of the city might have someplace in the city limits for gatherings of this kind," Livingston wrote in his book. "The city at the time had no fund available with which to improve the park, so in 1903, Joplin City Attorney Pearl Decker secured the passage of a bill through the legislature authorizing the city, by a vote of the people to levy a tax for park purposes. The matter was submitted to the people in the general election in 1904 and passed."

Livingston's book said Cunningham chaired one of Joplin's first park boards in 1903. That board included legendary Joplin names such as Charles Schifferdecker, William H. Landreth and James M. Leonard, each of whom eventually gave land which would make up the backbone of Joplin's park system.

"I'm reading a little bit into this, but, apparently, this leaves a lasting impression on them, serving on the board, and leads them to later give generous gifts of land back to the city," Belk said. "I just find that fascinating."

Before he became Mayor of Joplin in 1897, Cunningham helped establish two banks in the Joplin area, the Bank of Joplin in 1882, and the Bank of Carl Junction in 1892.

In 1911, Cunningham helped found the *Joplin Daily Tribune* newspaper.

Cunningham, who was married to Tabitha T. Cunningham, died in 1922 at the age of 77 and is buried in Fairview Cemetery in Joplin.

The Missouri Digital Heritage section on the Missouri Secretary of State's website features two postcards with pictures of Cunningham Park dated 1908. The description of the postcards say a group of ladies formed the Women's Park Association for Cunningham Park to carry out enhancements to the park.

"In May of 1909, the group unveiled an impressive nine-foot fountain with a nine-foot diameter octagonal base and a three-tiered waterfall," the website said. "Joplinites congregated at Cunningham Park for picnics and celebrations. Spacious lawns, beautiful walks, well-coiffed flowerbeds and a handsome bandstand provided pleasurable ambiance. By 1926, other amenities had been added — a screened-in shelter, children's playground, refreshment stand, swimming pool and bathhouse."

Joplin Parks Director Chris Cotten talked about that fountain at the six-month anniversary of the tornado on Nov. 22, 2011.

"For reasons lost to us through time, that fountain was removed in the 1920s, but the base was left behind," Cotten said. "For years and years it was used as a planter and, over time, its history as a fountain was forgotten.

"After the storm, its true history was again discovered, and today, some 80 years after its predecessor was shut down, water will again flow in this fountain basin. This time the water will flow from the top level in five streams, from 22 streams at the second level and finally from 11 streams at the third and last level. As City Manager Mark Rohr discussed, flowing water symbolized a regenerative spirit and this fountain symbolizes not only how the city will regenerate, but also shows that we will not forget."

The new Cunningham Park also features a memorial to volunteers in the northeast part of the park.

The memorial was designed over two months prior to the start of the Extreme Makeover: Home Edition build in October 2011.

Designed by architecture students at Drury University, the memorial features four concentric rings that represent different aspects of the work done by hundreds of thousands of volunteers — rescue, recovery, demolition and rebuilding. The rings feature bronze castings of different items and tools used in the rescue and rebuilding of Joplin, including hammers, wrenches, saws. It also incorporates debris from the storm.

Standing at the corner of the memorial is another ring, this one standing vertically and made of stainless steel.

It represents the "Miracle of the Human Spirit," the phrase used by Joplin City Manager Mark Rohr to describe how the city came together and how volunteers poured in from all over to help in that first week after the storm.

PHOTO BY ROSE FOGARTY

47. GOD BLESS THE PEOPLE OF JOPLIN, MISSOURI

By Rose Fogarty

My name is Rose Fogarty, and I am one of the founding members of the St. Lou Crew for Joplin. Along with my friends in the Crew, we have not only had the immense honor of meeting so many amazing people in the city of Joplin, but we have been able to witness first-hand their courage, strength and determination, rising up in the face of tragedy.

I wrote my first chapter in Randy Turner's first book *5:41 Stories from the Joplin Tornado* because I was lucky enough to be contacted by Randy after he read my personal story "How Will Norton Led Me to Joplin" on Facebook. I am so glad I shared that story because it was there that Randy found me and it is now documented forever. I was able to meet Randy at his book signing in December 2011 and I am honored that he asked me to write again about our efforts. Again, knowing that our experiences would be documented forever, I had to stop and write for him again in this anniversary edition.

The St. Lou Crew for Joplin has made four mission trips to Joplin as of May 2012. I was honored to have been present at three of those four trips. The first was June 3-4, 2011, just a few weeks after the tornado. What we saw and experienced shook every one of us to our core. We witnessed devastation beyond words, pain, suffering and courage. We also witnessed the most inspiring individuals, who still held onto their hope and faith in the face of adversity. These trips were difficult and trying at times. As one can imagine, trying to organize 50 plus strangers in a devastated city reduced to rubble, with no street signs to navigate can be challenging. However, once we all got to the point of really getting to work, we were all jolted in the reality of why we kept coming back to support this city.

Each time we got back to St. Louis after our trips, it was difficult to return to our normal lives after experiencing the sadness and devastation. Our first trip, the weekend of June 3-4, was captured in Randy's first book. I am writing today about our second trip, July 22-24 and beyond. This trip, I decided to take my eighth-grade daughter Lexei, who also fell in love with the people and city of Joplin. The night before we left, I told her and her friend Kelly, who was going with us, that they had to watch at least one hour of all of Will Norton's YouTube videos, so they could know who he was and how he inspired others. I am so glad that I did that, because they now had a purpose in connecting with Will and his story and were really looking forward to going.

As part of our July trip, we had a musical instrument drive in St. Louis to replace all of the instruments that were lost when the tornado hit Joplin High School. We were all so very thankful that the students were not in the high school that night for the graduation ceremonies, so our job was easy, to replace the instruments that were lost. Thanks to the help of the Play it Forward organization in St. Louis and the St. Louisans who once again came out to support our efforts, we collected close to 100 instruments and also filled an 18 wheeler (donated by McCarthy Holdings) full of donations to bring back to Joplin. I remember a very poignant moment as I watched the lines of volunteers unloading our truck at the warehouse, lined up one by one removing the instruments and donations. Watching each Crew member quietly and uniformly unloading piece by piece, reminded me of churchgoers lining up for holy communion. For me, in my mind, I saw each piece as a symbol of hope to distribute to the people of Joplin. It was very symbolic, and I was very proud of everyone in that warehouse. Filling a trailer full of random items, then backing it up to a warehouse garage and unloading as quickly as possible can be very difficult to manage. We tried our best to sort it appropriately and get it distributed to best help the families we found that so desperately needed assistance.

We delivered our first load to a storage shed. When we first pulled up, I was a little sad because I didn't think we could meet the family, which always made it more meaningful for us. Then, we saw Jennifer Hill, a young mother with her two young boys standing outside. They were so humbled and moved by our delivery that Jennifer told us she did not know what to say or do at the time except just watch and try to comprehend what was happening. We collected brand new furniture, which our crew members got donated from Carol House Furniture in St. Louis, plus many other items they needed as soon as they could get into a new home. As we unloaded a bike, the smile on her son's face meant everything to us. For him to have nothing and receive a bike with such elation and excitement really hit home for us that these kids had nothing left. They had no toys, no home, no household items or food. For every person who tried to tell us that we were in the way going to Joplin, we knew better, because we saw it firsthand, just like today. Joplin still needed help and we were listening.

Another group of us went to the second dropoff location to deliver to the next family. When we were walking in, we saw a young family with a baby, who had finally secured a place to live in an empty apartment. We were able to fill the empty space with couches, chairs and an entire baby room full of furniture. They had been living without furniture for a while and were so very grateful to have a home again and now finally furniture.

Our last stop on Friday was so incredibly amazing! We were ready to deliver instruments for the Joplin High School Eagle Pride Band. Joplin North Middle School was our dropoff point, since Joplin High School was destroyed by the tornado. The first group of the St. Lou Crew arrived early, so the rest of us were waiting on our truck. We waited and waited, looking at the time — then, just as God planned it – the truck full of the instruments we collected pulled up at EXACTLY 5:41 p.m. on Friday, July 22, two months to the date and minute of the tornado on May 22 at 5:41 p.m. It was definitely a sign and another little miracle from Will Norton, who is always present in my heart and mind on these mission trips. As our Crew carried each instrument, I saw each member proudly bring them into the school, in celebration, feeling like we had made an impact for the school. Once we got everything inside and saw how much our collection drive paid off, it was amazing to see the happiness and gratefulness on the band directors' faces as they saw what we delivered. Taking that picture amongst the instruments was certainly a memorable photo experience and one we all will never forget!

On the way back from this delivery, we decided to stop by a local bar, Sportsman's Park, located at St. Louis Avenue (ironically). We all needed a break and decided to pump some money back in the economy with some good old Bud Lights. We were all tired and weary, the group was unusually quiet and there were a lot of new people in the group who had not yet bonded. Then in walked a man who made the weekend really begin for us beautifully. He just happened to be in the bar and had heard we were in the room and wanted to stop by. His name was Gary Box and he was from the Joplin Chamber of Commerce. Gary wanted to personally thank us for helping the people of Joplin and said that wanted to be sure that we knew our work was appreciated and very much needed. As he stood in front of us toasting a Bud Light, with tears in his eyes, he spoke from his heart and told us what St. Louis (especially the Cardinals) meant to him, and how proud he was to see us there working in the community. Being St. Louisans and Cardinals fans, we just happened to have the patches the Cardinals gave us to bring down from the KC/STL Teams Unite for Joplin series and he was thrilled to receive them. At the same time, we could see the despair and sadness in his eyes. These people had lost hope, and seeing our group there working and giving back truly gave them inspiration for a new beginning and a feeling of not being forgotten. To this day, I am not sure if Gary realizes how much his words meant to us and still do. Gary looked like he had seen a lot of sadness… he looked tired and weary, yet had a sparkle of hope in his eyes as he spoke to our group. We were glad to help provide that hope and honored that Gary stopped in our room. His speech truly blew us all away. Gary if you are reading this, we thank you for your gift to us that day!

That evening we all sat around the campground sharing the stories from the day. An honorary member of our group, Pastor Dwight Seek, led us in prayer that evening. His words about volunteerism and teamwork inspired us and helped us prepare to face a new day. We were blessed to have met Pastor Seek at the warehouse on our first mission trip and he was

PHOTO BY ROSE FOGARTY

part of our group from the moment we met him. Tired from the day, we all turned in for the evening and could not wait to get to work the next day.

Saturday came and we all met at the volunteer operations at MSSU as we did on our first trip. However, there was something dramatically different this time. In June, there were thousands of people at the college, all wanting to help, from all over the country. At that time, we had to wait in lines to get on the buses to be transported to field. This time, sadly, we pulled up to an almost empty parking lot. How could this be just one month later? Gone was the media, gone were the volunteers, gone were the bountiful supplies. After speaking with a few people there, we were told that as the weeks went by, the volunteers dwindled right along with their hope. Hearing this only inspired our group even more, and we were determined to get to work.

We got on the bus and drove through the town. It looked different in that things were cleaned up, but Joplin still looked like a (destroyed) ghost town. Everything was still gone, no bark on the trees and we saw very few birds and animals. We got right to work and were assigned to remove debris at a home at 20th and Connecticut. For the new people to our group, the sight of the devastation was an awakening for them. For the people on their second mission, we knew the work that was ahead of us and could not wait to get back to it. As we sifted through debris we once again found clothes, dolls, purses, bibles (oh the bibles we found!) bank statements, and oddly enough hundreds of McDonald's cups and part of a Playland (we are still not sure where those originated or flew in from) ... The thing that was more difficult on this trip was the extreme heat. The first trip we made in June was hot, yet we were still able to last 3.5 hours in the debris field (which actually felt like eight). This trip was much more difficult. At 105 degree temperatures we only made it about two hours when people started getting weak. We had debris and dust in our eyes, dirt in our skin and cuts from moving metal and wood, but we all wanted to keep going. I personally had a severe case of poison ivy that kept getting worse by the minute and put me in the hospital, but I wasn't going to stop, that was for sure! For every piece of metal, wood and debris moved by the Crew, it was a step towards rebuilding the lives of Joplin residents and that is what we all wanted to help accomplish. I can assure you, that every piece was moved with love, heart and soul by all of our Crew members and we will never forget the work that we did in those fields.

After working in the debris field all day, a small group of us went to eat lunch at the local Schlotzsky's. We are all black and filthy, yet we still walked into the restaurant filled with people, I am sure we scared them a bit! As we started to eat, an elderly man and his wife came up to us with tears in his eyes. He said "Thank you for coming to help our city. So many people have left and we feel all alone." He shared some stories and talked about the sadness in people's hearts. He spoke about the media being gone, the volunteers dwindling and how it was going to take years to rebuild the city. He said he was not walking out of there without making a point to come up to our table and we were so glad he did, because it was so powerful and moving that we will never forget it. He asked me to be sure we keep coming back and we did. If that man is reading this right now, I want to say THANK YOU to him. As Pastor Dwight Seek told us so many times, no matter what we did when we were there, how big or how little, we will never truly know how we touched the people of Joplin, and our work was holy work, in God's name.

After the bus picked up our Crew we all went back to get ready for our

Get Away for the Day BBQ in Leonard Park. We had plenty of sponsors, including Hudson Security Systems and Kuna Meats, who saved the day for us with their donations. We made sure we got the word out and publicly invited the town. We promoted the BBQ around Joplin in the media so we were hoping people would come but we were still not sure if it would be a success. This time, we wanted to have a fun event to truly lift the spirits of the community. Everyone worked so hard to make it beautiful ... we covered the tables with bright colored tablecloths, wore leis and hula skirts (!), we had door prizes of gift cards to community stores to help the families get on their feet, and Craig Wicker our fearless leader spun the records as our DJ! Everyone made it incredibly special and it turned out that several hundred people showed up at different times throughout the day. They sat amongst us and shared their stories of the tornado. The BBQ lasted five hours and everyone truly enjoyed the day. Will Norton's family came to the BBQ, which meant so much to us to have them there, as we have come to know them as family.

Sunday, we woke up and everyone went about their business and headed home, yet I had one thing left to do. A small group of us went to pay respects to Will Norton. We left flowers at Will's grave with a note from the St. Lou Crew. As I stood above his temporary headstone, something struck me all in an instant and I was overcome with emotion. I had never met Will Norton in life, yet I do believe that he has worked through me and many others in his death. This was the closest I had physically ever been to him. I felt sad and crushed to be there as we were. Me at his feet and him beneath me. I thought of his mother and my own son. I could not help but cry. My daughter saw me crying and I know she didn't truly understand, but I know someday, when she is a mother, she will. The symbolism of our visit displayed that our work was being done in honor of all of the lives that were so tragically lost in this tornado. So many of us were drawn to Will's story, and standing there was extremely powerful for us, yet incredibly sad at the same time. Such a beautiful young man, who truly lived his life by God's will and word. He is a true inspiration to anyone who has been touched by him in his life and death.

As it happened on the first trip, when we got back to St. Louis it took a few days to get back to normal life, trying to leave Joplin behind in memory and not feel guilty enjoying the comforts of our own homes, which was nearly impossible. But the days go by, and this eventually happens.

However, our group still wanted to do more. If we could have gone to Joplin every weekend we would have and still would. Instead, we decided to make something happen in St. Louis. The St. Lou Crew members decided to make a small little miracle happen for two boys. On our very first mission trip back in June 2011 when we arrived at the warehouse to unload our donations, one of the very first boxes we opened was a train set from a little boy who wrote a note to whoever would end up receiving it in Joplin. In the note, he said his house burned down when he was five years old and people donated toys to him, so he wanted to give his train set back to someone who lost all their toys too. Through the diligence and persistence of our amazing members of the St. Lou Crew for Joplin, we identified a Joplin boy to give the train set to, and then found the Missouri boy who donated the set and brought the two together in St. Louis! Our crew members came together to make a special weekend for the two boys, including a courtesy overnight stay at the Ballpark Hilton, a tour of the Anheuser-Busch brewery and complimentary tickets to a Cardinals game, thanks to the St. Louis Cardinals. It was truly a special weekend for both families, the St. Lou Crew and the boys bonded and played together the entire weekend and we are sure they will remember it for the rest of their lives.

September came and a small group of members went down for their third trip. They attended the Joplin High School football game and were able to see the Joplin Eagle Pride band play that night with some of the instruments we replenished. The weekend pretty much got washed out due to rain, but the volunteers who went down spent their time wisely by helping with data entry, a mundane but much needed task.

November came, and the people of Joplin were still on our minds. We were thinking about all the kids who were not going to have toys for Christmas. Not only were they not going to get new toys, they had lost all of the toys they had in the storm. The St. Lou Crew decided to hold a toy drive around St. Louis, to culminate in a family event. We knew this was just the type of thing Will Norton would want us to do, so we appropriately named it in his honor. The Will Norton Memorial Toy Drive and Christmas Event was one we will never forget, for so many reasons. One of our Crew members, Rick Koser, flew in from California to help lead this trip. He did so much work from the West Coast, I jokingly named him our "Director of West Coast Operations!" He too was drawn to help Joplin through Will Norton's tragic story. This would be Rick's third trip with the St. Lou Crew. Rick found us on Facebook and is an honorary member of our group. Rick, being the amazing person that he is, just hopped on a plane in July and joined the mission, not knowing a single soul until his plan landed. That is truly the beauty and power of the internet, spreading the word all over the world and uniting others that would have never met before the computer age.

Once we started planning the December event, an old friend of mine, Mike Santangelo, asked how his organization, the St. Louis South Side Lions, could help. He asked if I would come and talk about the tornado and the efforts of the St. Lou Crew for Joplin at their next group dinner. Well, if I were going to do this, I was going to go big, so I built a huge PowerPoint presentation, complete with pictures from our mission trips. Amongst all the pictures of the tornado, I also knew it was so very important to talk about Will Norton and the man that he was and the man that he should have lived to be. Having now met his family and friends, I was able to talk about what he meant to those who loved him and the man he would have become had he lived. Mixed amongst the slides of photos of the devastation, I included photos of Will Norton, the son, the grandson, the brother, the friend and philanthropist. When I began telling his tragic story of losing his life on the way home from his high school graduation, being sucked out of the sunroof as his father was holding onto him, I looked around the room, which now became silent. I saw tears in the eyes of grown men around that table, most of whom were fathers. The next day I received a call from Mike informing me that our $200 donation from the South Side Lions had now turned into a $5,000 donation. The Lions then joined our mission and became our primary sponsor of the Will Norton Memorial Toy Drive.

As if things could not have fallen into place any better, Pat Hazzard and Dave Marty, high school friends of mine, donated their moving truck, time and storage facility to our mission. Hazzard Moving and Storage, was now on board and wanting to help as much as they possibly could. We set up drop off points around the St. Louis Area, including Kirkwood School District, Johnnie Brock's Dungeon, David Kodner Personal Jewelers, Jimmy John's at Baptist Church STL, Floyd Glass and Window and Wilson Means Salon. All of these people donated their time and resources to help the people of Joplin, Mo., and their toy collections truly made an impact on our mission.

Thanks to amazing news coverage from our St. Louis media friends at KSDK Channel 5, KTVI Fox 2, KMOX 1120 and News Talk 97.1, we were able to collect 5,000 toys for the kids in Joplin during our two-week collection. On Friday, December 10, the day before we left, we had a final collection at Kirkwood North Middle School. People drove by all day and dropped off toys which we loaded into the Hazzard Moving truck. Some didn't want to just drive by, they wanted to stay and give more. Total strangers went up to Manchester Road and collected more money, then went shopping for more toys. The school kids came out to help load the truck, truly displaying how Joplin has touched so many people's lives for the positive. It was an amazing, fun day and a great way for the kids in St. Louis to give back to the people of Joplin as well.

Saturday morning we headed out early for Joplin. I was happy to hear that my daughter wanted to come back with us again. Once we arrived the process began — and I do mean process! Not only did we have to sort over 5,000 toys by category, we then had to wrap and label them with all the names of the 500 kids that provided Santa with their wish list! Once wrapped and labeled, we had to take the list of 500 kids and line up the walls in sequential and alphabetical order by the time slots they were designated to arrive. We started working at around 10:30 a.m. and most of us did not go to sleep at all. We had to be ready when the families started arriving the next day at 10 a.m.! Once the families started arriving, it was so amazing to see all the kids walk through the winter wonderland, which was set up by Relief Spark. They also had plenty of Christmas treats donated, which made for a fun day as they walked through our event. As we watched the kids sit on Mrs. Claus and Santa's lap, our hearts filled with emotion, and we could all feel Will Norton's presence in the room. I heard so many people say that day "Will is here, I can feel him." Or "Will would have loved this." We had so many families stop and thank us, many with tears in their eyes, saying that their kids would not have had a Christmas if it were not for all the donations given for the Will Norton Memorial Toy Drive. Will is truly still helping kids by guiding us through our hearts.

After the Will Norton Memorial Christmas Event, there was, once again, one more thing to do before we headed back to St. Louis. We stopped by Will's grave with his grandparents, aunt and nephews, who are now considered family to me. Will's permanent headstone was now in place, a marble cross that stood as tall as Will did, at 6'3". We took photos of the cross and the flowers that we left. It wasn't until months later that I realized, as I was looking through our photos from that day, that my reflection was right there, standing within Will's cross. As soon as I saw it I started crying, because I knew that it was no accident and showed how Will was reflecting his love upon others and through our work. Truly amazing.

As we approach the one-year anniversary, I am thankful for my journey with the St. Lou Crew for Joplin and all of the ways it has affected me. This last year has been an amazing experience, and I have gained so much by meeting all the people I have met in Joplin, creating friendships that I will always cherish.

I personally have made lifelong friends in Joplin and will always consider it my second Missouri home. Kaleigh Reynolds, I am putting in writing that I will be at your wedding someday! I hope to be able to find the time to continue to go back and visit Joplin for the rest of my life. I look forward to watching it continue to grow and rebuild. I believe that all the souls that were lost that day were not lost in vain, as their spirits have guided others to do good works for those who survived that devastating day. For all of those who are still suffering, I wish you peace and hope for a better life, emotional and financial recovery, and the spirit to continue on, honoring the memory of those who died.

Thank you to all the people of the city of Joplin, Mo., for what you have given to the St. Lou Crew for Joplin was far greater than what we could have ever given to you. I pray that I always remember the city and experiences I had, even when I am and elderly woman. By that time, Will Norton will have been gone a very long time. Gone, but not forgotten, because his spirit will continue to live on through all the lives that he touched.

Thank you Randy Turner, for allowing me to once again write on behalf of the St. Lou Crew for Joplin, and the enormous gift we were given in our mission.

God Bless the people of Joplin, Mo.

48. REMEMBERING THE FORGOTTEN SCHOOL

By Randy Turner

During a recent teacher in-service day, staff members from Joplin East Middle School where I teach, left the warehouse where we are conducting classes for the 2011-2012 school year (and probably the next year or two) and returned to the building that we called our own for the last two years for a farewell ceremony.

I stayed at the warehouse.

It was not that I was making light of the planned ceremony. I am sure it helped some to find closure after the May 22 tornado that destroyed that building; I just did not have a strong connection. It was a brand new building, less than two years old, and while I had some wonderful memories in those two school years, I did not feel a need to say goodbye.

The building where I used to teach was an entirely different matter. Before moving into East Middle School, I taught at South for six years. It was an old building, one of those made in the 1920s that did not have a smooth transition into the computer era.

South did not have a gymnasium; it had an auditorium with an extended stage that was used for physical education classes. The computer lab was a converted boys bathroom. The classrooms, at approximately 500 square feet, were smaller than the ones in the warehouse and desks were jammed into every corner with a cruel efficiency.

An entire area of the basement was shut off due to asbestos. We had no playground area, just a fenced-in gravel lot with basketball goals and picnic tables that had been donated to us by our hard working parent-teacher organization.

By all definition, South Middle School was a dump compared to the spacious, modern school building we left it for prior to the 2009-2010 school year.

I loved that broken down building like no place I have worked in the past three and a half decades.

During the first year at the new East, I had to go to South during the school day on one occasion and it was not the same. The halls seemed darker, the laughter nearly non-existent. This was not my South. I made the mistake of stopping by Room 210, which had been home to me for six years. There were no traces of that home. It was just another classroom.

After serving as a temporary building for one of our other middle schools that year, the old South building was vacant last year for the first time in more than 80 years.

I did not even think about it until May 22. The same tornado that destroyed our state-of-the-art East Middle School, also ripped through the stately building with the grim, institutional look on 22nd Street.

I checked out East two days after the tornado. It took me more than five months to visit South. After I read that our board of education had awarded a contract to demolish South, I had to make one more pilgrimage to the place that had been such an important part of my life.

It was broad daylight Sunday when I parked my car in the gravel lot in the same parking place I used every morning at 6:45 a.m. during the school year.

As far as I could tell, I was the only one in a two-block area. The houses in this older part of town, the ones that survived the tornado, are mostly boarded up with prominent no-trespassing signs.

As 40-mile per hour winds whipped through my old school, despite the daylight, there was a sense that I was walking in another world.

Most of South's windows are gone, but the wind whipped through the blinds, all of which were intact, slamming them against the wall in a macabre symphony. Creaking metal sounds could be heard, every 10 seconds or so.

Sections of the building were gone and the front door, the one I had walked through thousands of times during those six years was covered by a sign warning of asbestos contamination.

I looked up at the second floor to the window of my room 210 and the ghosts of thousands of wonderful memories came back to me.

There was Jessica in her front row seat, working diligently on her Elks Lodge essay, filling in even the margins on her paper and then turning in 750 words for an essay that did not allow more than 250. After that, Jessica did a masterful editing job, eliminating 501 words and winning the contest.

There was Andrew causing people to roll in the aisles with laughter with his interpretation of a character during our reading of the play, The Diary of Anne Frank.

I could see Fox's always-empty seat, and then when I looked down at the floor, I saw her scribbling away in her notebook.

After thinking about those days for several, long minutes, I walked back to my car and left South Middle School for the final time.

I appreciate the public ceremony for East. I am sure it helped my fellow staff members deal with the loss of their workplace.

But to me, South Middle School was a home and a quiet, private goodbye was just what I needed.

49. A DAY IN THE LIFE OF A JOPLIN STUDENT

BY KARISSA DOWELL

OK, I just had to get this off my chest and throw this out there. I guess I just have survivor's guilt for not being in town, and not going through the tornado itself, and this is how I'm going to cope.

Everyday I wake up and walk out of my house to construction and destruction. I get in my car and drive through the tornado's path seeing destroyed houses and schools, and houses being built. Then I drive to our town mall for school, now, most people may say this isn't an ideal spot for a high school, and it's not, but, we have to make do with what we can get.

As you walk into the building at first the school may seem amazing and the laptops would interest anyone, but as school starts, you start to see how difficult it is to learn in a 21st century school. The classrooms are just big cubicles with 3/4 walls and movable giant whiteboard walls. As you try to learn, you hear classes from across the wall, or across the hall. As you take tests, you hear nothing but other classes having class or watching movies. It makes it very difficult to concentrate. Teachers get frustrated because when we take tests, students get their headphones out and listen to music to try and block everything else out. Now it may be said that's not a good way to learn, but we try to do what we can to earn the grade we need. The laptops crash and delete all your work, Word crashes and you can lose a whole report in a matter of seconds. People get on SharePoint and delete your work, or steal your work and copy it. Teachers sometimes don't receive your assignments, then you end up with missing or late assignments that you actually turned in on time.

Then there is the topic of we haven't gone one day without a "special visitor" or someone who is just curious to see how the school is, or how the students are doing now. We have had people come down to give us a special speech that they want us to pass on to the world. We always look at each other and ask, "of all the places to come to, why Joplin?" We have caseworkers and psychologists that check in on students periodically to make sure we are still OK.

As students, we feel like nothing but a zoo, or a tourist attraction, because you hear "and on your left you can see." As students we understand it is our duty to be proud and to show off our amazing accomplishments, but as juniors and seniors in high school, these are the times our grades need to be the best they can be to look great for college applications. This year, my grades have crashed because I cannot focus with all the noise and distractions going on around us, and teachers do not know how to teach with the laptops and most of the time you are told to "Google it" or "open your textbooks, but shut your laptops" now if only we could actually do that, what they don't understand is our textbooks ARE our laptops.

Now people have said, "I'd rather not be at an old rundown middle school." But, if you talk to almost any student at the Northpark campus, we would say "I would rather be there then here, because there has complete walls and you don't get a math and a history lesson while in Comm. Arts (English)." High school should be the best years of our lives, and because of this tornado we have had the best years taken away from us. We all had to mature way faster than we should, we had to grow up and learn what is actually needed in life. I'm proud to say I'm from Joplin, but I want to attend a school where it is actually school, and where we learn things other than life lessons.

We still try to make plans as friends, and to be normal teens, and we are like well let's go there. Oh yeah, it's not there anymore. It's hard to face and to remember what is and isn't there. We had to watch our high school be torn down. We all agreed it was hard to see it damaged and destroyed the way it was, but it is even harder to see it leveled, and no longer there. The building we grew up in, and the fields we watched our brothers and sisters play on, and then we were so glad to finally be on. The place where we always wanted to be, and finally attended there, the building we wanted to graduate from is gone. The place we were glad to call ours isn't there anymore.

After we leave the mall, we drive back to our houses, or go to work, where there are people constantly driving by and taking pictures, or stopping to ask questions. The other day we actually had a charter bus full of people drive through our neighborhood taking pictures. We feel trapped, because if we leave town we have the chance of being asked, "Oh, you're from Joplin?" Don't get me wrong, we are proud to say, "Yes, yes we are." But, when a disaster like this shakes a whole town and a whole world to an extent like this, it's hard. We can't even read our own town newspaper or get on our school's webpage without seeing the word "Tornado." We are not the town of Joplin anymore. We are the town of the "Tornado" and that is hard to face.

Karissa Dowell is a student at Joplin High School.

50. STUDENT TO STUDENT: SHARING STORIES

BY JOHN HACKER

For Dana Rodriguez and Carl Rankin Jr., from Marquette High School in Chesterfield, this year's spring break was about more than a few days off and hanging with friends.

It was a chance to meet new friends, like Nathan Parker and Mary Jean Miller, from Joplin High School and to help out fellow Missourians in Joplin as they continue to rebuild from the May 22 tornado.

A group of almost 100 students, teachers and other adults from one of the largest high schools in the St. Louis area spent their spring break, from March 18-23, volunteering in Southwest Missouri and living at the Church of the Nazarene in Carthage.

Although rainy weather limited the amount of work they could do outdoors in Joplin, they got a unique opportunity on March 20 to meet students their age who are directly dealing with the aftermath of that devastating storm.

The 85 Marquette students met with 30 or so members of the Joplin High School Key Club and National Honor Society who shared what it was like to be a kid and lose everything you own.

Marquette's Dana Rodriguez said, as a teenager, you don't think about losing everything all of a sudden

"Every person has taken things for granted before, because if you are asked before has anything like this ever come close to happening to you, we're like no," Rodriguez said. "We've had some tornado warnings, but you just can't believe how fast everything can get taken away. These kids from Joplin are talking about their friends dying and family members; they didn't know where they were. You feel it from them and for them when they're talking about how much fear and all the other different emotions that they went through."

Rankin said touring the damage path brought home to him just how bad things were in Joplin.

"We went down the path of destruction down by the hospital and looking at some of the area where everything was completely wiped out," Rankin said. "After all this time was just amazing to see and to think about how something so massive came through so quickly and took out all that stuff. You look at it and think, "wow, it's all gone," then you kind of think about how there were people and everything there.

Joplin High School's Nathan Parker survived even though the tornado tore down his home around him. He lived at 24th Street and Grand Avenue and had just come home from playing in the band at graduation ceremonies at Missouri Southern when the storm hit.

Parker, who appeared on the Fox News Network when school started at Joplin High School back in August, said he was honored to speak to the Marquette students.

"I feel honored to be given a chance to speak to volunteers who are coming and taking their own time to come and help Joplin," Parker said. "It's great, It makes you feel good, I don't know how to say it but thanks. I hope I would do that. I would like to do something like this. I hope they were able to learn from me that even though life is full of unexpected twists and turns there is always hope just beyond the corner."

Mary Jean Miller, president of the JHS Key Club, lives just south of the damage path and spent those frantic days after May 22 trying to make sure her friends were all right.

She spoke to the St. Louis students about coping with the new high school and the challenges of the new year.

"I was Key Club president for the past year and over the summer my board and I had to get together and figure out how we were going to do meetings," she said. "Our biggest concern was how are we going to have meetings when we're separated at two campuses. I've given this speech a bunch of times. We actually use Skype as our main means of communication. We use the laptops that the schools gave us to get on Skype so we can see the mall campus and the mall campus can see us."

51. COLLEGE STUDENTS FOREGO THE BEACH TO HELP WITH RECOVERY

BY JOHN HACKER

Joplin may not have sunny beaches or big parties, but that's not what a group of students from Penn State University were looking for when they were deciding what to do on their spring break.

More than 30 students and adults with the Christian Student Fellowship Group at Penn State came to Southwest Missouri March 4-10 to spend their spring break helping Joplin recover from the devastating May 22 tornado.

The group stayed at the Carthage First Christian Church and went to Joplin each day to receive their assignments from Americorps coordinators.

Many of the students spend much of their week helping the family of Kenny Huddleston in the 2600 block of Sargent Avenue rebuild their homes.

PHOTO BY JOHN HACKER

PHOTO BY JOHN HACKER

Kenny Huddleston, his wife and son and daughter, were on their way home from graduation ceremonies at Missouri Southern when they got caught up in the tornado. The truck they were in was slammed and twisted around a telephone pole and all the family members suffered some injuries. Emily Huddleston suffered a severe cut to her leg and spent months recovering in a hospital in Parsons, Kan.

The family's home and the homes of other family members in the same neighborhood were all destroyed, but many of the students from Penn State spent their week helping to put this family's lives back together.

"It's really pretty awesome," Kenny Huddleston said. "The folks next door really didn't have enough insurance and these students, coming down and helping do the drywall, build the deck, just shows the support people have for Joplin. There are a lot of caring people. I know it means a lot to the folks. It means a lot to us."

Buzz Roberts, Campus Minister with the Christian Student

PHOTO BY JOHN HACKER

Fellowship, said he has been to Joplin before, visiting Ozark Christian College for conferences for college campus ministers.

"I used to be a youth pastor up in Illinois and we used to come to Joplin all the time for the National Youth Minister's convention at Ozark Christian College," Roberts said. "The last time I was in Joplin was about four or five years ago, I was out in the Midwest speaking and I wanted to swing by and make some contacts with students at Ozark Christian College and try to persuade them to be campus ministers. I've always liked Joplin and I kind of remember some of the landmarks coming off I-44. This time, when I hit 26th Street, it was like, OK, I don't remember this."

Marilyn Lotito, a student at Penn State's campus in Du Bois, Penn., said she helped hang drywall and do other construction work one day, and another day she helped at the Salvation Army in Joplin,

"I heard that Joplin was pretty much leveled and I wanted to come because I always enjoy mission trips and there would be a lot of people who need help," Lotito said. "I love traveling to the different parts of the country and doing things I've never done before and learning new things. I'm so excited because I can finally nail decently. I wasn't very good at it last year, but I'm decent this year."

Spencer Brought, another Penn State student, said he had heard reports of how Joplin looked from volunteers from his church who came here last fall, but seeing it in real life put what happened here in a whole different light.

"We heard that there was still a lot of reconstruction being done and just the devastation in the town was still so great, so it seemed like a prime spot to come and help out," Brought said. "When we first got to Joplin, I was surprised at how much construction and demolition was still going on after a year. I didn't expect it. Definitely working here, you get an idea of how bad it was."

52. A NEW HOPE HIGH SCHOOL FOR JOPLIN

BY RANDY TURNER

THE FOLLOWING WAS WRITTEN THE DAY AFTER THE JOPLIN SCHOOL DISTRICT PASSED A BOND ISSUE TO BUILD NEW SCHOOLS TO REPLACE THOSE LOST IN THE TORNADO.

One of the lasting symbols of the May 22, 2011, Joplin Tornado was a makeshift sign that stood in front of the destroyed Joplin High School.

Where those who had passed the forlorn sight earlier had seen all but two letters blown off the sign, someone saw those two letters, an O and a P, added two homemade letters and turned a symbol of tragedy into one of hope.

That hope was realized tonight when voters in the Joplin School District, still reeling from the effects of the most deadly tornado to hit this nation in six decades, looked past their own difficulties and made the biggest step to not only recovery, but to moving the city of Joplin forward into the future.

Thanks to Joplin School District voters, the sign that had offered a hope for the future is now a guarantee. Sometime in the next three years, the city of Joplin will have a new high school, one that not only replaces the memory-filled building at 20th and Indiana, but one that will move the school firmly into the 21st Century.

The bond issue, which needed 57.4 percent to pass, only made it by a 45-vote margin, but in this case 45 votes were as good as 4,000.

It was a hard-fought battle for those in the Joplin community who saw the rebirth of a school system that had 10 buildings either completely destroyed or almost destroyed by the tornado.

Joplin High School students in grades 11 and 12 have been going to school in a converted anchor store at Northpark Mall, while those in grades 9 and 10 are attending classes in a converted middle school that was a high school three decades ago.

The children attending East Middle School, where I teach, are in what had been a spec building in an industrial park on the far outskirts of the district. Each day, they are greeted by the uninviting aroma of the nearby dog food plant. Students in some of our elementary schools are also in different locations, while even our administrative staff is a building that was formerly used by the Missouri Highway Department.

It is not easy to convince people to invest their faith in a type of school building that the Joplin area has never seen before, but the people of this school district learned something about our Superintendent C. J. Huff and the members of the board of education. When they make a promise, they deliver.

The first proof of that came shortly after the tornado. Huff, his staff, and district teachers began a quest to make sure that every student, every staff member was safe after the tornado. Though we lost students, including two from the high school and one from East Middle School, and a teacher at Franklin Technical School, which was also lost in the tornado, every person was accounted for before the next step began.

It was that next step that drew some disbelief from the people of Joplin, in fact the people of this nation. Huff promised, repeatedly, that school would start on time in the Joplin School District, only 87 days after 10 schools and about half of the buildings in the district had been hit.

While Huff was not the only community leader to provide inspiration in a time of desperate need, his unwavering commitment to helping a community heal by bringing its children back into the classroom served as a call to arms for Joplin.

Less than three months after the storm took more than 160 lives, faculty and staff returned to Missouri Southern State University for an opening day ceremony that was unlike any other ever held in this school district.

When we arrived on campus, we were greeted by hundreds of people from the community — the first time we had ever seen anyone but fellow school employees at this annual function.

Jay Nixon, the governor of the state, was also there to greet us.

Two days later, the children once again were in our classrooms. Some were at the mall, some were at a converted middle school, some were in a warehouse. But not one student in the Joplin School District had education delayed. The bells rang on time.

It was a bit hectic for us. All of the converted school buildings had one dignitary after another visiting. When a sixth grader at our school wanted to know directions to the front office, our science teacher, Mike Wallace answered, "Go down the hall and turn right at the governor."

After scaling one seemingly insurmountable height, Huff and the Board of Education set another, seemingly more impossible goal — passing a $62 million bond issue that would not only rebuild our schools, but make them far superior than before and also provide tornado safe rooms in each facility, not just for the staff and students, but for the community.

This second daunting task was termed "Operation Rising Eagle."

The obstacles were many. District officials and other bond issue supporters had to convince enough naysayers that it was vital to build schools of 2012 and beyond, and not just rebuild schools constructed decades ago.

They had to convince people who are already facing a heavy financial burden to make an investment in the future of the community.

Tonight, Operation Rising Eagle concluded with a victory, not a victory for C. J. Huff or the members of the Joplin Board of Education, or even the community steering committee that worked unceasingly to promote the issue, but a victory for the students of the Joplin School District, and students who have yet to be born.

When the tornado took this city's beloved high school May 22, all we had left was hope, as so memorably created on that broken sign.

Now that hope will become a reality.

53. A SEVENTH GRADER'S GIFT THAT KEEPS ON GIVING

BY RANDY TURNER

The most ugly, misshapen box I had ever seen was blocking my path as I walked down the hallway at Joplin East Middle School where I teach eighth grade English last month during the first week of school. As I executed what I thought was a crisp, evasive move to keep from tripping and falling flat on my face, our long-suffering secretary said, "Mt. Turner, you need to move your box."

I started to protest that it wasn't my box, but a quick glance at the recipient's address showed that whatever this cardboard mutation was, it was most definitely mine.

I started to lift it and found that to be an almost impossible task — it was heavy beyond belief so I managed to get it onto a dolly through a series of contortions and wheeled it to my room. I opened it and saw it was a box of books, one of many such gifts my school has received since our building was destroyed in the May 22 tornado that ripped through more than one third of our city.

Since that time, the misshapen box has sat in a corner of my room, sadly fitting in with the rest of my décor — until this morning. As I was unpacking a box of dictionaries I had received through the Adopt-A-Classroom program, I decided it was time to dive into the box and put the books on the shelves.

I was pleasantly surprised to see that the books were by some of the top authors for young people, and since I have my students do a third quarter research project on the American Civil Rights Movement, I was overjoyed to see eight copies of Rosa Parks' autobiography.

I was just about to throw away what was left of that misshapen box, when I saw an envelope peeking out from under rolled up paper shopping bag that had been placed between some of the books. The envelope was addressed to "Mr. Turner."

When I opened it, I was blown away by the message:

Dear Mr. Turner:

Hi! My name is Jane and I am from New York City. I am going into the seventh grade. When I heard about the tornado in Joplin, I felt awful. My mom thought it would be a great idea to help somehow. We found your blog about the damage to your school. The funny thing is that you are at East Middle School and I go to East Side Middle School. I thought that was a cool connection.

I put up signs in my building and left a box outside my door. Pretty soon, I received a bunch of books to donate to your school. I could not wait to send them. I hope that they help rebuild your library.

Have a good rest of the summer and a great school year.

Sincerely, Jane

P. S. I hope your class likes the books.

At the beginning of my classes today, my students will learn about the books seventh grader Jane Walsh contributed and learn a valuable lesson about what one person can accomplish when she sets her mind to something. In the not too distant future, Jane will receive thank-you letters from the people whose lives she has enriched through this simple, thoughtful gift.

For the last three months, the people at Joplin East Middle School and the rest of this community have seen over and over just how many good people are in this world. We have been overwhelmed by their kindness and generosity.

We have been introduced to thousands of people who have reached out their hands and hearts to this community. But for this teacher, in this eighth grade classroom, a seventh grader from New York City has catapulted to the top of the list.

Thank you, Jane.

*Pat Taylor, Marjorie Cooper, Ronnie Mayer, Joan Boyd and Janice Marqueard
attended the Peace Lutheran Church's Praise on the Parking Lot service on May
20, 2012, to mark one year since the Joplin tornado destroyed the church.*
PHOTO BY JOHN HACKER

54. AVENUE OF HOPE

BY JOHN HACKER

Peace Lutheran Church, located at 20th and Wisconsin Avenue was one of dozens of churches destroyed in the Joplin tornado of May 22, 2011.

Their church home was destroyed and members have been meeting in the Bethany Presbyterian Church at 20th Street and Virginia Avenue since then.

Twice, however, since the storm, they've held special services on the parking lot of their church. The first was on May 29, 2011, a service to affirm that they were still a church family one week after that family was made homeless.

The second was one year after the storm, on May 20, 2012, when they held a service they dubbed 'Praise on the Parking Lot,' in a tent near the concrete slab where their church home once stood.

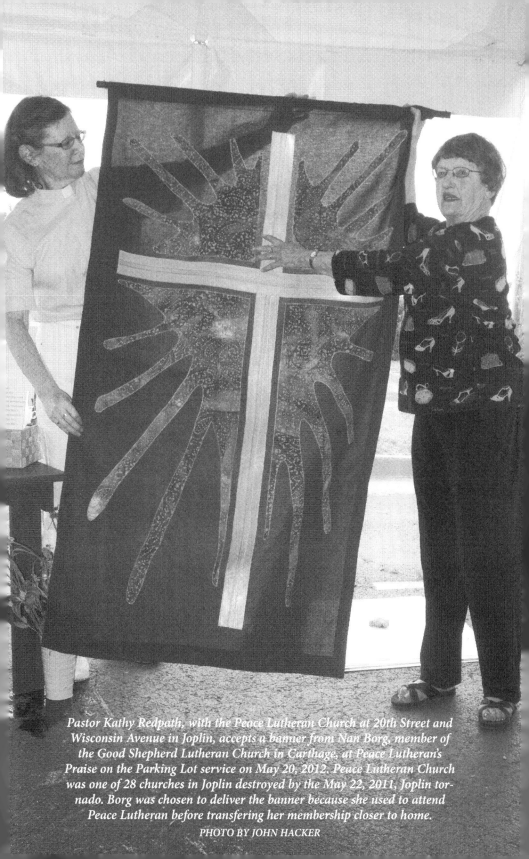

Pastor Kathy Redpath, with the Peace Lutheran Church at 20th Street and Wisconsin Avenue in Joplin, accepts a banner from Nan Borg, member of the Good Shepherd Lutheran Church in Carthage, at Peace Lutheran's Praise on the Parking Lot service on May 20, 2012. Peace Lutheran Church was one of 28 churches in Joplin destroyed by the May 22, 2011, Joplin tornado. Borg was chosen to deliver the banner because she used to attend Peace Lutheran before transferring her membership closer to home.

PHOTO BY JOHN HACKER

Pastor Bill Pape was interim pastor of the Peace Lutheran Church at 20th Street and Wisconsin Avenue on May 22, 2011, when the tornado destroyed the building. He led the church in a worship service in their parking lot one week after the tornado, then was replaced by Pastor Kathy Redpath in the summer of 2011. He returned to Joplin on May 20, 2012, for the church's Praise in the Parking Lot service marking the one year anniversary of the storm.

PHOTO BY JOHN HACKER

FORMER PASTOR RETURNS

Two pastors have played a big role in this church's existence since the tornado.

On May 22, 2011, Peace Lutheran Church was a church in transition. The pastor at the time, Bill Pape (pronounced Pop-pe), was an interim pastor, driving more than 240 miles each week from Kansas City to take care of church business and conduct services before returning home.

Pape was in Joplin when the tornado struck and would have been in the church at the time had he not made a fateful decision.

"I was in the building after the worship service," Pape said. "I was doing some writing and stuff, but it was such a pretty day ... I was going to go for a walk and come back but I got in the car and thought I can come back tomorrow. So I drove off or I would have been here when the tornado hit and wouldn't be here talking to you."

Pape conducted the first service for the battered congregation in the parking lot. The lot had to be cleared of debris before the service could be held on what turned out the be a cool day on Memorial Day weekend.

Most of the members responded and attended that service.

Pape was replaced in August by Pastor Kathy Redpath and returned to Kansas City, but he was back on May 20, 2012, for the "Praise on the Parking Lot" service.

"I came back to see all the people and to see the liveliness of the people," Pape said. "It was good to see how close they are to each other and how close they are to the God they worship."

"It was a congregation that I knew would come back."

Pape said the loss of the church building was a huge blow to the congregation and could have been a death blow, but it has not destroyed this family.

"It was a very big loss for the people," Pape said. "It was something (the congregation was) familiar with and liked. They are remembering baptisms, weddings, funerals, that were held there and now all of a sudden it's gone.

"All you see is a cement platform slab. I don't know if they will rebuild here or somewhere else. Once they get to the new building, eventually it will become who they are. "

Pape said it was important for him to come back and see how this church family was doing since he left. He said he's been back one time since August 2011.

"It was very important to be here," Pape said. "I was very pleased to be asked to come back. It was fun to see them again. I have enjoyed being here and it's great to see how well the congregation has done thus far, and know that they are going to take it the rest of the way. It was a good experience."

A MEMBER SURVIVES

Kathrin Elmborg lived across the street from Peace Lutheran Church, on Montana Place. She was a member of Peace Lutheran and the church played a huge role in her life.

Elmborg, who walked with a walker on May 20, 2012, because of recent knee surgery, grew up on a farm in Central Kansas and moved to Joplin 10 years ago from Kansas City.

She had just moved into her home at 102 Montana Place two months ago and was starting to feel at home.

"I had moved there to live next door to my granddaughter and her family, Elmborg said. "I was happy as a clam in my little house that I had fixed up. I lived right across the street from the church, then the tornado came and blew it all away.

"I was sitting, watching TV and my granddaughter called and wanted me to go to her in-laws to the basement and I said 'Ah, no, it's just another storm, I'll stay home.' All at once, the lights went out, my back door in my kitchen blew open so I thought I'd better shut my door or it will rain in. So I went to the backdoor and I tried to force it shut. Then the walls were tumbling down and the roof was gone and everything was falling down, and I was trying to close back door."

Elmborg believes God's hand was involved in her survival. She said she fell to the floor and the refrigerator and some cabinets fell and formed a tent over her that protected her.

"That's what kept me safe," she said. "I stayed there trying to close that door and when the tornado went over, I swirled around and sat down on the floor and then the refrigerator leaned a little bit and my cupboards leaned a little bit and there I sat, safe as if I had good sense. If I'd gone to the hall or bathroom I probably would have been killed."

Elmborg said members of her church family came and pulled her from the rubble of her home.

"I have no idea how long I was in there," she said. "I know it rained because by that time I was getting cold and wet and it was raining on me. I sat there for a while and pretty soon I heard our secretary's husband calling for me. They had come over here to see if the church was OK and they thought I was in my house so they called my name, and I answered him and he said he was so relieved to hear me answer him. So he and two other young men moved one of my walls and they pulled me straight up out of the rubble and rescued me.

"There was a couple here from church who put me in their car and they took me to another church member's home and she checked me out.

I had a few cuts and abrasions, glass cuts and things like that. Then they took me to their home and one thing I remember as we went north on Main to 171, all the emergency vehicles coming in already. It wasn't dark yet and there was all the emergency vehicles coming in. It was a steady stream.

"I had what I had on my back, and that wasn't much, so I had to borrow clothes. I knew the church was destroyed, we came out and could see that everything was destroyed. My granddaughter's home was completely demolished. It looked like a war zone and you can talk all you want, but until you see it, you can't understand it. My nephew from California came home maybe a month later to Kansas City to his mother's and they came down and he said I've seen the pictures and everything, but he said until you look at it, you don't understand the enormity of it."

Elmborg returned to her old neighborhood a few times during the week to try to salvage what she could from her home. She said the experience was a surreal mixture of terrible times and great fun.

"This was a couple of days after the tornado when we were sorting through junk," Elmborg said. "People would stop and work for a couple of hours, people we didn't know. We'd joke and laugh and I said, 'If this wasn't so horrible, it would be a lot of fun.' That's the way it was, it was a wonderful experience but it was the most horrible thing you could ever go through. If you can figure that out, I don't know.

"Young people would stop and ask, 'Can we help you for an hour or two?' As I said, we joked and had fun and it was horrible, but we were having a good time, which doesn't make sense."

Elmborg became even closer to her church family. In some ways, she symbolized the church's efforts to rebuild and stay positive in the wake of such horror.

Elmborg said coming back to the church after the tornado to worship in the parking lot was important.

"It just meant our family was still intact and we would survive," she said. "That service after the tornado meant a lot, it meant we're still here. Today's service, I thought was excellent, it was very upbeat and it meant we're here.

"The church is probably three-fourths of my life. We're like a family. I've been associated with lots of churches, but this little Lutheran Church is different. I've been a Lutheran all my life, but this is like family, everyone cares for everyone else.".

THE JOPLIN CROSS

During the May 20, 2012, service, Peace Lutheran members were reunited with pieces of their old church that had traveled the country since the tornado.

A cross, made of curved wood and standing on a thick wooden base covered with fragments of stained glass stood on the altar in front of them in the billowing white tent where they held that 'Praise in the Parking Lot' service.

On May 29, 2011, James Williams accompanied his wife the Rev. Janice Kibler to the service in the Peace Lutheran Church parking lot one week after the tornado did its work.

Williams, who works with wood, had an idea and a purpose for his visit. He wanted to make something to symbolize what had happened in Joplin.

He had no idea that some pieces of debris and 45 minutes worth of work on his part would take on the life that they have taken in the year since the tornado.

"I just went through the rubble and I was trying to find something we could make a little cross out of," Williams said. "We were thinking about something smaller but I was digging through the rubble and I found that piece. It was a piece of laminated interior beam and it had just been completely ripped apart because those beams were probably six or eight inches thick. This was just a piece of it that had ripped and it had the curve of the beam. It was about 10 feet long and I said 'That's it.' Then I saw the end of the pew laying in the rubble and the cross was made. It took 45 minutes for me to cut it up and screw it together.

"The stained glass was just pieces I picked up in the rubble and the brick isn't even attached, it has just traveled with it. It was one of the bricks in the building and it has stayed with the cross for a year. It's been to Orlando, it's been to Chicago for a Bishop's conference. It's going to two churches next week and the Sunday after, and then back to the Synod Assembly and then I know it has one more church and then I think it will come back to Joplin."

The cross almost didn't get made because Williams forgot the pieces

Pastor Janice Kibler, representing the Central States Synod of the Evangelical Lutheran Church, presents to the members of the Peace Lutheran Church in Joplin a cross made of wood salvaged from their destroyed church at their Praise in the Parking Lot service on May 20, 2012, marking one year after the Joplin tornado.

PHOTO BY JOHN HACKER

in his haste to get out of the neighborhood before it was shut down to allow President Barack Obama to tour the devastation on May 29, 2011.

"I had this stuff laid off to the side until the truck was empty, then the truck was empty and we took off," Williams said. "We got all the way to the highway and we were in a hurry to get out of town because Obama was coming. We went all the way out there and I realized, I forgot the wood. We turned around and came back and it took us two hours to get out of here.

"We were tempted to say, you know, maybe we don't need to make a cross, but we did. I'm glad we did too. I had no idea it would take on this life. With everybody wanting to see it, it has just gone all over."

Pastor Kathy Redpath said she first saw the Joplin Cross, as it was quickly dubbed, at the Synod Assembly in Kansas City, where it was displayed.

Kibler told the congregation about the cross at the May 20, 2012, service, where it was displayed in Joplin for the first time.

"This cross has been on a road trip," she said during the service. "We took it last year so we could have it at our Synod Assembly just two weeks after the tornado. From there, people at the assembly started asking, 'Can we take it home to our congregation so we can talk about hope and resurrection and life?' So it has been on quite a road trip through Kansas and Missouri. It even went to Orlando for the church-wide assembly. The presiding bishop, Mark Hanson, caught wind of this cross and said we want that at Orlando as well. So I brought it back for you today, but I'm going to take it again because the road trip isn't finished. You will get it back shortly. There's a notebook here, as it has gone to different congregations people have put in pictures and notes for you, notes of encouragement. So again, thank you for your witness. You are living through something that a lot of us are watching, observing and giving thanks to God for you."

Murlin Hintz, a member of the Peace Lutheran Church, gets emotional when talking about the group's destroyed building, but he was engrossed in the notebook that accompanied the cross.

He recognized the curve in the wood that made up the cross.

"What a surprise for us today that it was picked up by the Pastor's husband and brought back after being in so many places throughout the country," Hintz said. "This beam right here was actually one of the beams that was in the sanctuary and this is part of a pew and the stained glass and brick and it was just so cool to see this that I had to look through this book. Also in this book there are former members that were members of Peace Lutheran that have now moved someplace else and they wrote notes and things and wished us the best.

"It's just awesome. I just looked at it a little more thoroughly so I wouldn't miss anything and it's just neat to see all these names."

GOD'S LIGHT

Also at the May 20, 2012, service, Nan Borg, Carthage, a member of the Good Shepherd Lutheran Church in Carthage, returned to the church she called home for 17 years.

She brought with her a banner, created by members of the Good

Shepherd Lutheran Church as a gift to Peace Lutheran and its members.

"It displays the love of Jesus through the sun and through the cross on which he gave his life so we could live," Borg said. "Karen Moll is the head of the banner group at Good Shepherd and I didn't realize they were even making it, then at Bible study just this past Thursday, three days ago, they said 'We have a gift for you to take to Peace Lutheran,' because I am a former member. So I was just thrilled and it worked out beautifully that it could be presented at this particular service on this particular day. And even though it will be a while before it can hang, it certainly is a gift from one Lutheran Church to another."

Borg recalled her time at Peace Lutheran and the tornado that destroyed a church that held many fond memories for her.

"I was a member up until about two and a half years ago," Borg said. "It's so hard to think about May 22. We had a wedding that weekend and I came over and I couldn't find the church. The roads were so clogged and I was crying so hard, so I had to come back another day and pull up and be able to spend some time. I was a member here for about 17 years, taught adult Sunday school for the same amount of time and was very involved and this church is an extremely community-oriented church. I've always been very touched at how they reach out. Even when they're hurting, they reach out. In fact I think it was like a month after the tornado, they were having a bake sale so they could give to the literacy council. They are a precious group of people.

"It was very touching to be here today (May 20, 2012). And because I know these people and I've known them for so many years, they are very welcoming. So I was very glad to be able to present the banner."

Cliff Eighmy, a member of Peace Lutheran and a friend of Borg's from when she was a member, was moved by the gift from the Carthage church.

"It just makes you want to cry in happiness because people out there are thinking about us and they care," he said. "That's something that should be said, there's been so much support from people outside this community, donations and help from literally thousands of people, have come to this town and to our congregation to help."

Murlin Hintz was also moved by the gift.

"It means so much and there's been so much of that from all over the country that have poured in here, not just into Peace Lutheran but all of Joplin really," he said. "That is a very, very special thing for a church to do.

The lady that presented it to us, she used to be a member of this church so it was quite a surprise to her that they gave it to her to forward on to us.

"It's something that this church will always have after these decisions are made where to build, what to build, what kind of a building that kind of thing. Then there was another cross that was given to us from a church in Sedalia, Mo. There was a group in here that helped with the cleanup and they picked up a lot of the stained glass that was in the windows and they made this cross using the stained glass and it's all lit up. It is just awesome so that will be something that we'll always have in our new church as well."

NEW PASTOR

Pastor Kathy Redpath was appointed to take the leadership post of the church just weeks after the tornado struck and took over leadership in August 2011.

Redpath, who had been serving as pastor of a church in the tiny town of Mankato, Kan., described how she found out she was coming to Joplin and how a simple piece of art, dubbed the "Joplin Cross" played a role her discovering her future.

"I first saw that cross in the Synod Assembly in Kansas City, I was still serving in Mankato," Redpath said. "I had heard the news from Joplin but had no connection to it whatsoever. They explained it the first day of the assembly. The Synod Assembly is all the churches in Missouri and Kansas, Lutheran Churches, we gather once a year.

"I marveled at it and heard the story about it, and it was later that day that Pastor Janice Kibler talked to me. She knew I was looking for a new call and she said 'I have a seed to plant with you.' We were in a crowded, noisy hallway and I'm trying to hear what she's trying to say and she's talking about the Joplin tornado, and I thought I know about that, get to what you want to say. Then all of a sudden, I realized what she was saying. So I said, 'You want me to go to Joplin, is that it?'"

Pastor Kibler, who has been in Joplin many times, including the May 29, 2011, and May 20, 2012, services in the parking lot, did not know that she had chosen a pastor for Joplin who had experienced the power of a tornado before.

"I said, 'Are you aware that I lost my first home in Ohio in a tornado years ago?' and she did not know that piece," Redpath said. "While (the

Murlin Hintz, a member of the Peace Lutheran Church since 1979, reads over the guest book that arrived in Joplin with what has become known as the Joplin Cross, crafted of debris from the Peace Lutheran Church's building by Jim Williams, husband of Pastor Janice Kibler with the Central States Synod.
PHOTO BY JOHN HACKER

people of Joplin) will always identify with the 22nd of May, I will always think of the 10th of May because that was the date of ours. It was 1973 and we were living in a trailer. There was a tornado warning and we got out of the trailer, we got into a cement block building that had been put up there as a utility building. There were a dozen people in there and when we came out again, I fully expected to wash my dinner dishes. I never found my dinner dishes.

"We knew the man who had built (the utility building) and it turned out he, for no reason other than he wanted to do it, he put extra reinforcement in that building. There were at least a dozen people in there and we would have had nowhere to go if it weren't for that building. It wasn't an EF5. I don't know what it was, but it was not as devastating as Joplin. But in that trailer park, there had been 34 trailers and 31 of them were totally destroyed. The other three hung on by a thread, but they were gone and there were a couple of deaths there.

"That's the story I come out of, so I can identify with their stories and they can understand that at least I have some connection, even if it's not the same connection. I remember what its like to walk out there in the dirt and say, 'That's my grandmother's china in pieces.' I still get choked up about it and that's why I say, the stories will always be there. Whether we want them to be or not, they are there."

Redpath said taking over the church in the wake of such devastation has been tough, but she's had help.

"My first meeting with them was when we were deciding whether this was going to work out or not, there were about a dozen people gathered, part of what was supposed to be the core committee, the council, whatever they could gather that day, and I said to them, 'How does it feel to be a church without a building?'" she said. "And we reminded each other that church exists whether or not there's a building there."

Redpath said she has had to minister to people who have suffered extraordinary loss, but some of the ministry had already started before she got to Joplin.

"By the time I came and moved in in August, those people were on their way to dealing with it the best they could," she said. "That had to be done immediately and I wasn't here yet so that was done by other pastors or each other, whatever situation they found themselves in."

She said churches and groups from across the country have reached out to the Joplin community and to their church specifically.

"The list that the secretary has of all the individuals, congregations, Boy Scout troops, Girl Scout troops, just all kinds of groups that have sent things, financial gifts, blankets — we've had blankets galore — is amazing," she said. "We've had some unusual things. The one that sticks out in my mind is one church, I think it was in Pennsylvania, wanted to give us a Christmas tree. So they ordered from Home Depot or somewhere, and had it delivered, but then separately, they sent us a box of hand-made ornaments. Nobody duplicated that one."

At the May 20, 2012, service, Redpath received the banner from Nan Borg and the Good Shepherd Lutheran Church in Carthage.

Redpath said that gift was emblematic of many of the gifts they've received.

"That was huge," Redpath said. "The woman who presented it used to be a member here and now she's transferred her membership closer to where she lives, but her group decided they wanted to do that, so it's church to church and liturgical to liturgical. Actually, it's going to hang at Bethany, I'm quite sure, while we're there, and then it will be moved where ever we end up, whenever we end up.

A PROMISE TO REBUILD

The Peace Lutheran family continues to meet faithfully every week at the Bethany Presbyterian Church. Their former lot stands bare and cleaned of debris.

Church members continue to serve the community in many ways even without a building. The congregation has used some of its relief funds to buy new playground equipment for Parr Hill Park. It continues to support Crosslines in Joplin, and has held fundraisers for organizations such as Joplin Neighborhood Adult Literacy Action and the Freeman Chaplaincy Fund.

Members have formed a committee to decide whether they want to rebuild on the lot they own at 20th and Wisconsin or move to another location.

Hintz, who serves on that building committee, said the congregation is anxious, but it wants to make the right decision for its future.

"Some of us are getting kind of impatient," Hintz said. "It's been a year now and we don't have any building plans on their way yet and there are other churches that have been rebuilt. One of them had their first service Easter Sunday and they were located just over on the other side of the rail-road tracks. But we aren't rushing into anything.

"We need to look way ahead and this is where we're at with decisions now. Past memories are great, we never forget those but we need to look on ahead as to where is the best place for us to be for the future of Peace Lutheran Church here in Joplin and so these are the things we're dealing with now. Where can we best serve our mission to the community? This is what we're struggling with."

Redpath said the congregation is being deliberate in its decision because it is so important. She said the decision whether or not to build on their old location is a big hurdle.

"It's not ruled out, but it's also not decided," Redpath said. "I would like to think — in fact, I know — that we will be back. God will see to that."

55. GOD REMAINS WITH US IN JOPLIN

BY BILL PAPE

THE FOLLOWING ARTICLE WAS WRITTEN JUST AFTER PEACE LUTHERAN CHURCH HELD ITS JUNE 5, 2011, SERVICES IN THE PARKING LOT OF THEIR BUILDING, WHICH HAD BEEN DESTROYED IN THE MAY 22 TORNADO.

I have told the story many times since Sunday, a little over a week now, about Peace Lutheran Church, a congregation of the Evangelical Lutheran Church in America (ELCA) in Joplin, Mo. The church building was completely leveled by a tornado there May 22.

I have been told by a therapist-pastor that sharing that story is a way of living with guilt over what happened in Joplin and to me.

As the interim pastor of Peace Lutheran, I stay in Joplin only three days a week, commuting from my home in Kansas City, Mo. So I rode out the tornado in the motel basement. The motel was south of the storm's path.

But my therapist-pastor friend was right. I was experiencing what I had only often heard about and always thought I would never do: feel guilty about being alive.

I kept wondering, "Why did I decide not to go back to the church building?"

After seeing the destruction of the church, I am absolutely positive that I would not be writing this reflection today if I had gone back.

I'm dealing with this guilt. But as the days continue, I find that there are many things that just need to be done.

The Monday morning after the storm, as a number of us were walking through the rubble of the church building, we wondered: "Where are we going to hold worship on Sunday (May 29)?"

We decided to meet in the parking lot to let the world know what the people of Joplin know: we are still a congregation.

God is and will always be with us.

The service was chaotic, and it was spiritual. A number of newspapers, magazines, radio and television stations — local and national — came. I was wired up to six different stations. I don't even know who they all were, although I knew ABC, NBC and CNN were now part of my body.

The rains had finally left, so the weather was beautiful except for the 35-mile-an-hour winds.

But most importantly, God was there. You could just feel it among the 100 people who attended worship that Sunday morning.

The service itself, along with music (we had a keyboard loaned to us, hooked up to a battery, and a flutist), the prayers, the sermon and Holy Communion gave people a chance to celebrate and weep over lost homes, lost jobs, lost friends and families.

God was there.

Where does Peace Lutheran Church go from here? At this moment, we still don't have a place to worship for Sunday, June 5.

We know the parking lot is not going to work Sunday after Sunday. We have had two congregations offer to let us worship with them. But we have not yet had the time to sit down and decide where or how we might accept one of these generous offers. We are meeting tonight to begin the process.

We have no hymnals but have been offered some. No musical instruments, although we have been offered an organ. We have no risographs, copy machines, etc. We have lost all the past bulletins that would help us remember how we did certain worship services.

We have lost many other things that we just took for granted would be there every Sunday morning for us.

But what we do have are committed and dedicated members who are ready to do whatever is necessary for us to move forward.

What we do have is the ELCA Central States Synod in Kansas City, Mo., and ELCA members and congregations from all over the United States who have pledged to help us recover.

And, what we do have is the power and love of our God, Jesus Christ, and the Holy Spirit.

How can you not make it all happen when you have that kind of back-up team?

To God be the glory! Amen.

56. THANKS BE TO THIS EVER-PRESENT GOD

By Kathy Redpath

Pastor Kathy Redpath gave the sermon at Peace Lutheran Church, May 20, 2012, at the Praise on the Parking Lot service

From the moment that funnel cloud touched down on the edge of Joplin and churned its way across the city there began a time to weep, a time to mourn. This week, we mark the one-year anniversary of that day. I've heard people say things like "It's time to move on," or "we're not going to cry anymore over that." We're just going to move forward. Or we've had enough tears, let's just forget all that bad stuff and go back to life as it used to be. Don't we wish we could, just carry on as if it never happened.

But it did happen and because it happened, we are changed. We'll always find ourselves referring to before and after that tornado. We'll mark time by that day. We'll hear the date May 22, and into our minds will pop the Joplin tornado, and whether we like it or not, we will remember the events of that day.

But there's something else that we can remember. We can remember that God is with us, that God never left us during that time. Through it all, God was here. The storm was a product of the forces of the creation that God produced and God doesn't usually step in to alter those forces. But that never means that God is absent from them. From the moment that people began to crawl out from beneath the rubble, new stories came to light and God was in them. A family embracing family, neighbors helping neighbors. Strangers coming to the aid of strangers. God's presence was everywhere, in the acts of physical strength and raw courage and emotional connecting that took place up and down every street and in every neighborhood. From one side of the town to the other, God's spirit was here. Through stories of love and care and concern, through acts of heroism and self-sacrifice and devoted energy, through donations of everything, from clothing and blankets to food and toiletries, and as a friend of mine said, enough bottled water to fill a lake. All these are evidence of God at work among you and in you. God was here.

And God remains at work a year later as volunteers continue to pour in, and donations continue to be sent and needs continue to be addressed. God is here. As recovery begins to overshadow loss, and laughing begins to replace weeping, and building up becomes more evident than the tearing down, God is here. And God promises a future, a future based on hope and peace. In the waters of baptism and in the bread and wine of holy communion, we're reminded that God is with us for all season and for all times. God promises peace. In that peace, we will remember what came before. But we also will be able to turn to face the future knowing that God is here, God was here, God will be here. The congregation of Peace Lutheran Church continues to pray and discover where and how God is calling is to be engaged in mission to serve our community. Whether we eventually rebuild right here on this site, or whether we are led to start over again in a new location, we don't know that yet. But we do know this; God will be with us wherever we are, because God never left us. Thanks be to this ever-present God.

57. REJOICING, REMEMBERING AND REBUILDING

By Laela Zaidi

"But you are from Joplin. So you will remember, you will know, just how many people there are who see life differently; those who are guided by kindness and generosity and quiet service." -President Obama

I heard these words from President Obama during Joplin High School's graduation ceremony Monday night. Not on the television, but just some yards away from his podium in the stands of a local college's gymnasium. While I am not a member of the Class of 2012, I was still in awe with the crowd over our very own president standing before us. During his speech, I remember thinking: How did we get here? One year ago, President Obama spoke in Joplin to see the destruction left by an EF5 tornado and gave us hope. Last Monday, he came to rejoice with us in all that has been accomplished in just 12 months.

On May 22, 2011, Joplin was devastated by one of the seven deadliest tornadoes in the nation's history. Consider these numbers: 7,500 houses destroyed (including four houses of my relatives and my own childhood home), over 500 businesses demolished, 13 schools gone (with my high school among them) and more destruction that totaled nearly $3 billion in damage. The most unfortunate statistic of all, however, is the 161 lives lost. Of those who passed away, two of them, Lantz Hare and Will Norton, were students at Joplin High School. Will Norton was driving home from last year's high school commencement when the tornado ripped him from his father's arms.

For all of us in Joplin, May 22 gives a connotation of loss, fear, destruction, and pain. But every day presents newer statistics — different numbers that display the progress that has been made. Over 80 percent of Joplin's destroyed businesses have reopened their doors. Nearly 600 permits for new homes and almost 3,000 permits for rebuilding projects were issued by late April 2012. On Aug. 17, 2011, the school year began as scheduled, but our high school was split into two separate campuses across town. One of them, the 9/10 campus, is in a building formerly used as a middle school. The other, the 11/12 campus, is a temporary location built in an old Shopko store at the local mall. On my daily commute to the 9/10 campus, I notice more and more new homes spring out of the ground in the "tornado zone."

"In Joplin, the sun rises every day on a different place, and sets every night on a better place," said Governor Jay Nixon at the 2012 commencement.

His words rang true. Each day, whether I'm driving to the grocery store, school or simply around town, I'm reminded of what it takes to rebuild a community of 50,000.

In one year's time, pop sensation Katy Perry has sponsored senior prom, American Idol winner David Cook performed at homecoming, and the United Arab Emirates gave each Joplin High School student a laptop to replace the loss of textbooks. AmeriCorps members have been present in Joplin since hours after the storm. These individuals, along with other volunteers from all over the country, are helping with long-term recovery efforts, such as rebuilding homes. For their 200th and final episode, the popular television series Extreme Makeover: Home Edition completed the show's largest project ever in Joplin. A team of 21 builders and 13,000 volunteers accomplished building seven homes for seven families in one week.

Finally, thanks to the citizens of Jasper and Newton counties, a $62 million bond issue was passed to fund a brand new state-of-the-art high school, which celebrated its groundbreaking on the anniversary of the tornado with thousands in attendance. The groundbreaking was one part of a larger event called the "Walk of Unity." Joplin residents and supporters commemorated the anniversary of the tornado by treading through the heart of the tornado's path. Others stops on the walk included a steeple raising to recognize the 28 churches destroyed by the tornado, and a ribbon cutting at the opening of Kraft Insurance Services, to acknowledge last year's demolished businesses.

The list doesn't even begin to end there. Generosity has been given a new meaning for the people of Joplin. From across the nation and around the world, individuals have put their lives aside to take part in the efforts. Take for example, Zach Tusinger, a Joplin native who could have taken a higher-paying job at a law firm but instead decided to use his legal skills to assist those victims who are still facing legal challenges after the disaster. Mariah Hutchinson, who received her diploma Monday night, was so moved by the AmeriCorps volunteers that she signed up to volunteer for 10 months with the organization. She even applied for the FEMA Corps, a division of AmeriCorps that responds to natural disasters alongside FEMA. Of the thousands of volunteers who showed up in the days after the tornado, one man flew all the way from Japan. Toshiya "Toshi" Moto was so inspired by the efforts put forth by the U.S. following the 2011 tsunami that he decided to, in Obama's words, "pay it forward" and help American disaster victims.

"It's not just the sadness," Toshi explained. "You see the good side of people. I felt that in Japan and I feel that here."

The May 22 tornado brought tragedy, loss and devastation. I will never forget that "first look" of what the storm left behind, the feelings of being homeless, or knowing that I will never complete high school in a traditional building. Instead of letting those experiences define me, however, I have learned that it is how we respond to tragedy that makes us who we are. Just as President Obama stated, Joplin's citizens have seen a positive side to humanity that has forever changed us. Like Zach Tusinger, Mariah Hutchinson, Toshi and so many more, we will not sit aside when tragedy strikes others. Instead, we will understand and relate to those affected by the storm and use our talents to help them, just as we were, and continue to be, assisted by other generous souls.

Oscar-nominated actor Paul Giamatti used his acting skills to give a dramatic reading of the Book of Job during "Job for Joplin," an interfaith service held last weekend. A local group, "Restore Joplin," used all their profits from simple but popular t-shirt designs to meet the immediate needs of individuals and community service organizations in Joplin. A simple Facebook page and website created within hours of the tornado called Joplin Tornado Info provided a place for numerous relief organizations to send information to thousands of people.

Even though Joplin's restoration will take years, we will never forget the kindness of those who assisted us. I have learned all of us have the potential to make an impact on those around us, just as we were impacted by others. It can be by doing something as simple as making a Facebook page or designing a marketable product to flying halfway across the globe and volunteering. The extent of our impact doesn't matter, only that we attempt to make one and help others the best way we can. This is the very definition of the miracle of the human spirit. We will never forget May 22, but it is the continuing reconstruction — thanks to the generosity of others — that gives us a reason to rejoice, not just this year, but for many years to come.

Jennifer Nguyen, left, and Alyssa Wescoat console Megan Hickey immediately after the conclusion of the talent show/awards assembly.

PHOTO BY RANDY TURNER

58. TORNADO TEACHES TRUE MEANING OF SCHOOL

BY RANDY TURNER

THE FOLLOWING WAS WRITTEN SATURDAY, MAY 19, 2012

President Barack Obama will speak at the Joplin High School Graduation Monday night.

On Tuesday, the one-year anniversary of the tornado that destroyed one-third of this community and killed 161 will be observed with a unity walk that will cover the path of the tornado and end at Cunningham Park with a moment of silence at 5:41 p.m., the exact moment the tornado occurred.

Joplin will be the center of attention Monday, but on Friday, May 18, just three days before Air Force One arrives, the most important moment for 160 eighth graders at East Middle School where I teach had nothing to do with the anniversary or the president.

It was their last day of middle school and they were spending it in a converted warehouse, directly across from a dog food factory that continually offered an aromatic gift to the surrounding atmosphere.

The East Middle School building the children had attended for two years, what had been a brand new building, was just a memory. The auditorium, the gymnasium, and commons area were completely destroyed by the EF5 tornado; the rest of it was razed recently.

During the 2011-2012 school year, East students took physical education classes in a modular building and put on drama and musical productions in the auditoriums of the district's other middle schools, miles away.

Instead of the state-of-the-art auditorium that had been the pride and joy of the old East, students sat on the floor during assemblies and most of our last half day was dedicated to an East tradition — the annual talent show and awards assembly.

My Journalism Club students were set up at a table in the back of the cafeteria about 20 minutes before the program began. In front of them was an array of laptops that they would use to live blog the show, something we had never done before.

Darin was set up with the camcorder, while Jennifer, one of our two editors, Karly, Megan and Austen were on our blog website doing previews. Amy, the other co-editor, was on our Facebook page providing anyone who might have been online an opportunity to know what was going on this final day of the school year. Two sixth graders, Emma and Katy, were ready to take pictures.

At 9:30 a.m. the students began moving into the commons area, taking their seats on the floor.

For two and a half hours, I watched in awe as my students worked continually on a last day when their friends were relaxing. All of them had to leave their posts several times, either to accept awards for their academic accomplishments, or to perform.

It was a program filled with young girls singing Taylor Swift songs, or at least I think they were Taylor Swift songs, and students receiving awards for making the honor roll every quarter or for having perfect attendance.

The end of the program brought the teacher dance with faculty members showing their willingness to make fools of themselves (though a few of them are excellent dancers).

The final act was the concert choir's rendition of one of those goodbye songs that make the rounds this time of the year.

As I watched my journalism students, I saw the tears flowing. They knew this was their last day of middle school, but the song brought the point home.

And just like the high school graduation that will come Monday, the room was filled with young people who are ending one stage of their lives and preparing for the next.

A speculator on hug futures would have made a killing. I watched as three of my students shared a group hug, with Jennifer and Alyssa consoling Megan.

Hours after the final day of the 2011-2012 school year drew to a close, I received an e-mail message from Jennifer telling me she had posted a final story on our website. Since Jennifer is one of the best writers I have ever had the privilege of teaching, I quickly called up East Middle School Roundabout and read her story. It included the following passage:

I remember thinking for countless hours how I couldn't wait for summer. I couldn't wait to be out of school, to just be lazy! Many eighth graders were especially looking forward to the joys of high school! The time for relaxation and vacation was definitely anticipated ... and soon enough, the time came.

This school year went by like a breeze, and before we knew it, the end of school was soon approaching. This meant the end of middle school for the eighth graders, and the beginning of high school as freshmen. You would think we would be happy for summer, for a break.

Yes, we were happy, but we were also sad. The school year just went by too fast!

Too fast? We were in a warehouse, feeling forgotten in the nether regions of the school district. When the dignitaries came, they went to the mall high school, not to see this group of students who had been just as misplaced, just as much lost in the wake of the most horrifying incident of their young lives.

Too fast? Jennifer was right. The end of our educational adventure had come much too quickly.

Jennifer touched another emotional chord with her final words:

Tears spring to my eyes as I close with my final bid of farewell to East. Through all the good times and the bad, we have overcome and made this school truly unforgettable. This is why I will always remember you.

Goodbye East. I love you.

In her words, Jennifer hit on the reason why the Joplin Tornado could never bring East Middle School down. It was just a building that was destroyed, one that had packed many memories into its two years, but just a building.

Those unforgettable kids, the Jennifers, the Amys, the Megans, the Austens, the Darins, and all of the rest of them, the ones who sat in our makeshift classrooms and walked our warehouse halls this year and those who will be there next year as we wait for our new building to be built, they're the ones who make the school.

The circumstances that brought us together in this industrial park we call home were horrific, but what a wonderful school year.

59. JOPLIN HIGH SCHOOL 2012 PROM PHOTOS

60. DEATH DOESN'T GET THE LAST WORD; LIFE WINS

THE FOLLOWING IS THE TEXT OF REV. AARON BROWN'S SPEECH AT THE JOPLIN
TORNADO MEMORIAL SERVICE SUNDAY, MAY 29, 2011

FATHER JUSTIN MONAGHAN, ST. MARY'S CATHOLIC CHURCH: Heavenly Father, we take time to pause, reflect, and pray. Amidst the pain and heart of this devastation we have no doubt about your presence among us. You are infusing in each of us from near and afar a strength and resilience that is a special gift. You are calling our already close-knit community to new heights and determination and purpose. We hear the mission you have entrusted to us, and with your help we will put our hands to the plow.

We are grateful for the support you are sending us and for the backing of our governor and state and for the enormous support from our president and our country at this time of renewal and restoration. Father, we open to your will. Amen.

Please be seated.

REV. RANDY GARRIS, COLLEGE HEIGHTS CHRISTIAN CHURCH: Welcome and thank you for coming to today's memorial service.

Customarily, a greeting would include such words as "ladies and gentlemen" and "honored guests." But when there has been deep shared pain, when a community has suffered greatly and cried much together, and when the compassion and the kindness extended to one another has gone far beyond the scope of words, a more tender language than "honored guests" or "ladies and gentlemen" is heard. Words like "friends" and "neighbors" and "family" and "brothers and sisters." Words like "us." That's who gathers here today with us.

Thank you for your coming. Thank you for your role in each other's lives. Thank you for what you mean to one another.

A prayer which was led by Father Justin Monaghan who by the grace of God in a stout bathtub survived the destruction of the church of St. Mary's, a congregation of the Lord, on 26th Street. And physically and metaphorically the cross still stands. (APPLAUSE)

GARRIS: There's a three-fold purpose to this gathering. The first is to grieve. The loss of even one human life is a tragedy. And we have lost scores.

We also gather to pray God's blessings as we rebuild our lives, asking God to lead us as we rebuild around the things that matter most. And we gather to celebrate the kindness that people have and are giving to one another.

Our foundation has not moved. It's still in the same place. We still have a solid place to stand. In Romans, the eighth chapter, Apostle Paul wrote these, these words, "What, then, shall we say to these things? If God is for us, who can be against us? He who did not spare his own son, but gave him up for us all — how will he not also, with him, graciously give us all things?

"Who shall separate us from the love of Christ? Shall tribulation or distress or persecution or famine or nakedness or danger or sword?

"No, no. In all these things, we are more than conquerors through him who loved us. For I am confident that neither death nor life, nor angels nor rulers, nor anything present nor anything to come, nor powers, nor height or depth or anything else in all of creation will ever be able to separate us from the love of God in Christ Jesus, our Lord."

And now with the hymn of promise, the chancellor choir of the First United Methodist Church under the direction of Larry Sandburg (ph).

(CHOIR SINGING)

(APPLAUSE)

GARRIS: Pastor Aaron Brown has been a good friend of the four-state area, a faithful partner in the gospel, and a shepherd of St. Paul's United Methodist Church. It, too, is a congregation that has lost much, including its worship center. He'll have our message this afternoon.

REV. AARON BROWN, ST. PAUL'S UNITED METHODIST CHURCH: We're all trying to — trying to process our stories and understand them in the context of what's happened, and I thought I'd take the liberty of telling you about mine about Sunday. Our family lives south of the city of Joplin. And after the tornado, I drove as far as I could into town and ran to the home of one of my closest friends. His house was gone but he and his family were safe.

From there, I was able to run to our church on 26th and Monroe, and found that about a third of it was gone, and I just had to know if everybody inside was safe. And there was one person in the church at the time the tornado hit, and she was safe. She hid under a dishwasher in our kitchen.

I went out to the street and what I saw was that people were just running. I didn't know what else to do, so I just ran alongside people and I said, "Can I help you find somebody?" And I dug through houses. And I prayed with a young couple whose friends didn't make it out of their house. And across the street from there, there were two elderly people that had died in their own backyard. I don't know their names.

But there was just a lot of running and digging and hoping and praying. That's what I remember.

I got called back to the church and the kids' wing of our church miraculously was still standing and it became a triage center. It's ironic, the classrooms that the children had played that morning, laughed around and learned about Jesus around, they became the place where wounds were being treated, and broken bones were being set, and emergency surgeries were being performed. Tables where kids had been making crafts a few hours earlier became beds of comfort and rest for the wounded.

We have all spent the last seven days looking for family and friends. We've all had of moments of unbelievable relief at hearing somebody's voice, and we've all had those moments of heart-sickening pain and hearing that somebody that we know didn't make it.

Late Friday night, I deliver the news to Mark and Trisha Norton that their son Will, his body had been identified. Eighteen years old, absolutely overflowing with life and faith. He had just graduated from high school hours before he was killed. Will is one of — from what I've heard recently — one of 142.

What is the word of comfort for us today? The word of comfort today for Will's family and all of those grieving comes from the God of the universe, the God who took human form and walked among us. He suffered. He knows what it's like for us when we suffer.

And Jesus said this. He said, "Do not let your hearts be troubled. Trust in God. Trust also in me."

He said, "In my father's house, there are many rooms. If it were not so, I would haven't told you."

He said, "I'm going to prepare a place for you. And if I go and prepare a place for you, I will come back and take you to be with me, so that you also can be where I am."

He said, "Before long, the world will not see me anymore but you will see me. And because I live you also will live."

And then he also says, there's few verses later, he says, "Peace I leave with you, my peace I give to you. I do not give as the world gives, so do not let your hearts be troubled and do not be afraid."

To these families who died, I think God is saying right now is death does not get the last word. I think God is saying to those families right now, this is what I wanted you to see in the resurrection of Jesus, that death doesn't win ever. Even when you think it does.

(APPLAUSE)

BROWN: God is saying to you, families who lost someone, even if it looks like death wins, it doesn't get the last word. Life wins. Life wins.

(APPLAUSE)

BROWN: And I'll be honest. I don't know the faith stories of all those that have died. I don't know their faith stories.

But I know this — that God's grace is wider than we can ever imagine, that heaven is real, and that this life is not the only life that we see.

I need to be honest and confess, some of us are asking, why? Why did God do this? Why did god allow this, so much death so, much destruction?

But, listen — Jesus never promised to protect us from the storms of life. He never promised that life would be easy or convenient if we chose to follow him. In fact, almost all of his disciples, they were tortured to death.

What he did promise was very simple and powerful: to be with us. To be with us through the storm, to be with us as we grieve, to be with us as we stand at the grave site of our loved ones, to be with us and listen to us and guide us. And our challenge is: will we let him?

As hard as it may be, pray, as hard as it may be, talk to God. As hard as it may be, listen to his words. Let him love you. Let him love you.

Listen, God didn't do this to Joplin to punish us. Read the book. Jesus took our punishment for us. Read the book.

(APPLAUSE)

BROWN: This happened — this happened because life on this side of eternity is unpredictable. It's chaotic and it's broken. God says this, "For God so loved the world he gave his one and only son," and he hasn't stopped loving the world."

You may wonder at times, but the fact is that God loves you and God loves Joplin and God is walking through this tragedy today and he will make a way where it seems like there is no way. You know, when Jesus was crucified, everybody — I mean, everybody — they thought it was the end. The disciples had forgotten everything that he told them, that their world had come crashing down around them. There was this eerie darkness that covered the land. And for parts of three days, there was no hope.

But then, but then — then Easter. Death is swallowed up in victory. Light crushes the darkness. Life wins.

Life won then. And life wins now. And now, what do we do?

We get busy. Jesus didn't come back from the grave just to point us to heaven. He came back from the grave to give us a mission that those who call on his name would be the light of the world. His mission is for us to get busy, get busy serving, get busy rebuilding our city which I love.

And by the way, I think it is the center of the universe right here in Joplin, Mo.

(APPLAUSE)

BROWN: Let's get busy. Let's get busy loving more deeply than we ever have loved. Let's get busy taking care — you get busy taking care of your soul. Get busy connecting to God, the God who knows you by name and loves you more than you could ever imagine or believe.

And for those of you who have lost loved ones, get busy living out their legacy. They may have lost their lives, but none of them would want you to stop living yours. Get busy living.

We are not a people without hope. We are people from whom hope and light and life shines to the ends of the earth because God is good all the time. And all the time, God is good.

(APPLAUSE)

BROWN: In the name of Jesus, the Lord of life, and the Lord of light, and the Lord of hope, and the Lord of new beginnings, that is the good news, amen.

61. THE LONG JOURNEY

THE FOLLOWING IS THE TEXT OF GOVERNOR JAY NIXON'S SPEECH AT THE JOPLIN
TORNADO MEMORIAL SERVICE SUNDAY, MAY 29, 2011

Thank you, Pastor Gariss. To the families of those who were killed and injured; to the families of those who are still unaccounted for; to the people of Joplin who have endured this terrible tragedy; to the thousands of Missourians and citizens across the nation who have opened their hearts to help us heal; to the hundreds of firefighters and emergency responders who came without hesitation to climb over piles of rubble in search of survivors; to Pastor Garris, Pastor Brown, Father Monaghan, Lieutenant Colonel Kilmer, and the wonderful choir from First United Methodist Church of Joplin; and to President Obama who is with us today – thank you all for coming.

It is an honor to be here, joining the thousands of Missourians observing this special Day of Prayer. We stand on hallowed ground, to bear witness to the destructive power of Nature and the invincible power of faith.

We have come to mourn what the storm has taken from us, to seek comfort in community, and to draw strength from God to build anew.

It seems inconceivable that just one week ago, the people of Joplin were going about their daily lives, doing the ordinary things people do on a Sunday evening: Cooking supper. Watching TV. Walking the dog. Attending their sons' and daughters' graduation.

And then came the whirlwind. Nearly a mile wide and six miles long, with 200-mile-an-hour winds — churning and roaring, tossing cars and toppling trees, pounding homes, businesses, schools and churches to rubble.

But that storm, the likes of which we have never seen, has brought forward a spirit of resilience — the likes of which we've also never seen.

What our nation has witnessed this week is the spirit of Joplin, Mo. And we are humbled and awed by it.

You have given "Love thy neighbor" new meaning. The parable of the Good Samaritan in Luke, Chapter 10: verses 25 to 37, begins with a conversation between Jesus and a student of religious law. It starts with a legal question, and ends with a moral imperative.

The student asks Jesus, "What shall I do to inherit eternal life?" And Jesus turns the question around and asks: "What is written in the law?"

And the student, who is well-versed in the Talmud and the Torah, replies: "Thou shalt love the Lord thy God with all thy heart, with all thy soul, with all thy strength and with all thy mind. And thou shalt love thy neighbor as thyself."

And Jesus replies: "Thou hast answered right. This do, and thou shalt live."

But then the student, wanting greater clarity than the law provided, asks Jesus, "And who is my neighbor?" And Jesus tells him the story of the Good Samaritan.

From that parable, our charge is crystal clear. Good Samaritans do not pass by those who are suffering and in need. They show their compassion with action.

In Joplin, you see Good Samaritans everywhere you turn. You see them over in the gym at this university, where hundreds of volunteers make sandwiches every day.

You see them passing out blankets and pillows, sunscreen and flashlights to our neighbors made homeless by the whirlwind.

You need a flashlight. Because it gets pretty dark here at night – especially when you're standing in the street, staring at the lonely pile of matchsticks that was once your home.

If you had been in the ER at St. John's Mercy Medical Center last Sunday evening, mere moments after the tornado struck, you would have seen Good Samaritans rushing frantically to reach the wounded and the dying.

Shattered glass and bleeding patients everywhere, water and gas spewing from burst pipes, one doctor stumbled through the darkness with a flashlight in his teeth, following the wail of a wounded child.

You see Good Samaritans at every checkpoint in the destruction zone, where police officers and citizen soldiers of the Missouri National Guard keep watch over wet socks, teddy bears, cherished wedding photos and crumpled wheelchairs – all that is left of our neighbors' worldly goods.

You see them in the churchyard, men sleeping on cots under the stars, after driving all night to get here from Tuscaloosa. These men were so touched, so moved by the kindness of strangers in their hour of need, that they just had to come to Joplin. Good Samaritans – on a mission from God.

God has chosen us for a mission, too: to grieve together, to comfort one another, to be patient with one another, to strengthen one another – and to build Joplin anew. Not just to build it back the way it was, but to make it an even better place.

We know that all those who perished here are already in an even better place. But for us, the living, there is work to do. God says: "Show me." Show me.

The people of Missouri were born for this mission. We are famously stubborn and self-reliant.

Practical. Impatient. But whatever may divide us, we always come together in crisis.

And once our resolve is set, no storm, no fire or flood can turn us from our task.

In the pale hushed stillness before dawn, when the chainsaws have fallen silent, if you listen very closely — you can hear the sound of that resolve, like a tiny silver hammer tapping, tapping, tapping inside our heads.

In the days to come, the satellite trucks will pack up, leave town and move on. Joplin's story will disappear from the front pages. But the tragedy will not disappear from our lives.

We will still be here in Joplin – together – preparing for the long journey out of darkness into light. And we will need more hands, more tools, more Good Samaritans at every step.

This tragedy has changed us forever. This community will never be the same. We will never be the same.

The grief we share at this moment is overwhelming. That sorrow will always be part of us, a stone upon our hearts. But those we love – those we lost – are safe with God, and safe in our hearts. And in our hearts, the joy they gave us lives on and on. Nothing can take that from us.

We can, and we will, heal. We've already begun. Together, we can, and we will, rebuild – upon a granite foundation of faith. What we build on this hallowed ground will be a living monument to those we lost: mothers, fathers, our precious children.

It will be a monument to the will and determination of the hundreds of men, women and yes, even children, who helped their neighbors dig out of the ruins – a monument to the search and rescue crews who came swiftly to aid the quick, and the dead.

By God's grace, we will restore this community. And by God's grace, we will renew our souls.

One year from today, Joplin will look different. And more different still in two years, and in three years, and in five.

But as the years pass, the moral of our story will be the same: love thy neighbor. May God bless.

62. JOPLIN TAUGHT
THE WORLD

THE FOLLOWING IS THE TEXT OF PRESIDENT BARACK OBAMA'S SPEECH AT THE
JOPLIN TORNADO MEMORIAL SERVICE SUNDAY, MAY 29, 2011

THE PRESIDENT: Thank you. Thank you so much. Please, please be seated.

AUDIENCE MEMBER: I love you, Obama!

THE PRESIDENT: I love Joplin! (Applause.) I love Joplin.

AUDIENCE MEMBER: We love Joplin!

THE PRESIDENT: We love Joplin. (Applause.)

Thank you, Governor, for that powerful message, but more importantly, for being here with and for your people every step of the way.

We are grateful to you, to Reverend Gariss, Father Monaghan. I'm so glad you got in that tub. (Laughter and applause.) To Reverend Brown for that incredibly powerful message. (Applause.)

To Senator Claire McCaskill, who's been here, and Congressman Billy Long; Mayor Woolston. To Craig Fugate. It doesn't get a lot of attention, but he heads up FEMA, our emergency response at the federal level. He's been going from Tuscaloosa to Joplin and everywhere in between tirelessly doing outstanding work. We're grateful for him. Gail McGovern, the President of the National Red Cross, which has contributed mightily to the rebuilding efforts here.

Most of all, to the family and friends of all those who've been lost and all those who've been affected.

Today we gather to celebrate the lives of those we've lost to the storms here in Joplin and across the Midwest, to keep in our prayers those still missing, to mourn with their families, to stand together during this time of pain and trial.

And as Reverend Brown alluded to, the question that weighs on us at a time like this is: Why? Why our town? Why our home? Why my son, or husband, or wife, or sister, or friend? Why?

We do not have the capacity to answer. We can't know when a terrible storm will strike, or where, or the severity of the devastation that it may cause. We can't know why we're tested with the loss of a loved one, or the loss of a home where we've lived a lifetime.

These things are beyond our power to control. But that does not mean we are powerless in the face of adversity. How we respond when the storm strikes is up to us. How we live in the aftermath of tragedy and heartache, that's within our control. And it's in these moments, through our actions, that we often see the glimpse of what makes life worth living in the first place.

In the last week, that's what Joplin has not just taught Missouri, not just taught America, but has taught the world. I was overseas in the aftermath of the storm, and had world leaders coming up to me saying, let the people of Joplin know we are with them; we're thinking about them; we love them. (Applause.)

Because the world saw how Joplin responded. A university turned itself into a makeshift hospital. (Applause.) Some of you used your pickup trucks as ambulances, carrying the injured — (applause) — on doors that served as stretchers. Your restaurants have rushed food to people in need. Businesses have filled trucks with donations. You've waited in line for hours to donate blood to people you know, but also to people you've never met. And in all this, you have lived the words of Scripture:

We are troubled on every side, yet not distressed;

we are perplexed, but not in despair;

Persecuted, but not forsaken;

cast down, but not destroyed;

As the governor said, you have shown the world what it means to love thy neighbor. You've banded together. You've come to each other's aid. You've demonstrated a simple truth: that amid heartbreak and tragedy, no one is a stranger. Everybody is a brother. Everybody is a sister. (Applause.) We can all love one another.

As you move forward in the days ahead, I know that rebuilding what you've lost won't be easy. I just walked through some of the neighborhoods that have been affected, and you look out at the landscape, and there have to be moments where you just say, where to begin? How to start? There are going to be moments where after the shock has worn off, you feel alone. But there's no doubt in my mind what the people of this community can do. There's no doubt in my mind that Joplin will rebuild. And as President, I can promise you, your country will be there with you every single step of the way. (Applause.) We will be with you every step of the way. We're not going anywhere. (Applause.) The cameras may leave. The spotlight may shift. But we will be with you every step of the way until Joplin is restored and this community is back on its feet. We're not going anywhere. (Applause.)

That is not just my promise; that's America's promise. It's a promise I make here in Joplin; it's a promise I made down in Tuscaloosa, or in any of the communities that have been hit by these devastating storms over the last few weeks.

Now, there have been countless acts of kindness and selflessness in recent days. We've already heard the record of some of that. But perhaps none are as inspiring as what took place when the storm was bearing down on Joplin, threatening an entire community with utter destruction. And in the face of winds that showed no mercy, no regard for human life, that did not discriminate by race or faith or background, it was ordinary people, swiftly tested, who said, "I'm willing to die right now so that someone else might live."

It was the husband who threw himself over his wife as their house came apart around them. It was the mother who shielded her young son.

It was Dean Wells, a husband and father who loved to sing and whistle in his church choir. Dean was working a shift at the Home Depot, managing the electrical department, when the siren rang out. He sprang into action, moving people to safety. Over and over again, he went back for others, until a wall came down on top of him. In the end, most of the building was destroyed, but not where Dean had directed his coworkers and his customers.

There was a young man named Christopher Lucas who was 26 years old. Father of two daughters; third daughter on the way. Just like any other night, Christopher was doing his job as manager on duty at Pizza Hut. And then he heard the storm coming.

It was then when this former sailor quickly ushered everybody into the walk-in freezer. The only problem was, the freezer door wouldn't stay closed from the inside. So as the tornado bore down on this small storefront on Range Line Road, Christopher left the freezer to find a rope or a cord or anything to hold the door shut. He made it back just in time, tying a piece of bungee cord to the handle outside, wrapping the other end around his arm, holding the door closed with all his might.

And Christopher held it as long as he could, until he was pulled away by the incredible force of the storm. He died saving more than a dozen people in that freezer. (Applause.)

You see, there are heroes all around us, all the time. They walk by us on the sidewalk, and they sit next to us in class. They pass us in the aisle wearing an orange apron. They come to our table at a restaurant and ask us what we'd like to order.

Just as we can't know why tragedy strikes in the first place, we may never fully understand where these men and women find the courage and strength to do what they did. What we do know is that in a split-second moment where there's little time for internal reflection or debate, the actions of these individuals were driven by love — love for a family member, love for a friend, or just love for a fellow human being.

That's good to know. In a world that can be cruel and selfish, it's this knowledge — the knowledge that we are inclined to love one another, that we're inclined to do good, to be good — that causes us to take heart. We see with fresh eyes what's precious and so fragile and so important to us. We put aside our petty grievances and our minor disagreements. We see ourselves in the hopes and hardships of others. And in the stories of people like Dean and people like Christopher, we remember that each us contains reserves of resolve and compassion. There are heroes all around us, all the time.

And so, in the wake of this tragedy, let us live up to their example — to make each day count — (applause) — to live with the sense of mutual regard — to live with that same compassion that they demonstrated in their final hours. We are called by them to do everything we can to be worthy of the chance that we've been given to carry on.

I understand that at a memorial yesterday for Dean, his wife decided to play a recording of Dean whistling a song he loved — Amazing Grace. The lyrics are a fitting tribute to what Joplin has been through.

Through many dangers, toils and snares
I have already come;
'Tis Grace that brought me safe thus far
and Grace will lead me home...
Yea, when this flesh and heart shall fail,
And mortal life shall cease,
I shall possess within the veil,
A life of joy and peace.

May those we've lost know peace, and may Grace guide the people of Joplin home. God bless you, and God bless the United States of America. Thank you.

63. THE WORLD WILL NEVER FORGET WHAT YOU ACHIEVED

THE FOLLOWING IS THE TEXT FROM GOVERNOR JAY NIXON'S SPEECH FOR THE 2012 JOPLIN HIGH SCHOOL GRADUATION CEREMONY

Thank you. Good evening.

Over the past year, the Joplin Schools have faced — and overcome — many daunting challenges. That was possible because of the vision, leadership and dedication of Superintendent C.J. Huff.

With unwavering courage and unshakable resolve, C.J. has led the Joplin Schools forward. He has been an inspiration to us all. I'm proud to have worked closely in partnership with C.J., and I'm even more proud to call him my friend.

Mr. President, ladies and gentlemen, please join me in thanking one of Missouri's — one of America's — finest leaders and educators, Superintendent C.J. Huff.

Exactly one year ago, I stood on this same stage to address the college graduates of Missouri Southern State University.

It was a time of optimism. A time to mark a major milestone. A time to look ahead toward the bright horizon, with full hearts and soaring hopes.

The next day changed everything.

The next day changed all of us.

But what a difference a year makes.

And tonight, we gather together, as we have so many times in the past year, to celebrate another Joplin milestone.

Joplin High School Class of 2012, congratulations!

We are so proud of you.

All that you have achieved reflects your strength of character, hard work, and high aspirations.

It also reflects the character of this community.

This is a community of optimists.

This is a community of believers.

This is a community of fighters.

This is a community that never gave up, never gave in, and with HOPE in its heart and steel in its spine, has come back stronger and better than ever.

From Day One, your faith and your fight have shown the world that the spirit of Joplin is unbreakable.

Yes.

Joplin lost many things in the storm, but never lost its heart or its soul.

Because the schools are the heart and soul of Joplin, as they are across our great state and our great nation.

Our schools are a unifying force, a source of identity and pride. They are citadels of shared values, cherished hopes, and common dreams.

Public education is a bond not only between students and teachers.

It is a bond between generations, between a community's leaders and the children who, one day, will carry on their unfinished work.

Joplin schools became the rallying point for this community.

With classes set to resume on Aug. 17, there wasn't much time. But with each passing day, as the storms of spring gave way to the heat of summer, Joplin's army gained ground.

And Joplin became a rallying point for a much larger community. A community of people so inspired by your remarkable story that they needed to be part of it.

They came by the thousands, from all faiths and all walks of life, from Alaska to Florida, from Sweden to Japan.

Brick-by-brick and board-by-board, Joplin rose from the rubble.

In Joplin, the sun rises every morning on a different place, and sets every evening on a better place.

And so, just 87 days after the most devastating tornado in our history, Joplin schools opened — just as Dr. Huff promised — on Aug. 17.

That is the spirit of Joplin, and each one of you is part of it.

This class, this school, and this community will forever stand as a symbol of the best of our nation, and the best in us.

Tonight, we look toward the bright horizon stretched before the Class of two thousand and twelve.

With full hearts and soaring hopes, we celebrate the parents and grandparents, aunts and uncles, brothers and sisters, friends and neighbors who have loved and supported the Class of 2012 since they were in kindergarten.

The faith and values you have instilled in these young adults are the bedrock they will build their lives on. That foundation cannot be moved.

We celebrate the faculty, staff and administration of Joplin High School.

In a year like no other, you put your personal needs aside, and always put your students first.

For your abiding compassion and devotion, we will be forever in your debt.

We celebrate each and every member of the Joplin community who gave so selflessly, worked so tirelessly, to ensure a bright future for your children.

They will carry on your unfinished work.

Most of all, we celebrate you — the Joplin High School Class of 2012.

The world will never forget what you achieved here.

You have been tried and tested, and are stronger for it, smarter, too.

You are now ready to take all that you've learned at Joplin High, and use it to pursue your dreams — to become a doctor or a dancer, a soldier or a scientist, an engineer or an entrepreneur.

You have learned — perhaps too soon — that life is a fragile thread that binds us together. Never take a single moment for granted.

You know — because you have lived it — that from great adversity, great blessings flow.

And with teamwork, tenacity, and the grace of God, all things are possible.

Congratulations, and God bless.

Just a few days after the tornado struck, President Obama came to Joplin. As we walked the ravaged streets, he spoke with many of our families, folks who had lost everything.

He prayed with us, remembering the courage of those who gave their lives protecting others, and asked the Lord to watch over us and guide us through the difficult days ahead.

The President pledged that our country would be with us, and stay with us, at every step, as Joplin recovered and rebuilt.

And he has kept that commitment, as a true partner and a true friend of Joplin.

Please join me in welcoming back to Joplin, the President of the United States of America, Barack Obama.

64. BECAUSE YOU ARE FROM JOPLIN

The following is the text from President Obama's prepared speech for the 2012 Joplin High School Graduation

Good evening Superintendent Huff, Principal Sachetta, faculty, parents, family, friends, the people of Joplin, and the class of 2012. Congratulations on your graduation, and thank you for allowing me the honor of playing a small part in this special day.

The job of a commencement speaker – aside from keeping it short and sweet – is to inspire. But as I look out at this class, and across this city, what's clear is that you're the source of inspiration today. To me. To this state. To this country. And to people all over the world.

Last year, the road that led you here took a turn that no one could've imagined. Just hours after the class of 2011 walked across this stage, the most powerful tornado in six decades tore a path of devastation through Joplin that was nearly a mile wide and thirteen long. In only 32 minutes, it took thousands of homes, hundreds of businesses, and 161 of your neighbors, your friends, and your family members. It took Will Norton, who had just left this auditorium with a diploma in his hand. It took Lantz Hare, who should've received his diploma next year.

By now, most of you have probably relived those 32 minutes again and again. Where you were. What you saw. When you knew for sure that it was over. The first contact you had with someone you love. The first day you woke up in a world that would never be the same.

And yet, the story of Joplin is the story of what happened the next day. And the day after that. And all the days and weeks that followed. As your city manager, Mark Rohr, has said, the people here chose to define the tragedy "not by what happened to us, but by how we responded."

That story is part of you now. You've grown up quickly over the last year. You've learned at a younger age than most that we can't always predict what life has in store for us. No matter how we might try to avoid it, life can bring heartache. Life involves struggle. Life will bring loss.

But here in Joplin, you've also learned that we have the power to grow from these experiences. We can define our own lives not by what happens to us, but by how we respond. We can choose to carry on, and make a difference in the world. And in doing so, we can make true what's written in Scripture – that "tribulation produces perseverance, and perseverance, character, and character, hope."

Of all that's come from this tragedy, let this be the central lesson that guides you and sustains you through whatever challenges lie ahead.

I imagine that as you begin the next stage in your journey, you will encounter greed and selfishness; ignorance and cruelty. You will meet people who try to build themselves up by tearing others down; who believe looking after others is only for suckers.

But you are from Joplin. So you will remember, you will know, just how many people there are who see life differently; those who are guided by kindness and generosity and quiet service.

You'll always remember that in a town of 50,000 people, nearly 50,000 more came to help in the weeks after the tornado – perfect strangers who've never met you, and would never ask for anything in return. One of them was Mark Carr, who drove 600 miles from Rocky Ford, Colo., with a couple of chainsaws and his three little children. One man traveled all the way from Japan, because he remembered that Americans were there for his country after last year's tsunami, and he wanted the chance to pay it forward. Many were AmeriCorps volunteers who have chosen to leave their homes and stay here until Joplin is back on its feet.

There was the day that Mizzou's football team rolled into town with an 18-wheeler full of donated supplies. Of all places, they were assigned to help out on Kansas Avenue. While they hauled away washing machines and refrigerators from the debris, they met Carol Mann, who had just lost the house she lived in for eighteen years. Carol, who works part-time at McDonald's even as she struggles with seizures, told the players that she had even lost the change purse that held her lunch money. So one of them went back to the house, dug through the rubble, and returned the purse with $5 inside.

As Carol's sister said, "So much of the news you hear is so negative. But those boys renewed my faith that there are so many good people in the world."

That's what you'll remember. Because you are from Joplin.

You will remember the half million dollar donation that came from Angelina Jolie and Missouri native Brad Pitt. But you'll also remember the $360 that was delivered by a nine-year-old boy who organized his own car wash. You'll remember the school supplies donated by your neighboring towns, but also the brand new laptops that were sent from the United Arab Emirates – a small country on the other side of the world. When it came time for your prom, make-up artist Melissa Blayton organized an effort that collected over 1,000 donated prom dresses, FedEx kicked in for the corsages, and Joplin's own Liz Easton, who lost her home and her bakery in the tornado, made 1,500 cupcakes for the occasion.

There are so many good people in the world. There is such a decency, a bigness of spirit, in this country of ours. Remember that. Remember what people did here. And like the man from Japan who came to Joplin, make sure to pay it forward in your own life.

Just as you have learned the goodness of people, so have you learned the power of community. As you take on the roles of colleague and neighbor and citizen, you will encounter all kinds of divisions between groups – divisions of race, and religion, and ideology. You'll meet people who like to disagree just for the sake of being disagreeable; who prefer to play up their differences and instead of focusing on what they have in common, or where they can cooperate.

But you are from Joplin. So you will know that it's always possible for a community to come together when it matters most.

After all, a lot of you could've spent your senior year scattered throughout different schools, far from home. But Dr. Huff asked everyone to pitch in so that school started on time, right here in Joplin. He understood the power of this community, and the power of place. And so teachers worked extra hours, and coaches improvised. The mall was turned into classrooms, and the food court became a cafeteria – which sounds like a bit of an improvement. Sure, the arrangements might have been a little noisy, and a little improvised, but you hunkered down, and you made it work. Together.

Together, you decided that this city wasn't about to spend the next year arguing over every detail of the recovery effort. At the very first town meeting, every citizen was handed a Post-It note, and asked to write down their goals and their hopes for Joplin's future. More than 1,000 notes covered an entire wall, and became the blueprint that architects are following to this day.

Together, the businesses that were destroyed in the tornado decided that they weren't about to walk away from the community that made their success possible. Even if it would've been easier. Even if it would've been more profitable to go somewhere else. Today, more than half the stores that were damaged on the Range Line are up and running again. Eleven more are planning to join them. And every time a company re-opens its doors, people cheer the cutting of a ribbon that bears the town's new slogan: "Remember. Rejoice. Rebuild."

I've been told that before the tornado, many of you couldn't wait to leave here once high school was finally over. Your student council president, Julia Lewis, said, "We never thought Joplin was anything special; but seeing how we responded to something that tore our community apart has brought us together. Everyone has a lot more pride in our town." It's no surprise, then, that many of you have decided to stick around, and go to colleges that aren't too far from home.

That's the power of community. That's the power of shared effort. Some of life's strongest bonds are the ones we forge when everything around us seems broken. And even though I expect some of you will ultimately end up leaving Joplin, I'm convinced that Joplin will never leave you. The people who went through this with you; the people you once thought of as simply neighbors or acquaintances; classmates or even friends – the people in this auditorium tonight – they are family now.

They are family.

In fact, my deepest hope for all of you is that as you begin this new chapter in your life, you will bring that spirit of Joplin to every place you travel and everything you do. You can serve as a reminder that we're not meant to walk this road alone; that we're not expected to face down adversity by ourselves. We need each other. We're important to each other. We're stronger together than we are on our own.

It is this spirit that's allowing all of you to rebuild this city. It's the same spirit we need right now to help rebuild America. And you, class of 2012, will help lead this effort. You're the ones who will help build an economy where every child can count on a good education; where everyone who is willing to put in the effort can find a job that supports a family; where we control our own energy future and we lead the world in science and technology and innovation. America will only succeed if we all pitch in and pull together – and I'm counting on you to be leaders in that effort.

Because you are from Joplin. And you've already defied the odds.

In a city with countless stories of unthinkable courage and resilience over the last year, there are some that still stand out – especially on this day. By now, most of you know Joplin High senior Quinton Anderson, who's probably embarrassed that someone's talking about him again. But I'm going to talk about him anyways, because in a lot of ways, Quinton's journey has been Joplin's journey.

When the tornado struck, Quinton was thrown across the street from his house. The young man who found him couldn't imagine that Quinton would survive such injuries. Quinton woke up in a hospital bed three days later. It was then that his sister Grace told him that both their parents had been lost to the storm.

Quinton went on to face over five weeks of treatment, including emergency surgery. But he left that hospital determined to carry on; to live his life, and to be there for his sister. Over the past year, he's been a football captain who cheered from the sidelines when he wasn't able to play. He worked that much harder so he could be ready for baseball in the spring. He won a national scholarship as a finalist for the High School Football Rudy Awards, and he plans to study molecular biology at Harding University this fall.

Quinton has said that his motto in life is "Always take that extra step." Today, after a long and improbable journey for Quinton, for Joplin, and for the entire class of 2012, that extra step is about to take you towards whatever future you hope for; toward whatever dreams you hold in your hearts.

Yes, you will encounter obstacles along the way. Yes, you will face setbacks and disappointments.

But you are from Joplin. And you are from America. No matter how tough times get, you will be tougher. No matter what life throws at you, you will be ready. You will not be defined by the difficulties you face, but how you respond – with strength, and grace, and a commitment to others.

Langston Hughes, the poet and civil rights activist who knew some tough times, was born here in Joplin. In a poem called "Youth," he wrote,

We have tomorrow
Bright before us
Like a flame.
Yesterday
A night-gone thing,
A sun-down name.
And dawn-today. Broad arch above the road we came.
We march.

To the people of Joplin, and the class of 2012:

The road has been hard. The day has been long. But we have tomorrow, and so we march. We march, together, and you are leading the way. Congratulations. May God bless you, and may God bless the United States of America.

CENTERS FOR DISEASE CONTROL REPORT ON FUNGAL INFECTIONS FROM JOPLIN TORNADO

On May 22, 2011, at 5:34 p.m. a tornado with winds >200 mph struck Joplin, Missouri, injuring approximately 1,000 persons and causing 159 deaths. On June 3, a local physician notified the Springfield-Greene County Health Department and the Missouri Department of Health and Senior Services (MODHSS) of two patients hospitalized with tornado injuries who had suspected necrotizing fungal soft-tissue infections. MODHSS initiated active surveillance for such infections at hospitals and laboratories serving patients injured in the tornado, and CDC began assisting MODHSS with identification of fungal isolates. By June 10, eight patients with necrotizing fungal soft-tissue wound infections caused by Mucormycetes (formerly Zygomycetes) were identified. On June 14, a CDC field team arrived in Missouri to assist with the onsite investigation.

As of July 19, a total of 18 suspected cases of cutaneous mucormycosis had been identified, of which 13 were confirmed. A confirmed case was defined as 1) necrotizing soft-tissue infection requiring antifungal treatment or surgical debridement in a person injured in the tornado, 2) with illness onset on or after May 22, and 3) positive fungal culture or histopathology and genetic sequencing consistent with a Mucormycete. No additional cases have been reported since June 17.

The field team reviewed medical charts to describe the 13 confirmed cases. The median age of the patients was 48 years (range: 13–76 years); seven were female, and all were white. Injuries sustained during the tornado included lacerations (12 patients), fractures (11), and blunt trauma (nine). The 13 patients had an average of four wounds documented in the medical chart when they were examined at the emergency department. Post-trauma wound management included surgical debridement for all 13 patients and removal of a foreign body from six. Wooden splinters were the most common foreign body, found in the wounds of four patients. Two patients had diabetes, and none were immunocompromised. Ten patients required admission to an intensive-care unit, and five died.

CDC received 48 clinical specimens, including 32 fungal isolates and 16 tissue blocks collected from wounds for microscopic evaluation, immunohistochemical staining, and DNA sequencing; specimens from all 13 patients yielded the Mucormycete Apophysomyces trapeziformis. Further laboratory and epidemiologic studies are ongoing, including case-control studies to evaluate risk factors for infection.

Cutaneous mucormycosis is a rare infection caused by fungi of the order Mucorales, which typically are found in soil and decaying wood and other organic matter. Although cutaneous mucormycosis often is opportunistic, affecting patients with diabetes, hematologic malignancy or solid organ transplant (1), A. trapeziformis often is associated with immunocompetent hosts after traumatic implantation of fungal spores (2). The case-fatality rate for cutaneous mucormycosis has ranged from 29% to 83%, depending on severity of disease and underlying medical condition of the patient (1). Early diagnosis, aggressive surgical debridement, and administration of systemic antifungals have been associated with improved outcomes (1).

Cutaneous mucormycosis has been reported after previous natural disasters (3,4); however, this is the first known cluster occurring after a tornado. None of the infections were found in persons cleaning up debris.

Health-care providers should consider environmental fungi as potential causes of necrotizing soft-tissue infections in patients injured during tornadoes and initiate early treatment for suspected infections. Additional information is available at http://www.cdc.gov/mucormycosis.

NWS Central Region Service Assessment
Joplin, Missouri, Tornado – May 22, 2011

U.S. DEPARTMENT OF COMMERCE

National Oceanic and Atmospheric Administration

National Weather Service, Central Region Headquarters

Kansas City, MO

July 2011

Cover Photographs

Left: NOAA Radar image of Joplin Tornado. Right: Aftermath of Joplin, MO, tornado courtesy of Jennifer Spinney, Research Associate, University of Oklahoma, Social Science Woven into Meteorology.

Preface

On May 22, 2011, one of the deadliest tornadoes in United States history struck Joplin, Missouri, directly killing 158 people and injuring over 1,000. The tornado, rated EF-5 on the Enhanced Fujita Scale, with maximum winds over 200 mph, affected a significant part of a city with a population of more than 50,000 and a population density near 1,500 people per square mile. As a result, the Joplin tornado was the first single tornado in the United States to result in over 100 fatalities since the Flint, Michigan, tornado of June 8, 1953.

Because of the rarity and historical significance of this event, a regional Service Assessment team was formed to examine warning and forecast services provided by the National Weather Service. Furthermore, because of the large number of fatalities that resulted from a warned tornado event, this Service Assessment will provide additional focus on dissemination, preparedness, and warning response within the community as they relate to NWS services.

Service Assessments provide a valuable contribution to ongoing efforts by the National Weather Service to improve the quality, timeliness, and value of our products and services. Findings and recommendations from this assessment will improve techniques, products, services, and information provided to our partners and the American public.

Lynn P. Maximuk
Director, Central Region
National Weather Service

July 2011

Executive Summary

On May 22, 2011, one of the most devastating tornadoes in the nation's history directly killed 158 people and injured over 1,000 in Joplin, Missouri. From a National Weather Service (NWS) perspective, this was essentially a "warned" event in that advance notice of the tornado was given, critical information was communicated and received, and most people sought the best shelter available to them. The timely actions of the "weather enterprise" (NWS, media, emergency management), and the eventual response of local businesses, churches, schools, and the general public undoubtedly saved many lives.

The NWS Springfield Weather Forecast Office was wellprepared and performed in an exemplary manner in both its provision of services and its application of scientific expertise. The professionalism and dedication of the staff members is clearly a credit to the communities they serve.

Still, to learn what more can be done to help reduce fatalities from strong and violent tornadoes, the assessment team examined relevant issues ranging from internal NWS warning operations to dissemination strategies to public warning response. To help accomplish this, nearly 100 interviews were conducted in Joplin with tornado survivors, local businesses, media, emergency management, NWS staff, city officials, and others.

Many of the key findings within this report involved societal aspects of warning response and risk perception. Responding to warnings is not a simple act of stimulus-response, rather it is a non-linear, multi-step, complex process. Relationships between false alarms, public complacency, and warning credibility are highly complex as well.

The vast majority of Joplin residents did not immediately take protective action upon receiving a first indication of risk (usually via the local siren system), regardless of the source of the warning. Most chose to further assess their risk by waiting for, actively seeking, and filtering additional information.

The reasons for doing so were quite varied, but largely depended on an individual's "worldview" formed mostly by previous experience with severe weather. Most importantly, the *perceived* frequency of siren activation in Joplin led the majority of survey participants to become desensitized or complacent to this method of warning. This suggests that *initial* siren activations in Joplin (and severe weather warnings in general) have lost a degree of credibility for most residents – one of the most valued characteristics for successful risk communication.

Instead, the majority of Joplin residents did not take protective action until processing additional credible confirmation of the threat and its magnitude from a non-routine, extraordinary risk trigger. This was generally achieved in different ways, including physical observation of the tornado, seeing or hearing confirmation, and urgency of the threat on radio or television, and/or hearing a second, non-routine siren alert.

This report suggests that in order to improve warning response and mitigate user complacency, the NWS should explore evolving the warning system to better support effective decision making. This evolution should utilize a simple, impact-based, tiered information structure that promotes warning credibility and empowers individuals to quickly make appropriate decisions in the face of adverse conditions. Such a system should:

a. provide a non-routine warning mechanism that prompts people to take immediate life-saving action in extreme events like strong and violent tornadoes

b. be impact-based more than phenomenon-based for clarity on risk assessment

c. be compatible with NWS technological, scientific, and operational capabilities

d. be compatible with external local warning systems and emerging mobile communications technology

e. be easily understood and calibrated by the public to facilitate decision making

f. maintain existing "probability of detection" for severe weather events

g. diminish the perception of false alarms and their impacts on credibility

While the weather enterprise was generally successful in communicating the Joplin tornado threat in a timely manner, current communication and delivery mechanisms are not seamless and are somewhat antiquated. Specifically, many warning dissemination systems are not fully compatible with specific warning information provided by storm-based warning polygons—occasionally resulting in untimely gaps and confusion during dissemination. To improve the warning dissemination system and provide a more coordinated warning message, the NWS should continue to advance the development and cultivate the use of GPS-based mobile communications technologies and Emergency Alert System/NOAA Weather Radio upgrades.

Last, an important impediment to heightening the urgency of the severe weather message from the Weather Forecast Office was the WSR-88D Volume Coverage Pattern strategies available to forecasters. Low level rotational intensification and tornado genesis occurred very rapidly as the storm approached Joplin. Limited scans (every 5 minutes) at the lowest elevations slices likely impacted the WFO ability to quickly ascertain the magnitude of the event. To enhance the ability to monitor rapid tornado genesis, the NWS should develop and implement additional Volume Coverage Pattern strategies that allow for more continuous sampling near the surface (e.g., 1-minute lowest elevation sampling).

Table of Contents

1. Introduction and Background

On May 22, 2011, one of the most devastating tornadoes in the nation's history directly killed 158[1] people and injured over 1,000 in Joplin, Missouri. The Joplin tornado was the first single tornado to result in over 100 fatalities since the June 8, 1953, Flint, Michigan, tornado.

The tornado was rated EF-5 on the Enhanced-Fujita Scale, with its maximum winds estimated at more than 200 mph. The path of the entire tornado was 22.1 miles long and was up to 1 mile in width. The EF-4/EF-5 damage path was roughly 6 miles long from near Schifferdecker Avenue along the western portions of Joplin to near Interstate 44 east of Joplin, and generally ½ to ¾ of a mile wide along the path (Figure 1).

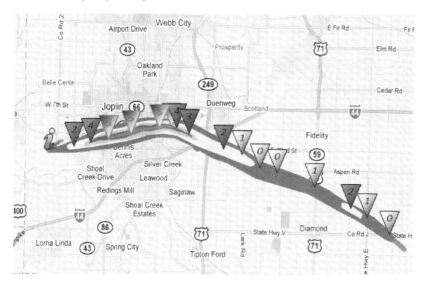

Figure 1: Storm Track and Intensities for May 22, 2011, Joplin Tornado

Because this was a warned event with an unusually high number of fatalities, this Service Assessment was initiated for the primary purpose of learning what more could be done to further limit fatalities and injuries from EF-4/EF-5 tornadoes. To this end, the assessment focus was on communication, dissemination, community preparedness, and the public warning response leading into and during the event. The assessment team interviewed over 60 survivors; local emergency management for Joplin and surrounding areas; local print, radio, and television media; NWS employees; Joplin city officials; fire and law enforcement dispatchers; and employees and patrons from area businesses, schools, and hospitals. In total, this was nearly 100

---

[1] As of the date of this report, there were 158 direct fatalities and 4 indirect fatalities (updated 12/5/2011 to reduce direct fatalities by 1).

interviews. This report attempts to synthesize the most common responses, and occasionally highlight other responses that offer important insights.

Not surprisingly, there was a full spectrum of responses on most key interview points, especially on issues concerning how people perceived and responded to warnings. For example, some people took shelter in appropriate locations, but did not survive. Others mistakenly drove their vehicles into the tornado path, but somehow lived to tell of it.

Also, while these interviews and the assessment efforts sought insights on how to reduce violent tornado fatalities, it is worth noting that the actions of the "weather enterprise"[2], local businesses, churches, schools, and the general public undoubtedly saved many lives on May 22, 2011. Generally speaking, advance warning of the tornado was given, information was communicated and received, and most people sought the best shelter available to them. It is difficult to quantify these impacts and place them in historical context with other comparable tornadoes.

Several key decision points along the warning and response timeline are referred to throughout this report. As background, these are listed below in Table 1, Figure 2 (tornado warning polygons) and Appendix A (radar observations).

130 pm CDT – NWS/SPC Tornado Watch issued for Southwest Missouri in effect until 900 pm CDT
509 pm CDT - WFO Springfield Tornado Warning Polygon #30 issued for Western Jasper County MO (including northeastern Joplin) in effect until 600 pm CDT
511 pm CDT – Initial 3 minute siren alert sounded for Jasper County and Joplin
517 pm CDT – WFO Springfield Tornado Warning Polygon #31 issued for southwest Jasper County MO (and Joplin), northwest Newton County MO and southeast Cherokee County (KS) in effect until 600 pm CDT
534 pm CDT – Approximate initial Tornado touchdown ½ mile southwest of JJ Highway and Newton Road (southwest of Joplin City limits)
538 pm CDT – Second 3 minute siren alert sounded for Jasper County and Joplin. EF-4 Damage begins as tornado approaches Schifferdecker Avenue in western Joplin
548 pm CDT – WFO Springfield Tornado Warning Polygon #32 issued for southern Jasper County MO (including Joplin), northern Newton County MO and western Lawrence County MO in effect until 630 pm CDT

Table 1: Key Timeline of Events for Joplin Tornado Event

---
[2] Throughout this report, "weather enterprise-'" refers collectively to NWS, media, and emergency management.

2

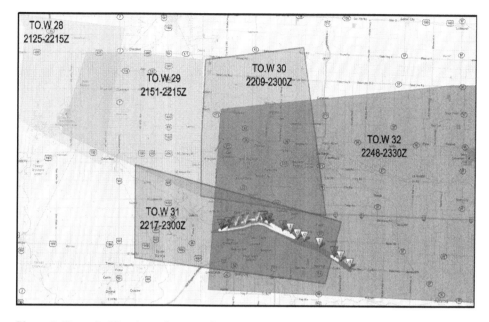

Figure 2: Tornado Warning polygons prior to and during the Joplin tornado and the tornado damage path

2. Societal Aspects of Risk Perception and Warning Response

A major portion of the Joplin Tornado Service Assessment was dedicated to understanding the societal response to NWS warnings and external local warning systems. The Service Assessment team went to Joplin, Missouri, between June 7-9, 2011, to interview residents about how they received, processed, and responded to the warnings leading up to the May 22 tornado.

Finding #1: *Recent NWS Assessments have addressed societal impacts of warnings, most notably the "Super Tuesday Tornado Outbreak of Feb. 5-6, 2008" and the "Mother's Day Weekend Tornado Outbreak of 2008." Many of the societal impacts uncovered in previous Service Assessments were also evident in Joplin, suggesting the NWS should take a more aggressive stance in addressing warning response.*

Recommendation #1: *For future Service Assessments, NWS should plan a more structured approach to collecting information on societal aspects of warning response. This should include developing subteams well-versed in social science and NWS warning operations that can be quickly deployed to the field following any given severe weather disaster.*

a. METHODOLOGY

In order to meet the Assessment objectives, the team utilized ethnographic methods or techniques commonly used by social scientists to scientifically describe cultures and the people within these cultures[3]. In particular, the team strove to understand residents' points of views regarding the process of warning reception to warning response, and how decisions were made.

The team carried out a series[4] of semi-structured interviews with residents and local businesses: in-person, over the phone, or in group settings. Semistructured interviewing is a method of inquiry based on the use of an interview guide to provide consistency between interviewers, providing a menu of questions or topics that need to be covered in a particular order.This method is useful in situations where interviewers have only one opportunity to conduct an interview. Questions for this Assessment were formulated in such a way as to minimize the influence of the interviewer, and perhaps most importantly, to allow each person to define the content of the discussion they felt was important.

The findings in this Service Assessment represent a local case study, meaning that the societal responses to warnings that are described in this Assessment are meant to reflect the trends present in this particular sample. Because of limited sample size and distribution, interview responses are largely characterized in general terms, and occasionally in specific terms to highlight useful insights.

b. RISK SIGNALS: RECEIVING AND UNDERSTANDING THE WARNING

Response to severe weather warnings is a complex, non-linear process depending on perception of risk. Perception of risk is influenced first and foremost by the method in which the risk is communicated. The warnings, or risk signals[5], that aroused Joplin residents' attention, prompted their belief in the threat of the tornado and informed their decisions to act included, in no particular order: broadcasts made on television and radio, NWS watches and warnings obtained via commercial and government web pages, the activation and deactivation of the 1st siren, the activation of the 2nd siren; text messages, posts to social media networking sites, information transmitted over NOAA Weather Radio (NWR), observations of the physical environment, and messages from family, friends, neighbors, and coworkers. Each of these signals, independently or in combination, were processed in varying ways over differing amounts of time, heightening

---

[3] Spradley, James P. (1979) *The ethnographic interview*. New York: Holt, Rinehart and Winston (17)

[4] The results shared in this section of the report are based on the perspectives of 54 residents of Joplin. Nine of the 63 interviews were not included because they were either second-hand accounts, wind interfered with the audio recording, or the interview did not contain relevant data.

[5] Kasperson, Jeanne X., Roger E. Kasperson, Nick Pidgeon, and Paul Slovic (2003). The social amplification of risk: assessing fifteen years of research and theory. In The Social Amplification of Risk. N. Pidgeon, R. E. Kasperson and P. Slovic. (eds). Cambridge, UK: Cambridge University Press. Pp. 13-46.

or diminishing perceptions of threat.

Finding #2a: *For the majority of surveyed Joplin residents, the first risk signal for an imminent severe weather threat came via the local community siren system. As a result, there was a significant degree of ambiguity associated with the first alert regarding the magnitude of the risk, the seriousness of the warning, and its potential impact.*

This did not necessarily mean that residents exclusively relied on these systems for their weather information, only that the sirens were their first indication of a risk.

In Joplin, it is community policy to sound sirens when either a tornado is reported to be moving toward Joplin or severe thunderstorm winds are expected to exceed 75 mph. These triggers may or may not be associated with an NWS warning, and the Jasper County/Joplin Emergency Manager has discretion and uses professional judgment on when to activate sirens. These types of local warning system policies are by no means unique to Joplin.

Once the decision is made to activate sirens, they are sounded in one, 3-minute burst and then shut off. For those that used the sirens as the initial alert tool, there was no way to immediately discern the magnitude and nature of the threat, or its potential impact. This lack of information makes it difficult for warning recipients to calibrate the severity of the situation, thus delaying their response. Also, several of those interviewed expressed confusion associated with the single 3-minute siren alert, thinking the threat was over once the sirens had ceased.

Conceptually, warnings could be defined broadly as the number and combination of risk signals each person received and processed prior to their decision to take protective action.
The interviews indicated that individuals received anywhere between two and nine risk signals from the time they were aware of the possibility of severe weather to the time they engaged in protective action. This drastic difference is explained by a) the differing lengths of time that passed from first indication of threat to taking protective action, b) the differing ways individuals received risk signals and interpreted the situation as threatening, and c) the effect of conflicting risk signals.

The number of signals between first indication of severe weather and protective action markedly increased as information became conflicted or unclear. In the most extreme example, one resident's interview indicated nine risk signals identified before taking protective action:

1. Aware that thunderstorms were probably going to happen
2. Noticed the weather changing outside
3. Heard the 1st siren while driving to restaurant (approximately 30-minute lead time)
4. Restaurant shut doors and disallowed entry
5. Drove to a 2nd restaurant where business was carrying on as usual
6. Noticed the weather changing
7. Reports came from TV and radio

8. Patron indicated tornado in Joplin
9. Management instructed protective action

In this example, signals 4 and 5 are significant in that they heightened and diminished this resident's perception of risk, respectively. Once the restaurant shut its doors and refused entry, this resident perceived the threat of severe weather as real and commented during the interview that he did not want to be in his car. Upon arriving at another restaurant close by, however, his perception of threat was diminished because business at this second establishment was carrying on as normal: he was escorted to a table and ordered a meal.

c. PERCEPTION, PROCESSING AND PERSONALIZING THE THREAT

Finding #2b: *The majority of surveyed Joplin residents did not immediately go to shelter upon hearing the initial warning, whether from local warning sirens, television, NWR, or other sources. Instead, most chose to further clarify and assess their risk by waiting for, actively seeking, and filtering additional information.*

In order to gain a sense for how social models of understanding influenced perceptions of risk and warning response, particular attention was paid to the "worldviews" held by residents. Worldview[6] is defined as an overall perspective of how people interpret their environment or the world around them – and is generally informed by things like one's experience, education, and cultural values.

Interviews showed aspects of worldview that influenced risk perception and warning response included: previous experiences with tornadoes, apathy, familiarity with seasonal weather patterns in southwest Missouri, optimism bias, perceived frequency of siren activation in Joplin, social networks as mechanisms for warning dissemination, avid fear of tornadoes, and the number of deadly tornadoes earlier in the year.

Previous experiences with tornadoes were shown to have an influence in the way residents perceived their risk and responded to the warnings. As one resident indicated, the tornado he experienced prepared him mentally for appropriate response action during this event. Another resident commented that time spent in Oklahoma City made him complacent to the possibility of a tornado in Joplin.

Similarly, familiarity with seasonal weather in southwest Missouri played a major role in risk perception and warning response. Most individuals commented that severe weather in southwest Missouri during spring is common; however, tornadoes never affect Joplin or themselves

---

[6] Roncoli, Carla, Keith Ingram, Christine Jost and Paul Kirshen (2003) "Meteorological Meanings: Farmer's interpretation of seasonal rainfall forecasts in Burkina, Faso." In Weather, climate, culture. S. Strauss and B. Orlove (eds). Oxford; New York: Berghahn Books. Pp. 181-200.

personally. It was common in the interviews to hear residents refer to "storms always blowing over and missing Joplin," or that there seemed like there was a "protective bubble" around Joplin, or "there is rotation all the time, but never in Joplin.". One city employee stated, "… don't think it can't happen in your community, because that's what I thought." This sense in which people believe their personal risk from a hazard is less than the risk faced by others is referred to as optimism bias and can lead to diminished perceptions of threat and influence response.

Although not as common, social networks as mechanisms for warning dissemination were found to generally amplify perceptions of risk and lead to warning response. For example, one woman reported eating dinner with family, receiving a text message about the tornado, and then receiving a phone call shortly after informing her of a storm travelling through Joplin. This heightened the woman's belief that a threat existed and prompted her and her family members to take shelter at the restaurant.

Similar to seasonal weather patterns, the perceived frequency of siren activation (false alarms) led a large number of participants to become desensitized or complacent to this method of warning. Many noted that they "hear sirens all the time[sirens] go off for dark clouds," they are "bombarded with [sirens] so often that we don't pay attention," "the sirens have gone off so many times before," "sirens are sounded even for thunderstorms," and "all sirens mean is there is a little more water in the gutter."

The diminished severity or absence of a threat (complacency) held by Joplin residents can be understood as resulting from their normalization of the threat. Normalized responses toward severe impacts are likely to occur in groups frequently exposed to hazardous weather[7]. The same could be said for residents in Joplin who, based on their perceived frequent exposure to local warning systems (and NWS warnings) during spring, normalized their reactions to the activation of the first siren and characterized it as just another aspect of springtime in Joplin.

Finding #2c: *Familiarity with severe weather and the perceived frequency of siren activation not only reflect normalization of threat and or desensitization to sirens and warnings, but they also establish that initial siren activation has lost a degree of credibility for many residents. Credibility is considered to be one of the most valued characteristics for effective risk communication[8].*

---

[7] Bankoff, Greg (2007) 'Living with risk; coping with disasters: hazard as frequent life experience in the Philippines'. Education about Asia. 12(2): 26-29

[8] Trumbo, Craig W., and Katherine A. McComas (2003) "The functionality of credibility in information processing for risk perception." Risk Analysis 23(2): 343-353.

It should be noted that stakeholders in the warning process, such as media or Emergency Managers, were less likely to think over-warning or desensitization to NWS warnings was an issue. During interviews, Emergency Managers in particular felt the frequency of warnings was appropriate, while media staff were split with some saying "most warnings were 'cry wolf,'", while others emphasized the importance of advance warning for all tornadoes regardless of false alarms. In general, these groups have a sense of obligation for the safety of their constituents which influences their worldview of the warning process and risk perception.

TRIGGERS FOR DECISIONS TO ACT

Though risk signals tended to elevate awareness, there were certain signals that stood out, added important credibility to the warning, and acted as triggers in prompting a belief in the threat and taking protective action.

Finding #2d: *The majority of surveyed Joplin residents did not take protective action until receiving and processing credible confirmation of the threat and its magnitude from a non-routine trigger.*

While searching for additional information concerning the severe weather threat constitutes "taking an action," the actions many residents described taking were not the immediate life-saving measures desired with the issuance of a tornado warning. In most cases, these life-saving actions, or the decision to find shelter, were associated with additional extraordinary risk signals. This was generally achieved in different ways, including:

a. Physical observation of the environment (seeing the tornado approach).

   While significant numbers of people actually did this, the approach was complicated by having a "rain-wrapped" tornado that made the tornado more difficult to recognize until it was very close. There were numerous accounts of people running to shelter in their homes just as the tornado struck, despite significant advance warning of the risk.

b. Seeing or hearing confirmation of the threat on radio or television, seeing the large tornado on the air, or hearing on-air instructions to "take cover now."

   When the tornado began moving into Joplin, most local electronic media switched to "wall-to-wall" coverage of the event, which included live video from tower-cams. As coverage quickly evolved, and the magnitude of the event became clear, on-air commentators implored those in the path to take cover immediately. This kind of media coverage helped convey the seriousness and urgency of the situation, and prompted many listeners and viewers to find shelter.

c. Hearing a second, non-routine, siren alert at approximately 538 pm CDT.

It is the Joplin emergency management policy to sound the sirens onetime for a severe weather alert. Because of the length of time that had elapsed since the initial siren alert, and as reports came into central dispatch of a tornado moving into Joplin, the Emergency Manager made the decision to activate the local warning sirens a second time. This second siren activation came about 20 minutes after WFO Springfield issued the Tornado Warning for southwestern Jasper County, including Joplin (issued at 517 pm CDT). A large number of those interviewed noted that this non-routine second siren alert raised their level of awareness, confirmed the alert, indicated the seriousness of the warning, and prompted them to get to the best available shelter.

It is unclear how many of those killed in the tornado failed to take shelter, or if a change in response time and behavior would have impacted survival rates. In the case of the Joplin tornado, it was somewhat fortunate that the tornado was moving at a relatively slow forward speed (~20 mph), and the initial siren alert occurred more than 20 minutes before the tornado struck the city.

Lastly, several of the people interviewed indicated a desire for different levels of warning (applied to local siren policies) as a means to clarify the seriousness/magnitude of the threat. Specifically, these comments spoke to some desired differentiation in warnings and siren tones between life-threatening emergencies and threats to property. These persons noted, "maybe there should be two levels of warning... a regular warning and a panic button warning for when it will be really bad," "I wonder if there shouldn't be different types of sirens for different types of warnings," and another noted that there is a difference between a warned big event and a warned small tornado or funnel cloud.

TAKING PROTECTIVE ACTIONS

After processing a variable number of risk signals and reaching a decision to act, the majority of surveyed Joplin residents took shelter in the most appropriate location available to them. This included basements, interior rooms or hallways, or crawl spaces. This suggests campaigns to promote severe weather safety practices are effective.

Even if this action was taken in the last available seconds, in many cases it was a life-saving measure. Unfortunately, due to a number of factors, below ground shelters (basements) are not common in the Joplin area, and some people likely still found themselves in situations that were not survivable. It is unclear to what degree this contributed to the tornado mortality in Joplin. Preliminary analysis done by the Joplin Globe newspaper revealed that most fatalities occurred in residences (54%), followed by non-residential buildings (32%), and in vehicles or outdoors (14%). This type of analysis is beyond the scope of the Service Assessment and is being addressed in separate studies by both the National Institutes of Standards and Technology and Federal Emergency Management Agency.

The majority of businesses interviewed had a plan for receiving warnings and sheltering patrons. While lives were lost in these non-residential buildings, the toll certainly would have been much higher if not for the action plans and employees in these businesses.

In addition, a significant number of fatalities in Joplin occurred in vulnerable populations such as the elderly, infirm, or disabled. These populations typically require additional time and/or assistance to get to the best available shelter.

Best Practice #1: *NWS outreach and severe weather safety education programs should continue to emphasize and assist area businesses with severe weather safety action plans via the StormReady program or other similar mechanisms. This kind of outreach and planning assistance should also be extended to vulnerable populations in nursing homes, group homes, hospitals, etc.*

d. CONCLUSIONS

Responding to warnings is not a simple act of stimulus-response, rather it is a non-linear, multi-step, complex process. Relationships between false alarms, public complacency, and warning credibility are highly complex as well. While residents of Joplin addressed these in terms of local warning siren systems, they also relate directly to the content and skill of NWS warnings and the weather enterprise as a whole. As a rudimentary evaluation of NWS warning skill, severe weather verification statistics were compiled for the period from 10/1/2007 to 4/1/2011. These are listed in Table 2.

	Probability of Detection	False Alarm Rate	Initial Lead Time
All Tornado	70%	76%	12.5 minutes
All Severe	83%	46%	18.6 minutes
EF0-1 Tornado	68%	NA	11.9 minutes
EF2-5 Tornado	84%	NA	16.3 minutes
EF3-5 Tornado	94%	NA	17.8 minutes

Table 2: NWS Severe Weather Warning verification statistics from 10/1/2007–4/1/2011

Finding #2e: *Nationally, 76% of all NWS Tornado Warnings, in their totality, are false alarms. This means 24% of all tornado warnings are eventually associated with an observed tornado – indicating limited skill in differentiating between tornadic and non-tornadic events; however, 68% of EF0-1 tornadoes receive advance warning of near 12 minutes, while 94% of EF3-5 tornadoes receive advance warning of near 18 minutes, indicating an ability to better detect strong/violent tornadoes.[9] Just over half (54%) of all severe weather warnings coincide with a*

---

[9] Because NWS warnings do not differentiate between weak and strong/violent tornado warnings, a calculation of false alarm rate for strong/violent tornadoes is not possible.

severe weather event, indicating moderate skill in distinguishing between severe and non-severe thunderstorms.

While there are no guarantees that simply decreasing false alarms will significantly impact warning response behavior, the results of the Joplin residents interviews appear to indicate a relationship between perceived false alarms, degree of warning credibility, and complacency in warning response. Nonetheless, as indicated by the report findings, there are a number of ways NWS can explore to improve effective decision making within the warning response process.

Recommendation #2: *To improve severe weather warning response and mitigate user complacency, the NWS should explore evolving the warning system to better support effective decision making. This evolution should utilize a simple, impact-based, tiered information structure that promotes warning credibility and empowers individuals to quickly make appropriate decisions in the face of adverse conditions. This structure should:*

a) *lessen the number of risk signals processed before protective action is taken (finding 2b)*
b) *provide a non-routine warning mechanism that prompts people to take immediate life-saving action in extreme events like strong and violent tornadoes (finding 2d).*
c) *be impact-based more than phenomenon-based for clarity on risk assessment (finding 2a)*
d) *be compatible with NWS technological, scientific, and operational capabilities (finding 2e)*
e) *be compatible with external local warning systems and emerging mobile communications technology (finding 2a)*
f) *be easily understood and calibrated by the public to facilitate decision making (finding 2a)*
g) *maintain existing "probability of detection" for severe weather events (finding 2e)*
h) *diminish the perception of false alarms and their impacts on warning credibility and response (finding 2c)*

3. Warning Communications, Dissemination, and Community Preparedness

The communication and dissemination of warning information during the Joplin tornado event was complex and involved the cooperation of several partners, as well as a variety of different systems. For this portion of the assessment, numerous interviews were conducted with local media, emergency management, local fire and law enforcement dispatch, and WFO Springfield staff. Also, as part of the evaluation, a well-attended media round-table meeting was held at the local Joplin television stations. These entities constitute much of the local weather dissemination enterprise, or weather enterprise.

STORM-BASED WARNINGS AND LOCAL WARNING DISSEMINATION SYSTEMS
While the weather enterprise was generally successful in communicating the threat in a timely

manner for the Joplin tornado, current communication and dissemination mechanisms are not seamless and are somewhat antiquated. This can lead to untimely gaps and confusion during dissemination.

Storm-based warnings are an important feature of the warning process, and are designed to limit the "false alarm area" associated with severe weather warnings. All of the partners interviewed preferred storm-based warnings (also referred to as warning polygons), because of the more specific information they provide; however, while more specific, communicating storm-based warning information comes with challenges within the current dissemination infrastructure.

Finding # 3: *Many current warning dissemination systems are not fully compatible with specific warning information provided by storm-based, warning polygons.*

Recommendation # 3: *The NWS should continue to collaborate with partners who disseminate weather information to advance GPS-based warning dissemination systems that are compatible with more specific storm-based warning information. This change should include cultivating use of mobile communications technologies (text messaging, smart phone apps, Commercial Mobile Alert System, etc.) and technological upgrades of the Emergency Alert System (EAS) and NWR.*

One local media outlet in Joplin reported some success using text messaging and social media (e.g., Facebook) as a method of disseminating warning information and receiving storm reports from residents. In addition, most television stations reported using their Facebook accounts to deliver and receive weather information, including warnings and storm reports; however, among residents interviewed in the field, only a small number stated that this was how they primarily received the warnings.

Many current dissemination systems are based on geo-political boundaries and jurisdictions (e.g., counties), including EAS and NWR. This can inadvertently project a sense of over-warning or confusion for the general public when warning polygons overlap or multiple warning polygons are issued for a county. For better or worse, NWR and EAS alerted Jasper County (and Joplin) residents twice within a 10-minute period for tornado warning polygon #30 at 509 pm and polygon #31 at 517 pm CDT (Figure 2).

These same considerations can impact other dissemination modes as well. Some NWS partners in the Joplin area have adapted their local warning systems in an attempt to be more specific, avoid confusion, and avoid possible warning fatigue created by multiple polygons over the same geographic area. Emergency Managers in Jasper and surrounding counties have local warning instructions that are based on reports and local discretion, and are not necessarily tied to NWS warnings.

For Joplin specifically, sirens were activated twice, based on reports rather than NWS warnings.

According to the Emergency Manager, the first 3-minute siren activation, at 511 pm CDT, resulted primarily from funnel cloud reports to the west of Joplin in southeastern Kansas. This activation roughly coincided with the 509 pm CDT issuance of tornado warning polygon #30 for a different thunderstorm cell affecting western Jasper County (and northeastern Joplin). According to some interviews, slight confusion was created because of this overlap. Residents heard the initial siren activation and then the warning details for polygon #30, and assumed the activation was for the area to the north.

In one example, a man was clearly confused by the string of warning information he received and processed from various sources.

1. Heard first sirens at 511 pm CDT (estimated 30-35 minutes before tornado hit).
2. Went to the TV and heard NWR warning from TV override that indicated tornado near airport drive 7 miles north (polygon #30) of his location.
3. Went on porch with family and had a cigar. Looked like a regular thunderstorm.
4. Heard second sirens (estimated 27 minutes later).
5. Thought something wasn't right so went inside and turned local TV stations on.
6. Saw on TV several colored counties for tornado warnings, but regular programming was still on and thought the threat was still to the north.
7. Heard his wife yell "basement," grabbed the cat and told son to put his shoes on.
8. Tornado hit as they reached the top of the basement stairs, destroying their home.

NWS tornado warning polygon #31 was not issued for southwest Jasper County, including all of Joplin proper, until 517 pm CDT. Yet, because the sirens already had been sounded once, there was hesitation to do so again. Once reports were received of a tornado on the ground, the sirens were reactivated in Joplin at 538 pm CDT. While this prompted many people to action, by that time, the tornado was moving into western portions of the city and had started to produce EF-4 damage.

Additionally, television meteorologists combined polygon warnings on air in an attempt to simplify the warning situation. Since tornado warning polygons #30 and #31 overlapped, covered portions of Jasper County, and both expired at 600 pm EDT, local television meteorologists combined the multiple tornado warnings into a broadcast summary. While the television meteorologists also prefer the specific information associated with warning polygons, they sometimes find it difficult to communicate the threats when multiple polygons overlap (Figure 2).

Finding # 4: *Partners adapt weather and warning information in their local warning systems in an attempt to communicate risk simply and unobtrusively. The result is sometimes a poorly coordinated warning message across the weather enterprise that can lead to confusing or mixed* *messages.*

Recommendation # 4: *The NWS should collaborate with partners throughout the weather enterprise to provide a better coordinated warning message. Guidance should be developed to assist partners in the development of local warning system and siren strategies that work in conjunction with NWS warnings rather than independent of them.*

Because of compatibility issues between NWS warning strategies and antiquated dissemination systems, NWS forecasters also need to remain cognizant of the service issues that occasionally may arise from their warning polygons.

NWSCHAT AS A COORDINATION TOOL

Many NWS partners, particularly Emergency Managers and television media, emphasized the interaction with WFO Springfield during the storm using NWSChat. They almost unanimously commented on how the interaction with WFO Springfield and surrounding WFOs was enhanced by the chat room and provided valuable information during the event. This communication link enabled them to make timely, accurate decisions at the local level.

Best Practice #2: *NWSChat should continue to be supported and encouraged as a valuable communication tool amongst the weather enterprise team members.*

Finding #5: *Because the Joplin/southwest Missouri area lies near the intersection of multiple NWS County Warning Areas , there was some difficulty noted by NWS partners in following chats from many different offices.*

Recommendation #5 : *The NWS should continue to improve collaboration tools for our partners. Partners requested improvements to the current NWSChat display to include a "dashboard" interface to allow them to more easily monitor multiple offices at the same time.*

COMMUNITY PREPAREDNESS

By most all accounts, WFO Springfield has a solid working relationship with various partners in and around the Joplin area. This relationship has been enhanced from the roughly two dozen outreach and spotter training events in the last year that were conducted in Joplin and surrounding areas.

The city of Joplin is also a StormReady community. The Emergency Manager and city officials were interviewed about the StormReady process and the application was reviewed with them. In general, the StormReady program was a positive experience for the city and aided them in preparation for this storm event. The process highlighted the need for community leaders to help develop severe weather plans for businesses, schools, hospitals, and other entities. Several large businesses and public venues were struck during this tornado, with each facility having a varied degree of preparedness. The StormReady program could be a useful vehicle for facilitating increased interaction with local businesses and public venues to develop severe weather plans within communities.

Finding #6: *The StormReady renewal application for the city of Joplin had some discrepancies and incomplete information. WFO Springfield does not have a StormReady Advisory Board that consists of any individuals outside the local office.*

Recommendation #6: *NWS needs to maintain a credible structure to the StormReady program, including local advisory boards, and adhere to established criteria for StormReady certifications.*

4. WFO Springfield Products and Services

WFO Springfield issued a well-integrated product and service suite before, during, and after the tornado. These products and services allowed for advance planning by the general public and emergency management community, provided for effective and accurate warnings well in advance of the tornado, and undoubtedly saved numerous lives.

Hazardous Weather Outlooks (HWO) were issued frequently on Friday, May 20, and Saturday, May 21, and were consistent in notifying NWS users of potential severe thunderstorms for Sunday, May 22, for the Joplin area. A consistent message was also delivered on Friday and Saturday mornings via multimedia web briefings (MMWB) and website graphics. At that point, WFO Springfield was focused on large hail and damaging straight-line winds as the main severe weather threats, although isolated tornadoes were mentioned in all of the products.

The Area Forecast Discussion (AFD) issued at 235 am CDT on Sunday, May 22, included an excellent section addressing the expected severe thunderstorm development and evolution for the afternoon and evening hours. In this AFD, forecasters continued to focus on very large hail as the primary threat for later in the day, but continued to maintain a small tornado probability. The main objection to widespread tornado development was unfavorable lower level wind speed and direction forecast guidance. Once again, similar forecast and reasoning information were presented via HWO, MMWB and web graphic products created early Sunday morning.

By shift-change Sunday morning (8 am CDT) WFO forecasters recognized an increased threat for a more substantial severe weather outbreak later in the day and reflected that thinking with HWO and MMWB updates through the remainder of the morning hours. During this time, an important decision was made not to conduct a conference call with county and city Emergency Managers and media. WFO policy states that conference calls should be conducted when moderate or high confidence exists for a high impact event, such as widespread wind damage from derechos, or the possibility of damaging or otherwise long-track tornadoes. While confidence was high that very large hail would occur with some severe thunderstorms, forecaster confidence that significant tornadoes would occur was too low to justify a conference call. The Emergency Managers and members of the media interviewed following the tornado all agreed that conference calls held by WFO Springfield prompt them to increase their awareness and preparation for anticipated severe weather events and result in a greater dissemination of information throughout the community. All groups stressed that conference calls raise awareness more than MMWBs and suggested that WFO Springfield initiate calls for moderate or higher risks of severe weather. Although the content is essentially the same in the MMWB, the personal contact provided by the conference calls conveys a greater sense of urgency to weather situations.

Finding #7: *Conference calls provided by WFO Springfield play a critical role in heightening the preparedness levels of NWS partners and are requested by partners for scenarios with SPC Moderate Risk or greater.*

Recommendation #7: *The NWS should ensure that tools and procedures are in place for WFO operational staff to easily conduct conference calls with NWS partners. These calls should be provided in a consistent manner and associated with SPC Moderate Risk or greater.*

A series of complex meteorological events and interactions took place during the afternoon hours of May 22 that eventually resulted in the devastating EF-5 tornado. Forecasters at WFO Springfield discussed the ongoing and expected mesoscale evolution with an AFD issued at 107 pm CDT with a headline of "Mesoscale Convective Discussion." Shortly thereafter, Tornado Watch #325 was issued at 130 pm CDT for all of southwest Missouri. A routine AFD was issued at 237 pm as well as another "Mesoscale Convective Discussion AFD" issued at 347 pm, which also discussed the results of a special 19Z radiosonde observation (RAOB). These afternoon discussions were timely, well-written and did a good job of keeping all users up to date with the latest meteorological reasoning on imminent storm development and convective mode. Forecaster focus remained on very large hail as the main severe weather threat, but isolated tornadoes were also deemed a possibility due to the very unstable air mass in place and sufficient low level wind structure. Updated HWOs were also issued at 114 pm CDT and 347 pm CDT that included an upgrade in tornado probabilities.

Best Practice #3: *WFOs should issue non-routine AFDs to discuss ongoing and expected mesoscale feature evolution when severe thunderstorms are anticipated.*

The first thunderstorms of the day developed between 200 pm and 300 pm CDT over southeast

16

Kansas and quickly became severe, prompting Severe Thunderstorm Warnings from WFO Springfield. As severe storms moved east, forecasters became increasingly concerned about their tornado potential and issued the first Tornado Warnings of the day at 425 pm and 451 pm CDT for portions of Cherokee and Crawford Counties in southeast Kansas, west of Joplin. At 433 pm CDT, forecasters briefed the Jasper County (which encompasses Joplin) Emergency Manager on the severe storms to the west. Additional thunderstorms then developed to the east near the Kansas and Missouri border and also rapidly became severe. These were identified by forecasters as having high tornado potential. Tornado Warning #30 was issued for one of these storms at 509 pm CDT for western Jasper County, including the northeast part of the city of Joplin but was for a different storm than the one that eventually hit the city. This alert was followed by Tornado Warning #31 at 517 pm CDT for the next storm to the south for southwestern Jasper County and portions of neighboring counties which included all of Joplin. Another coordination call was made to the Jasper County Emergency Manager at 525 pm CDT to update him on the Tornado Warning and latest information concerning the storm. At this point, the severe thunderstorm west of Joplin had become the dominant thunderstorm in the region and was poised to produce a violent tornado.

Based on storm surveys and radar imagery, it was estimated that initial tornado touchdown occurred just west of Joplin at 534 pm CDT, moved into western portions of Joplin around 536 pm CDT and crossed Schifferdecker Avenue around 538 pm CDT. Thus, WFO Springfield issued Tornado Warning #31 with 17 minutes of lead time for touchdown and 19 minutes lead time before entering Joplin. The entire path of the tornado was encompassed by warning polygons.

Tornado Warning (#30) for Joplin was first updated with a Severe Weather Statement at 530 pm CDT that indicated the storm had a history of funnel clouds. The first indication of a confirmed tornado was issued via another Severe Weather Statement at 539 pm CDT that stated, *"At 534 pm CDT...trained weather spotters reported a tornado near Galena"* and that *"This storm is moving into the city of Joplin."* At 542 pm CDT, WFO Springfield issued another Severe Weather Statement that stated, *"At 538 pm CDT...trained weather spotters reported a tornado near Joplin."* This statement was followed by another Tornado Warning for southern Jasper County at 548 pm CDT in effect until 630 pm. This warning stated, *"At 543 pm CDT...trained weather spotters reported a tornado near eastern Joplin"* and *"damaging and multiple vortex tornado was reported with this storm."* This warning was followed with one Severe Weather Statement as the tornado moved southeast of Joplin and eventually dissipated around 612 pm CDT. Additionally, numerous Local Storm Reports were issued as the tornado moved through the city.

Despite being focused mainly on very large hail as the primary severe weather threat prior to thunderstorm development, warning forecasters did an outstanding job of recognizing the tornado potential of the storm that moved through Joplin and issued an accurate Tornado

Warning with sufficient lead time for people to take life-saving action. Unfortunately, the tornado developed rapidly on the southwestern outskirts of a densely populated area and had moved through much of the city before the size and violence of the tornado was apparent to warning forecasters. Thus, they did not issue a Severe Weather Statement with a "Tornado Emergency"[10] headline for Joplin proper; however, radar imagery by 540 pm CDT certainly indicated a well-defined hook echo over Joplin accompanied by a very large and distinctive debris ball. Warning forecasters on duty at that time noted that this was their first indication of the size and strength of the tornado. It follows that the Severe Weather Statement issued at 542 pm CDT and Tornado Warning issued at 548 pm CDT should have been more strongly worded and portrayed a greater sense of urgency. Instead the statement and warning were worded very much like previous warnings and statements issued that day. A quote from the Service Assessment for the Super Tuesday Tornado Outbreak applies here: *"During tornadic episodes where the forecasters have a high level of confidence an immediate and widespread response is critical, statements such as 'this is an extremely dangerous and life threatening situation' would increase the level of significance of these products."*

Finding #8: *After the significance of this event was apparent, Tornado Warnings and Severe Weather Statements lacked enhanced wording to accurately portray that immediate action was necessary to save lives with this tornado.*

Recommendation #8: *WFO warning forecasters should use wording that conveys a sense of urgency in warnings and statements when extremely dangerous and life threatening weather situations are in progress.*

5. SPC Products and Services

SPC forecasters correctly anticipated a threat of severe weather for Joplin more than 48 hours in advance, and anticipated a significant severe weather threat more than 24 hours in advance. As time progressed, SPC forecasters increasingly focused on the possibility of supercells with very large hail and tornadoes and issued a Tornado Watch about 4 hours prior to the Joplin tornado. A progression of pertinent SPC graphical forecasts is depicted in Figure 3.

A slight risk of severe thunderstorms was mentioned by SPC for a broad area of the eastern United States, stretching from northeast Texas to the eastern Great Lakes, beginning with the Day 3 Convective Outlook issued during the early morning hours of Friday, May 20. This outlook also mentioned a 30% chance of severe weather for southwest Missouri, including the city of Joplin. The outlook text stated, *"...isolated supercells...a couple which may be capable of producing tornadoes..."* would be possible on Sunday, May 22.

---

[10] NWS Directive NWSI 10-511, Section 4.3.4, allows this product for rare situations when reliable sources confirm, or there is clear radar evidence, of a damaging tornado.

This reasoning continued with the Day 2 Convective Outlooks issued on Saturday, May 21. A slight risk of severe thunderstorms (30% probability) was maintained for southwest Missouri in both outlooks issued that day. Additionally, the afternoon update mentioned significant severe weather for Sunday, May 22, in a narrow swath from south Texas to southwest and central Missouri. At this time, very large hail was expected to be the primary threat; however the outlook text also stated, *"low level winds are expected to back later in the day...in response to southwestern U.S. trough...with a tornado or two possible."*

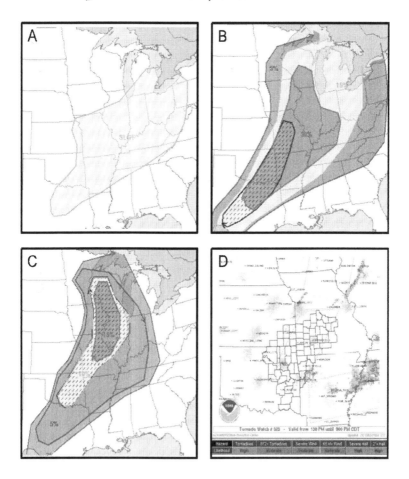

Figure 3: (A) SPC Day 3 Categorical Outlook issued 20/0730z valid 22/12z – 23/12z
(B) SPC Day 2 Combined Probability Outlook issued 21/1724z valid 22/12z – 23/12z
(C) SPC Day 1 Tornado Probability Outlook issued 22/1255z valid 22/13z-23/12z
(D) Tornado Watch #325 valid 22/1830z-23/0200z

SPC upgraded a portion of the severe thunderstorm slight risk area to a Moderate Risk with its Day 1 Convective Outlook issued at 755 am CDT on Sunday, May 22. Joplin was included in the Moderate Risk area and was also in an area that was forecasted to have a 10% chance of a EF2-EF5 tornado. The severe weather mode and locations of highest severe weather probabilities continued to be fine-tuned by SPC through the morning and early afternoon hours. An update to the Day 1 Convective Outlook, issued at 1117 am CDT, stated, *"Currently the highest probability for diurnal thunderstorm development appears to be from northeastern Oklahoma into Missouri where area will be influenced by left exit region of upper jet streak stretching from the southern Rockies into southern plains."* A Mesoscale Discussion was issued at 106 pm CDT for southwest Missouri (and surrounding areas) which stated, *"...and although low level shear is a bit marginal...it will be more than sufficient for tornadoes given extreme instability."*

Tornado Watch #325 was issued by SPC (after coordination with WFO Springfield and other affected offices) at 130 pm CDT which included Joplin. The text of the watch indicated *"explosive thunderstorm development"* with a *"strong tornado or two possible."* This watch provided about 4 hours of lead time prior to the tornado moving through Joplin. Another Mesoscale Discussion issued by SPC at 348 pm CDT specifically mentioned the possibility of cyclic tornadoes.

Interviews with partners and stakeholders, including WFO forecasters, media, and Emergency Managers, found SPC products and services very useful. In this particular case, the progression to a moderate risk on the morning of the 22nd was especially noted. All local television meteorologists stated they directly monitor and use SPC products frequently. Local Emergency Managers were more likely to get their convective outlooks and watch information through WFO products like the HWO.

Amongst the general public, the majority of residents had little idea there was a threat of severe weather prior to Sunday, May 22. About half of those interviewed, reported learning of the possibility of severe weather in the hours leading up to the tornado. Just less than half reported their first indication of a severe weather threat was in the moments just prior to the tornado.

6. WFO Springfield Warning Operations

WFO Springfield operations are well-established for severe weather and, from all accounts, those on duty performed in an exemplary manner, both in the provision of services and the application of scientific expertise. The station duty manual (SDM) contains several detailed plans for varied severe weather scenarios. The WFO has modeled its severe weather operations using the Incident Command System which creates a flexible structure that can be expanded depending upon the significance of the event.

For the Joplin tornado event, the WFO was staffed initially with six employees, and added an additional employee midway through the event. The Meteorologist in Charge and Warning Coordination Meteorologist were called in shortly after the Joplin impacts were known. The staffing profile was modeled after a moderate event detailed in the planning section of the Severe Weather SDM. WFO Springfield utilized two Radar Operators for this event as well as a coordinator, meso-analyst and a Verification/Communication Specialist. The office configuration was excellent and fostered good communications between the severe weather team. The severe weather team was placed in a cluster within a corner of the operations area and was self-contained. Warning forecasters and radar operators were situated next to each other with the Severe Weather Coordinator behind them.

The office maintains a situational awareness display that is in clear view of the warning operations team. The display is composed of two ceiling mounted projectors and screens. It is flexible and can display information from any of the Advanced Weather Interactive Processing Systems units as well as personal computers in the operations area. The WFO also recently added to its Situational Awareness Display a large screen television with access to various news outlets. This addition proved valuable during the Joplin tornado event because staff was able to follow, in real-time, local and national news accounts of the storm aftermath.

The Verification Specialist was at a workstation across from the Radar Operators. The dedicated position of Verification/Communication Specialist is designed to encompass use of all of the avenues of social media including NWSChat, Facebook, and Twitter as well as collecting and disseminating real-time ground truth reports. This position was praised by the user community as an invaluable resource for rapid communication during severe weather. Local media in particular commented on the importance of rapid dissemination of real-time reports via chat and Local Storm Report products. At the time of the event, WFO Springfield had just recently activated its Facebook page, and this portion of verification/ communications position was not fully developed.

Best Practice #4: *WFO Springfield employed a dedicated Verification/Communication Specialist position to communicate using chat and social media during the event.*

The primary radar operator at WFO Springfield made excellent use of "Bunkers Storm Motion Vectors"[11] and other mesoscale tools early in the event. These techniques, in combination with observed storm behavior, suggested the storm motions were more deviant than originally anticipated. This fact signaled that localized low-level helicity was beyond values suggested by the available analyses, indicating an increased risk for tornadoes. This degree of situational awareness was extremely critical for anticipating the evolution of the tornado threat. This awareness, along with recognition of a cell merger over southeast Kansas, led directly to the

---

[11] Bunkers. et. al. (2000). "Predicting Supercell Motion Using a New Hodograph Technique. Bunkers." *Weather and Forecasting.*

early warning of the Joplin tornado.

Once the primary Radar Operator recognized a significant storm was developing, WFO Springfield staff sectored radar responsibility. The primary Radar Operator maintained surveillance of the storms associated with the Joplin tornado and passed the remaining storms off to the secondary Radar Operator. While WFO Springfield did an excellent job of sectoring radar operations, one common WFO severe weather practice they did not employ is working in radar/warning teams of two. This requires more personnel to implement, but it allows one forecaster to concentrate on radar interrogation and the other to concentrate on the warning message and product composition at the text workstation, typically resulting in an improvement to both. Employing such a strategy may have led to enhanced product wording as suggested in Recommendation #8.

The initial Tornado Warning decision for the Joplin tornado was made based on a combination of radar data from the WFO Tulsa (KINX) and WFO Springfield radar (KSGF). See Appendix A (Figure 4).

Finding #9: *Radar data acquisition was compromised across key geographic locations, mainly, owing from Volume Coverage Pattern (VCP) selection at both KSGF and KINX. In this case, velocity data was obscured on KSGF upstream of Joplin near a critical warning decision point and KINX velocity data was obscured over Joplin during the height of the tornado event.*

The VCP 211 scanning strategy was employed at KSGF for the duration of the event. There are three notable impacts from this selection. First, the scanning strategy takes approximately 5 minutes to complete versus 4.2 minutes for VCP (2)12. Over the course of the 90 minutes leading up to and including the tornado, there were roughly 4 fewer volume scans available for use. The reduced data frequency leads to a greater lag in sampling the rapid increase in the tornado circulation intensity. Second, the VCP (2)11 scanning strategy is less effective at capturing data in the lower portions of thunderstorms, especially at ranges comparable to Joplin from KSGF. Finally, velocity data was unnecessarily compromised from both KSGF and KINX during key times. In reference to the VCP selections at both sites (KSGF 211, KINX 212), the 2XX series of VCPs presents substantial degradation in low-level velocity data at fixed ranges from the radar site, a direct result of employing a fixed Pulse Repetition Frequency (PRF) on the lowest elevation scans.

Recommendation #9: *WFO warning operations should make use of the more effective/adaptable VCP 12 and manually select appropriate PRF to remove range obscured velocity data and mitigate compromised radar datasets.*

Also, concerning sampling frequency, it is very apparent that near surface processes responsible for both tornadogenesis and intensity escalation occur on time scales much shorter than the radar observes. Re-emphasizing, the average tornado exists on time scales shorter than one complete WSR-88D volume scan. Use of Federal Aviation Administration Terminal Doppler Weather Radar (TDWR) has exposed NWS field offices to a more effective means of gathering radar data at the lowest elevation level where time criticality is the greatest. The TDWR scanning strategy samples at the lowest elevation every minute while completing a volume scan, thus attempting to capture rapid changes near the surface.

Finding #10: *Low-level rotational intensification and tornadogenesis occurred very rapidly with the Joplin tornado from 529 pm CDT to tornado touchdown around 534 pm CDT and the beginning of EF-4 damage around 538 pm CDT. Limited scans at lowest elevation slices during this time impacted the WFO's ability to quickly ascertain the magnitude of the tornado.*

Recommendation #10: *To enhance the ability to monitor rapid tornadogenesis and tornado intensification, NWS should develop and implement additional hybrid WSR-88D VCP strategies that allow for more continuous sampling near the surface (e.g., 1-minute lowest elevation sampling).*

Lastly, WFO Springfield continued to issue warnings and statements in a timely and effective manner even with the increased workload following the Joplin disaster. The office implemented a Public Information Officer position to handle the increased media calls and developed talking points for incoming staff. Storm survey teams were developed next day after the event to survey the tornado tracks. In response to the increased workload within the office, staffing was increased in the short term to meet the demand. Due to the magnitude of the event, the increased workload and demands on the staff became increasingly more difficult to manage. During this phase, the Central Region Headquarters Regional Operations Center deployed two additional staff members and an onsite Incident Meteorologist to assist with WFO operations and provide support for the local Emergency Operations Center.

Best Practice #5: *NWS offices should have a post-disaster plan and work closely with Regional Operations Centers on strategies for staffing and resource allocation after high profile weather events.*

Appendix A - Radar Imagery

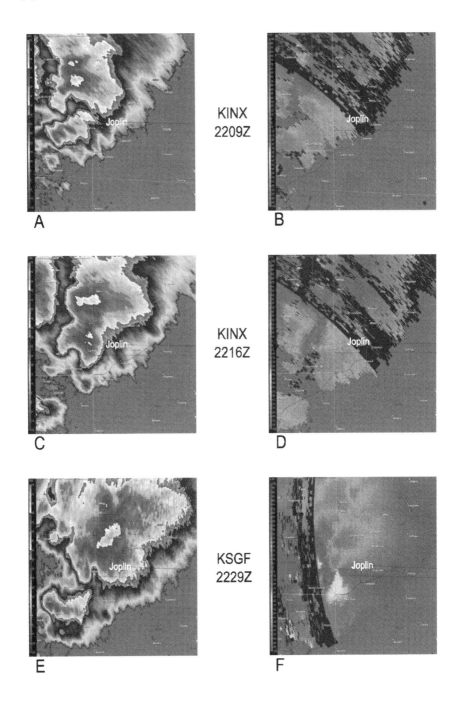

KINX
2209Z

KINX
2216Z

KSGF
2229Z

A
B
C
D
E
F

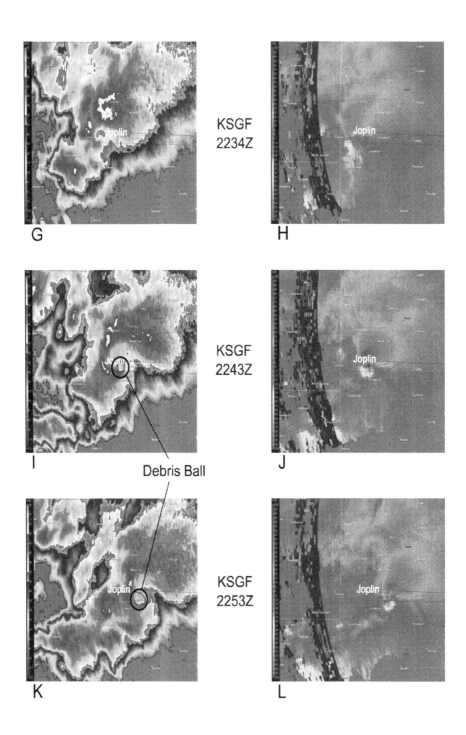

G

KSGF
2234Z

H

I

KSGF
2243Z

Debris Ball

J

K

KSGF
2253Z

L

Figure 4:

(A) KINX 0.5° Base Reflectivity valid 2011 May 22, 2209Z

(B) KINX 0.5° Storm Relative Velocity valid 2011 May 22, 2209Z

(C) KINX 0.5° Base Reflectivity valid 2011 May 22, 2216Z

(D) KINX 0.5° Storm Relative Velocity valid 2011 May 22, 2216Z

(E) KSGF 0.5° Base Reflectivity valid 2011 May 22, 2229Z

(F) KSGF 0.5° Storm Relative Velocity valid 2011 May 22, 2229Z

(G) KSGF 0.5° Base Reflectivity valid 2011 May 22, 2234Z

(H) KSGF 0.5° Storm Relative Velocity valid 2011 May 22, 2234Z

(I) KSGF 0.5° Base Reflectivity valid 2011 May 22, 2243Z

(J) KSGF 0.5° Storm Relative Velocity valid 2011 May 22, 2243Z

(K) KSGF 0.5° Base Reflectivity valid 2011 May 22, 2253Z

(L) KSGF 0.5° Storm Relative Velocity valid 2011 May 22, 2253Z

Appendix B - Upper Air Observations

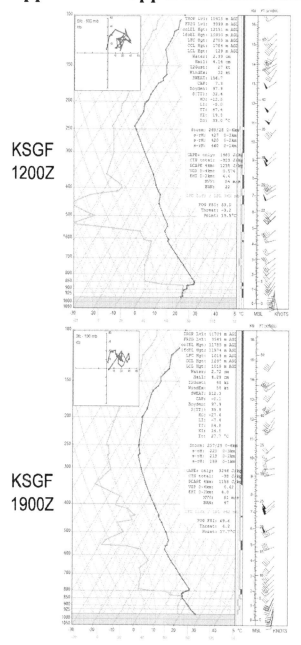

KSGF
1200Z

KSGF
1900Z

Figure 5: Skew-T/log-P from Springfield, Missouri, at 1200z and 1900z

Appendix C - Operational EF Scale

EF Number	3 Second Gust (mph)
0	65-85
1	86-110
2	111-135
3	136-165
4	166-200
5	Over 200

Appendix D - Findings, Recommendations, and Best Practices

Findings and Recommendations

Finding #1: *Recent NWS Assessments have addressed societal impacts of warnings, most notably the "Super Tuesday Tornado Outbreak of Feb. 5-6, 2008" and the "Mother's Day Weekend Tornado Outbreak of 2008.". Many of the societal impacts uncovered in previous Service Assessments were also evident in Joplin, suggesting the NWS should take a more aggressive stance in addressing warning response.*

Recommendation #1: *For future Service Assessments, NWS should plan a more structured approach to collecting information on societal aspects of warning response. This should include developing sub-teams well-versed in social science and NWS warning operations that can be quickly deployed to the field following any given severe weather disaster.*

Finding #2a: *For the majority of surveyed Joplin residents, the first risk signal for an imminent severe weather threat came via the local community siren system. As a result, there was a significant degree of ambiguity associated with the first alert regarding the magnitude of the risk, the seriousness of the warning, and its potential impact.*

Finding #2b: *The majority of surveyed Joplin residents did not immediately go to shelter upon hearing the initial warning, whether from local warning sirens, television, NWR, or other sources. Instead, most chose to further clarify and assess their risk by waiting for, actively seeking, and filtering additional information.*

Finding #2c: *Familiarity with severe weather and the perceived frequency of siren activation not only reflect normalization of threat and or desensitization to sirens and warnings, but they also establish that initial siren activation has lost a degree of credibility for many residents. Credibility is considered to be one of the most valued characteristics for effective risk communication.*

Finding #2d: *The majority of surveyed Joplin residents did not take protective action until receiving and processing credible confirmation of the threat- and its magnitude- from a non-routine trigger.*

Finding #2e: *Nationally, 76% of all NWS Tornado Warnings, in their totality, are false alarms. This means 24% of all tornado warnings are eventually associated with an observed tornado —*

indicating limited skill in differentiating between tornadic and non-tornadic events; however, 68% of EF0-1 tornadoes receive advance warning of near 12 minutes, while 94% of EF3-5 tornadoes receive advance warning of near 18 minutes, indicating an ability to better detect strong/violent tornadoes. Just over half (54%) of all severe weather warnings coincide with a severe weather event, indicating moderate skill in distinguishing between severe and non-severe thunderstorms.

Recommendation #2: *To improve severe weather warning response and mitigate user complacency, the NWS should explore evolving the warning system to better support effective decision making. This evolution should utilize a simple, impact-based, tiered information structure that promotes warning credibility and empowers individuals to quickly make appropriate decisions in the face of adverse conditions. This structure should:*

a) *lessen the number of risk signals processed before protective action is taken (finding 2b)*
b) *provide a non-routine warning mechanism that prompts people to take immediate life-saving action in extreme events like strong to violent tornadoes (finding 2d).*
c) *be impact-based more than phenomenon-based for clarity on risk assessment (finding 2a)*
d) *be compatible with NWS technological, scientific, and operational capabilities (finding 2e)*
e) *be compatible with external local warning systems and emerging mobile communications technology (finding 2a)*
f) *be easily understood and calibrated by the public to facilitate decision making (finding 2a)*
g) *maintain existing "probability of detection" for severe weather events (finding 2e)*
h) *diminish the perception of false alarms and their impacts on warning credibility and response (finding 2c)*

Finding # 3: *Many current warning dissemination systems are not fully compatible with specific warning information provided by storm-based, warning polygons.*

Recommendation # 3: *The NWS should continue to collaborate with partners who disseminate weather information to advance GPS-based warning dissemination systems that are compatible with more specific storm-based warning information. This change should include cultivating use of mobile communications technologies (text messaging, smart phone apps, Commercial Mobile Alert System, etc.) and technological upgrades of the Emergency Alert System (EAS) and NWR.*

Finding # 4: *Partners adapt weather and warning information in their local warning systems in an attempt to communicate risk simply and unobtrusively. The result is sometimes a poorly coordinated warning message across the weather enterprise that can lead to confusing or mixed messages.*

Recommendation # 4: *The NWS should collaborate with partners throughout the weather enterprise to provide a better coordinated warning message. Guidance should be developed to assist partners in the development of local warning system and siren strategies that work in conjunction with NWS warnings rather than independent of them.*

Finding #5: *Because the Joplin southwest Missouri area lies near the intersection of multiple NWS County Warning Areas (CWA), there was some difficulty noted by NWS partners in following chats from many different offices.*

Recommendation #5: *The NWS should continue to improve collaboration tools for our partners. Partners requested improvements to the current NWSChat display to include a "dashboard" interface to allow them to more easily monitor multiple offices at the same time.*

Finding #6: *The Storm-Ready renewal application for the city of Joplin had some discrepancies and incomplete information. WFO Springfield does not have a StormReady Advisory Board that consists of any individuals outside the local office.*

Recommendation #6: *The NWS needs to maintain a credible structure to the Storm-Ready program, including local advisory boards, and adhere to established criteria for Storm-Ready certifications.*

Finding #7: *Conference calls provided by WFO Springfield play a critical role in heightening the preparedness levels of NWS partners, and are requested by partners for scenarios with SPC Moderate Risk or greater.*

Recommendation #7: *The NWS should ensure that tools and procedures are in place for WFO operational staff to easily conduct conference calls with NWS partners. These calls should be provided in a consistent manner and associated with SPC Moderate Risk or greater.*

Finding #8: *After the significance of this event was apparent, Tornado Warnings and Severe Weather Statements lacked enhanced wording to accurately portray that immediate action was necessary to save lives with this tornado.*

Recommendation #8: *WFO warning forecasters should use wording that conveys a sense of urgency in warnings and statements when extremely dangerous and life threatening weather situations are in progress.*

Finding #9: *Radar data acquisition was compromised across key geographic locations, mainly owing from Volume Coverage Pattern (VCP) selection at both KSGF and KINX. In this case, velocity data was obscured on KSGF upstream of Joplin near a critical warning decision point and KINX velocity data was obscured over Joplin during the height of the tornado event.*

Recommendation #9: *WFO warning operations should make use of the more effective adaptable VCP 12 and manually select appropriate Pulse Repetition Frequencies (PRF) to remove range obscured velocity data and mitigate compromised radar datasets.*

Finding #10: *Low level rotational intensification and tornadogenesis occurred very rapidly with the Joplin tornado from 529 pm CDT to tornado touchdown around 534 pm CDT and the beginning of EF-4 damage around 538 pm CDT. Limited scans at lowest elevation slices during this time impacted the WFO's ability to quickly ascertain the magnitude of the tornado.*

Recommendation #10: *To enhance the ability to monitor rapid tornadogenesis and tornado intensification, NWS should develop and implement additional hybrid WSR-88D VCP strategies that allow for more continuous sampling near the surface (e.g., 1-minute lowest elevation sampling).*

Best Practices

Best Practice #1: *NWS outreach and severe weather safety education programs should continue to emphasize and assist area businesses with severe weather safety action plans via the Storm Ready program or other, similar mechanisms. This kind of outreach and planning assistance should also be extended to vulnerable populations in nursing homes, group homes, hospitals, etc.*

Best Practice #2: *NWSChat should continue to be supported and encouraged as a valuable communication tool amongst the "weather enterprise" team members.*

Best Practice #3: *WFOs should issue non-routine AFDs to discuss ongoing and expected mesoscale feature evolution when severe thunderstorms are anticipated.*

Best Practice #4: *WFO Springfield employed a dedicated Verification Communication Specialist position to communicate using chat and social media during the severe weather event.*

Best Practice #5: *NWS offices should have a post-disaster plan and work closely with Regional Operations Centers on strategies for staffing and resource allocation for high profile weather events.*

Appendix E - Acronyms

AFD	Area Forecast Discussion
CDT	Central Daylight Time
EAS	Emergency Alert System
EF	Enhanced Fujita Tornado Scale
HWO	Hazardous Weather Outlook
KINX	Tulsa, Oklahoma Radar
KSGF	Springfield, Missouri Radar
KS	Kansas
LSR	Local Storm Report
MMWB	Multi Media Web Brief
MO	Missouri
mph	miles per hour
NOAA	National Oceanic and Atmospheric Administration
NWS	National Weather Service
PRF	Pulse Repetition Frequency
RAOB	Rawindsonde Observation
SDM	Station Duty Manual
SGF	Springfield, MO
SPC	Storm Prediction Center
TDWR	Terminal Doppler Weather Radar
VCP	Volume Coverage Pattern
WFO	Weather Forecast Office

Appendix F - Team Members

Richard Wagenmaker	Meteorologist in Charge	NOAA/NWS Detroit, MI
Justin Weaver	Meteorologist in Charge	NOAA/NWS Lubbock, TX
Gary Garnet	Warning Coordination Meteorologist	NOAA/NWS Cleveland, OH
Bethany Hale	NOAA Central Region Collaboration Team Coordinator	NOAA/NWS Kansas City, MO
Jennifer Spinney	Research Associate	University of Oklahoma, Social Science Woven into Meteorology

Other Contributors

Bill Davis	Meteorologist in Charge	NOAA/NWS Springfield, MO
Steve Runnels	Warning Coordination Meteorologist	NOAA/NWS Springfield, MO
Dr. Greg Mann	Science and Operations Officer	NOAA/NWS Detroit, MI

ABOUT THE AUTHORS

 RANDY TURNER is an eighth grade English teacher at East Middle School in Joplin and spent more than two decades as a reporter and editor for southwest Missouri newspapers. He has written two novels and two non-fiction books.

 JOHN HACKER is the managing editor of *The Carthage Press* and has covered Missouri and Kansas news for two decades. A graduate of Missouri Southern State University, Hacker has won numerous awards for reporting and photography.

Turner and Hacker co-authored *5:41: Stories from the Joplin Tornado.*

25814879R00218

Made in the USA
Lexington, KY
05 September 2013